DATE DUE

DEC 0 7 1994	
MAR 2 2 1996	
APR 2 2 1996	
MAY 1 0 1996	
DEC 1 3 1996	
DEC 1 2 1997	
JUL 3 0 1999	
MAR 2 0 2000	
NOV 1 0 2005	
APR 1 7 2006	
APR 0 5 2011	

BRODART.   Cat. No. 23-221

Sexing the
Millennium

Sexing the Millennium

WOMEN AND THE
SEXUAL REVOLUTION

Linda Grant

GROVE PRESS
New York

An earlier version of this book was published in Great Britain in 1993 by HarperCollins Publishers.

Published simultaneously in Canada
Printed in the United States of America

FIRST EDITION

Library of Congress Cataloging-in-Publication Data

Grant, Linda, 1951–
    Sexing the millennium: women and the sexual revolution /
Linda Grant.—1st ed.
    "Earlier version of this book was published in Great Britain in
1993 by HarperCollins"—t.p. verso.
    Includes bibliographical references and index.
    ISBN 0-8021-1549-7
    1. Sex customs.   2. Sex role.   I. Title.
HQ16.G73   1994   306.7—dc20   93-41427

Design by Laura Hough

Grove Press
841 Broadway
New York, NY 10003

10 9 8 7 6 5 4 3 2 1

For some sexual revolutionaries who had dinner at Florent:
Rowena Rowling,
Barbara Zitwer,
Ruth Ammon

Acknowledgments

A large number of people helped me along the way—by agreeing to be interviewed, providing contacts or facilities, lending or giving me books, making inspired suggestions, reading the manuscript, or providing beds for me in New York—and I here most gratefully thank them: Annette Ramírez de Arellano, Andrew Billen, Alma Birk, Lola Bobbish, Brian Braithwaite, Helen Gurley Brown, Janet Briggs, Peter Brawne, Mic Burton, Louise Chunn, Larry and Joan Constantine, Dilys Cossey, Hermine Demoriane, Margaret Drabble, Betty Dodson, Udi Eichler, David Elstein, Carolyn Faulder, Michael Fish, Margaret Forster, Carla Gaspasian, Michele Grant, Patricia Gossell, Mark Hoffman, Jim Holt, David Housham, Laurence Hughes, Marek Kohn and Sue Matthias Kohn, Grace Lau, David McConnell, John McGahern, Blake Morrison, Mandi Norwood, Michelle Olley, Michael O'Regan, Jefferson Poland, Jay Rayner, Robert and Erma Rimmer, JoAnne Robertson, Adeline Pendleton Satterthwaite, Barbara Seaman, Ska, Buff, Bet, and Day, Jeff Selth, Joan Smith, Eleanor Stephens, Gay Talese, Colm Tóibín, Rebecca Tomlinson, Anthony Wall, Francis Wheen, Lucy Whitman, Hugo Williams, Richard Wilson, Alice Wolfson, Helen Zahavi.

I'm particularly indebted to Richard Ogar, my guide to Berkeley and Haight-Ashbury in the sixties, for putting his life on the line, so to speak. I also here acknowledge a deep gratitude to three people who must remain anonymous and who bravely agreed to bear witness.

Thanks are also due to Michael Fishwick, Lucinda McNeile, Rebecca Lloyd, Betty Palmer, and Annie Robertson at HarperCollins U.K. I am very grateful to my U.K. agent, Derek Johns, whose calm efficiency and attention has guaranteed a very smooth transition from manuscript to book, and to Ellen Levine for all her hard work on bringing this edition into being. Allison Draper, at Grove Press, has demonstrated beyond all doubt the value of a good editor. Her suggestions have in every way improved the U.S. edition.

Finally, my deepest debt is to my former agent, Imogen Parker. She knows what she did.

The disappearance of utopia brings about a static sense of affairs in which man himself becomes no more than a thing. We would then be faced with the greatest paradox imaginable, namely, that man, who has achieved the highest degree of rational mastery of existence, left without any ideals, becomes a mere creature of impulse.

Karl Mannheim, *Ideology and Utopia*, 1936

Sex is important! Sex is profound! Sex is funny!

Cynthia Heimel, *Sex Tips for Girls*, 1983

Contents

Sexing the

Millennium

What Sexual Revolution?

Therefore the question I would put to proponents of the anatomy-is-destiny theory is this: are you happy *with this state of affairs? Can you shrug off the fact that women are routinely denigrated, despised, segregated, raped, mutilated and murdered? Are you saying, in fact, that it is* natural *for men to hate and fear women?*

Joan Smith, *Misogynies*

For two years women have been saying to me, "I hear you're writing a book. What's it about?" I would reply, "The sexual revolution." And then it would come—archly, provocatively, sadly, or with a world-weary moue of disillusion, "Really? Has there *been* a sexual revolution?" For the first few months this perplexed me. I could be standing there talking to a thirty-eight-year-old lawyer who had lived with her partner for ten years and was just about to have her first child (with benefit of nanny, cleaning lady, and nursery), and she would still say, "Has there *been* a sexual revolution?"

I had my facts. Did she realize that until the mid-1960s it was virtually impossible for a single woman to furnish herself with birth control? That in some British family-planning clinics, where contraception would be prescribed to the engaged, the receipt for the wedding dress was required as proof that the applicant was free from intentions of immorality? That until the licensing of the Pill in 1960 it was men who took charge of contraception? Did she not remember the burden that virginity placed on girls, who had to be permanently vigilant against its accidental loss or theft? That premarital sex led, invariably, to pregnancy? That landlords would not rent to unmarried couples? That abortion and homosexuality were illegal and the divorce laws trapped people in violent or loveless marriages? That there was no sexual persona for the post-nubile single woman? That women married or had a career, but if they did the latter they would be sexless, repressed—spinsters whom, by implication, no man wanted or loved?

It was a smug litany, and irrefutable. It silenced any listener. And yet, they said. And yet. They had expected more. A sexual revolution that had eroticized women's lives and given them solid (and hard-won) liberties had somehow failed them nonetheless. Sexual freedom had once been the shape of their dreams.

The idea of the future has been a controlling metaphor for this century, for modernism. For women born in the last fifty years, the sexual revolution had the same meanings the Russian Revolution held for a generation of socialists. It promised to demolish the old socio-sexual order of women servicing men's physical needs with little hope or even knowledge that their own could be fulfilled. It would be an egalitarian answer to the old double standard. But the sexual revolution had turned out to be a history of radical ideas repackaged for the mass market, co-opted by the sex industry and tabloid newspapers. For many women there had been only a betrayal. If anyone had benefited, it was often asserted, it was men. Where before there had existed a restraining morality that put wives, mothers, virgins, and children off-limits, a double standard that could work in women's favor, now all women were fair game.

If there had been a sexual revolution, why did women still fear rape whenever they stepped outside their houses? Where was the totally safe, totally effective birth control we had been promised? How could teenage girls who slept with their boyfriends stop being called sluts by their friends? Where were all the thirtysomething men for the thirtysomething women to have sex with? Why was abortion still under threat? Why was there a multimillion-dollar silicone-breast-implant industry—if women and men were sexually equal, why did women feel such anxiety about their attractiveness? And if women were so free, so liberated, so unbuttoned-up about lust, why did the top-shelf magazines with their pneumatic bimbettes make them feel so uncomfortable? Why were they on the side of censorship in this matter and no other? *Why* had female desire not transformed the world?

Since the sexual revolution, relations between men and women seem to have turned murderous. In 1991, two books were published in the same month in Britain. The first was Bret Easton Ellis's *American Psycho*. Ellis's anti-hero, Patrick Bateman, dressed to kill in Giorgio Armani, Gianni Versace, Ralph Lauren, and A. Testoni, teeth cleaned with a faux-tortoise-shell toothbrush and rinsed with Cepacol, hair enriched with Vivagen and aerated with Mousse à Raiser, skin moisturized by Clinique, soothed by Pour Hommes, anti-aged by Baume des Yeux, traverses New York killing people and often eating portions of his victims served as meatloaf. Bateman inserts rats up a woman's vagina. He saws off arms and cuts out tongues. He makes a necklace of vertebrae and wears it, humming softly, in the bath. He loves bodies: "Free weights and Nautilus equipment relieve stress. My body responds to the workout accordingly. Shirtless, I scrutinize my image in the mirror above the sinks in the locker room at Xclusive. My arm muscles burn, my stomach is as taut as possible, my chest steel, pectorals granite-hard, my eyes white as ice. In my locker in the locker room at Xclusive lie three vaginas I recently sliced out of various women I've attacked in the past week. Two are washed off, one isn't. There's a barette clipped to one of them, a blue ribbon from Hermès tied around my favorite."[1]

The second book was *Dirty Weekend* by Helen Zahavi. Its heroine, Bella, emerges from a basement flat in Brighton to murder men. This is brought on by an obscene phone call she receives from a neighbor: "I can tell by the way you move that you know I'm watching you," he says. "You've got a kind of look-at-me way of moving. It's naughty of you, to move like that, when you know I'm watching."[2] He tells her his fantasies: he fucks her on the bathroom floor; he fucks her until she pukes and she loves it, she loathes it. One day she has had enough unsolicited phone sex; masked, armed, and unafraid, she breaks into his flat and beats him to death with a hammer. Later that weekend she smothers with a plastic bag a man who tries to pick her up in a hotel bar. She shoots several drunken yuppies who are beating up a tramp. "If you see a woman walking," Zahavi writes, "if she's stepping quietly home, if you see her flowing past you on the pavement. If you would like to break her brittle bones, and you want to hear the hopeless pleading, and you want to feel the pink flesh bruising, and you want to taste the taut skin bleeding ... Think on ... For unknowingly, unthinkingly, unwittingly you might have laid your heavy hand on Bella."[3]

Helen Zahavi is a gentle young woman from Brighton, a translator. "I knew liberals wouldn't like this book," she says. "It's not a liberal book, it's not saying, 'understand these men,' it's saying, 'eliminate them' and that's a very frightening idea for many people, very foreign. I believe that if the State doesn't protect the weakest members of society, they have a complete right to protect themselves. If someone climbed in through the window in the middle of the night, I would feel completely justified in blowing his head off. Any woman who is sleeping in her bed can imagine her paralysing fear of an intruder and she knows if she cannot defend herself she's lost. And they come in because they know a woman cannot defend herself. Feminine behaviour is rooted in fear of offending the male, bruising his ego and arousing him to violence. I wanted to reverse that situation."

In 1991 and 1992 there were some interesting killings. A mother of three served her husband with a drugged Chinese stir-fry before beating him to death with a rolling pin and, with the help of her daughter, burying the body in the garden, where it lay undetected until a neighbor began digging to put up a fence.[4] A jealous husband drove his car into his wife at sixty miles an hour.[5] The wife of a major in the British armed forces killed her husband's German mistress by knocking her down and running her over with her car.[6] A man killed his wife by throttling her and immersing her in a vat of hydrochloric acid.[7] A former nun stabbed her husband seventeen times with a kitchen knife.[8] Another woman strangled the man she lived with and chopped him up. She kept the head in the house for eighteen months until she threw it out with the rubbish.[9] A pensioner of seventy-nine battered his wife to death with a hammer.[10] A female serial killer in the United States was found guilty of murdering seven middle-aged men. She picked up her victims on Florida highways, robbing them of their money and jewelry, which she gave to her female lover. A

.22-caliber handgun was used for the killings. As the seven-woman, five-man jury pronounced their verdict, she shouted at them, "I was raped. I hope you get raped, scumbags of America."[11] In Rostov-on-Don, in Russia, police finally caught a middle-aged teacher who had slaughtered dozens of boys and girls.[12] A Japanese man went on German television to inform an enraptured audience how he killed and ate his Dutch girlfriend when they had both been students in Paris.[13] The list is, of course, misleading in one way. In the year ending September 30, 1991, 299 men were in prison in Britain for killing their spouse or lover. Only twenty-two women were serving sentences for the same offense.[14]

While feminists and anti-censorship libertarians were debating the effects of pornography, I went to the former Yugoslavia to examine claims that up to fifty thousand Muslim women in Bosnia had been raped in camps dedicated to sexual torture. War creates its own fog of propaganda and disinformation. Rape has always been one of the spoils of war, the officers claiming the paintings and jewelry, the men making do with more temporary pleasures. But Bosnia was the first postmodern conflict, the first without sides defined by communism and capitalism, the first to be formed in part by mass communications (all parties hired public-relations companies). The Serbian irregulars who swept through the eastern part of Bosnia in April 1992 were under the control of Vojislav Seselg, a failed sociologist and anticommunist dissident who had revived the Chetniks, a far-right party of the Second World War. Imprisoned in the mid-1980s, Seselg recruited a paramilitary organization of ex-convicts or men still serving their sentences who were promised their freedom in exchange for a stint in his army. The prospects for rape and pillage were excellent, the men were informed. Many were junkies and were only able to summon up the courage to go into battle tanked up on Ecstasy and other drugs.

Since Tito's death in 1980, video porn had been freely available in Yugoslavia, and not just in the cities. Every village had its video store with its mandatory top shelf of X-rated lovelies. The most likely explanation for the extent and horror of rape in Bosnia is that rape camps became porn studios without cameras where sexual fantasy was freed from the prison of the imagination. A Dutch gynecologist on the European Community's investigative mission into rape in Bosnia reported an account of a man whose penis had been amputated, cut up, and forcibly fed to his wife and daughter. The *Croatian Medical Journal* carried a photograph of a corpse mutilated in this way.

At the same time that *American Psycho* and *Dirty Weekend* were published, the film *Silence of the Lambs* was released. The press found in it the ultimate shock, designer cannibalism. Hannibal Lecter and his entrée of human kidneys with fava beans, washed down with a good Chianti, was the New York foodie's black joke. But in Thomas Harris's book, Lecter was a minor character. At its heart is Buffalo Bill, a man of indeterminate sexuality who kills women to collect their skins, which he sews into a woman-suit. Buffalo Bill wants to be a woman. And he believes that the outward characteristics—breasts, vagina, slim waist, wider hips, soft thighs—*are* women. The insides—ovaries like walnuts, uterus like a cantaloupe, organs, brain, bones, estrogen pumping from the thalamus—he throws away. This is, for me, the most resonant and most murderous symbol of the manipulation of female sexual identity into product. It is the ultimate postmodern image—the final discarding of content in favor of form. Anyone can possess a woman now, through sex, through pornography, through suburban transvestism. I see Buffalo Bill everywhere I look: on billboards, in the triumphant survivors of sex-change operations, most of all in Margaret Thatcher and Madonna, who said for herself, and perhaps for Thatcher too, "Pussy rules the world but I have a dick in my brain."

From this midnight we recall that what had characterized the sixties was optimism. Men and women were confident that they could do anything they liked: go to the moon, solve the population crisis, end hunger and inequality. They thought they could make a sexual revolution because they believed in the future. When they stopped believing, they continued to fuck. But removed from the context of history, of a sense of past, present, and future in which sexual freedom was the most personal expression of revolutionary change, sex became an isolated event, turned inward. It acquired a new meaning. In our plague years, sex is the site not only of desire but of passions tipped over the edge of the rough-and-tumble of intercourse into beatings and mutilation. Sadomasochism, which has always existed in rooms and clubs, in small ads and back pages, has become *the* postmodern spectacle, a new kind of safe sex that enacts violence in a timeless theatrical tableau.

In the 1980s, as many people have noted, it was money rather than the body that was suffused by eroticism. In health-conscious America, sex was as dubious as additives or cholesterol. When newspaper editors and publishers said that a story or a title or a cover was "sexy," they meant that it was heightened by a kind of racy populism. Cultural studies, the Trumps' divorce, were "sexy." That was what did us for sex. There has never been a time this century in which sex has not been associated with modernity. It has been inseparable from the discourse of liberation. But in the eighties, sex was sunk into a silence almost as grave as that out of which it emerged, bawling its head off in around 1963, the time of the Profumo scandal and the mass availability of the Pill. The sexual revolution dwindled into the vulgarity of the porn industry, of middle-aged men still plaintively asking, "Do you swing?" As late as 1992, a British journalist discovered the new chastity:

> It was happening all around me. People were giving up sex—from fear, of course, from a sense of responsibility, from ideological propriety or the pursuit of purity. . . .
>
> It was at a dinner party that I finally realized the seriousness of the issue. I had just recounted a rather sordid tale of my promiscuous male misdemeanours, the punchline of which was my conquest's confession that the episode was the first time she had had sex in two-and-a-half years. This had shocked me, frightened and surprised me. Silence, not laughter, greeted my conclusion. The smooth swish of noses being swiftly upturned was unmistakable. The disdain was definite.
>
> To these modern citizens I was infected with sex, practically rabid with the need for sex. In the age of the New Man, the New Sense, the New Reason, the return to decent values, I was a social leper, a cultural dinosaur, a sex junkie, someone who not only had sex but wanted it, someone so sick with sex he admitted it and felt no shame about it.[15]

Ninety-nine percent of politics is good luck, and the Right in the eighties was truly blessed by AIDS. Without it, how would conservatives have sustained the moral backlash and panic that has thwarted our lives for the past ten years? The eighties were a sickening refutation of sixties optimism, of the *idea* of progress. Sexuality was the battleground on which the 1984 presidential campaign in the United States was fought and won, an election in which the Democrats had as a major policy initiative reproductive rights, which Reagan successfully repudiated.

Many people have noted that because the erotic is the place where the classes, races, and generations meet, it is the focus for anxieties about the collapse of social and economic order. Desire and pleasure are lawless and undisciplined. Therefore the manipulation of morality has been an important weapon in maintaining social control. It has been useful to the Right that the campaigns to which feminism has devoted some of its greatest attention are those against rape, pornography, prostitution, incest, and child abuse. Andrea Dworkin, the major figure in eighties feminism, found in sex a nightmare of pain, mutilation, violence, and enslavement. In November 1992, she told the London *Evening Standard,* "The fact is women do not like intercourse very much. Our lack of orgasms is proof enough; we think we like sex as some slaves may have thought they liked picking cotton."[16] The sight of sections of the women's movement in alliance with the new puritan Right has unsettled and confused many feminists, myself included. Feminism has always been accused by libertarians of being anti-erotic because it refuses the scripts that men have written for our sexuality—we have, even, walked right off the stage into another play. But those campaigns that have drawn the widest support and attracted greatest attention from the media, have uncovered a stubborn and pervasive belief among a sullen, silent majority of women that sex is little more than male violence. For several years there has been a great silence from feminism about sexual relations between women and men. In 1970, Germaine Greer could write:

> Revolutionary women may join Women's Liberation Groups and curse and scream and fight the cops, but did you ever hear of one of them marching the public street with her skirt high crying, "Can you dig it? Cunt is beautiful!" The walled garden of Eden was CUNT. The mandorla of the beautiful saints was CUNT. The mystical rose is CUNT. The Ark

of Gold, the Gate of Heaven. CUNT is a channel drawing all towards it. Cunt is knowledge. Knowledge is receptivity, which is activity. Cunt is the symbol of erotic science, the necessary corrective of the maniacal conquest of technology. Skirts must be lifted, knickers (which women have only worn for a century) must come off forever. It is time to dig CUNT and women must dig it first.[17]

Twenty-one years later, in her book *The Change,* she embraced her own menopause, grateful for the liberation it gave her from physical desire. At fifty-two she chose the role of hag or crone, with its rescued status of Wise Woman, and railed against "the men whose names appear on hundreds of learned papers every year, elaborating the possibilities of eliminating menopause and keeping all women both appetizing and responsive to male demand from puberty to the grave, driving the dreaded old woman off the face of the earth forever."[18] The profoundness of the feminist No invades and infects feminist culture. The feminist Women's Press published, as its contribution to the debate on the sexual revolution when the nineties began, *Anticlimax* by Sheila Jeffreys, for whom "Heterosexuality is the institution through which male-supremacist society is organized, and as such it must cease to function."[19] Jeffreys castigated women for succumbing to desire for men, an "unwelcome resurgence within feminism"[20] based on the eroticization of power difference, each heterosexual act being an exercise in female masochism.

Only in the academic field of gender studies have feminists and gay men continued to debate the sexual revolution, and there should be an honorable mention for Lynne Segal, Elizabeth Wilson, and Jeffrey Weeks, whose patience and determination to abandon neither socialism nor feminism have provided readers with a sustained analysis of sexual politics that has continually questioned the discourse of censorship. But despite the wealth of work on gender politics that has emerged in the last ten years, much of it has been characterized by a love affair with theory. The influence of Jacques Lacan has rendered a great deal of this subject matter incomprehensible to the lay reader lacking a thorough grounding in psychoanalysis.

It is gay men who have been the heroes of our times for their refusal to accept their silencing by the Right, though large numbers of them were being literally silenced forever. They forced themselves to political attention. Queer politics is a revolutionary refusal of liberalism. The campaign in Britain to have the homosexual age of consent lowered to bring it into line with the heterosexual has been the only attempt since the sixties to extend sexual freedom rather than conserve or limit it. Lesbians, initially the group least affected by AIDS, have been free to launch a dazzling attempt to deconstruct *and* reassemble the female persona. Dykes have emerged to become the most powerful and resonant image of future sexuality. Throughout the years of moral panic, it was lesbians who challenged the institutionalized forms of the erotic, attempting to define a female-centered sexuality in lesbian porn magazines like *On Our Backs*. To lesbians (and gay men), what they did in bed was central to their identity and culture. They were lesbians because of a *sexual* preference, and while the moral backlash threatened their liberty, it was impossible to sit it out for the duration, as heterosexuals did. There are lesbians who wear leather jackets, boots, and stick-on mustaches and mock the narrow prescriptions of clone style. In the photographs of the lesbian photographer Della Grace we find not a gallery of postmodern references to camp icons of "glamour" but what one critic has described as an expansion of "the catalogue of qualities associated with feminism, admitting toughness, aggression and the hooligan stare into the female thesaurus."[21]

It was not only AIDS that produced the reaction against the sexual revolution. There is no doubt that by the beginning of the eighties people were bored silly with sex. The generation that had been freed to fuck was now confined to the tepid pleasures of the marriage bed. The tactics of the pickup were replaced by the strategies of relationships. In the Reagan-Thatcher years, desire meant "gimme," "I want." Desire was a gaping jaw that was passive even beyond the activity of acquisitiveness. Desire could be fulfilled in many forms—food, clothes, furnishing, vacations. But almost as quickly, we began to gag on all those *things*. We wanted something else shoved down our throats. The boredom threshold of a generation really does seem to be about a decade long. For the marginal (and there are many who do not fit into the culture of family values—gays, single and divorced people, the young) taking a walk on the wild side is the way we differentiate ourselves. And so the moral panic has proved to be pretty short-lived. As soon as it became apparent that heterosexuals were not dying in anything like the same numbers as gay men (at least not in Europe and America), when the recession braked the spending spree, when babies as designer accessories proved not to have a volume control, let alone a remote channel changer permanently locked onto smiling and gurgling, sex was back. Madonna opened her mouth and we were shocked by how much we had forgotten.

But even during those black days of the eighties (that is, when everyone wore black), there was a phenomenal rise in the number of women undergoing plastic surgery to "augment" their breasts. In America, faced with the prospect of a ban by the Food and Drug Administration, they formed a pro-choice movement parallel to the abortion campaign of the sixties and seventies. After the *faux* natural look of the sixties, there was a revival in cosmetics and perfume and lingerie, in a cult of beauty as artifice. In part this reflected the consumer boom of the period. But one of the onuses feminism had placed on women was to be strong, independent, gutsy. In the mass media, this translated into a call for newly toned bodies and that dick in the brain, which allowed women to compete in the workplace but undermined their sense of their own femininity. The power-dressing suit imposed a masculine form on women's bodies. To compensate, they had to re-balance their gender. If big breasts were the most outward form of sexiness and femininity, and if they also denoted maternity, then muscle would have to vie with voluptuousness. The uniform of the eighties career woman was a long, dark jacket, short skirt, dark, sheer stockings, high heels, all worn over a lace teddy with a drenching of Opium just to make sure. A real woman has curves with attitude.

So far I have been talking about a generation of women and men who directly experienced the sexual revolution, whose desires, whether they realize it or not, were transformed by its promise and who later witnessed the partial closing down of the freedoms it granted. But they are not alone. There is another generation, born since the sixties, for whom Madonna is the cultural icon, the comic-book autonomous Bitch Queen, consumer greed turned back again to the true site of desire, the sexual organs that women have not yet named: "cunt," "snatch," "beaver," "pussy." Madonna's sexual confidence has filled the void that feminism's preoccupation with male violence left to her. The postmodernist, postfeminist sexuality of the video generation, coming of age during a period of reaction and fear, yet without the real repression of the fifties, is sex formed of images and styles. It is consumerist: witness the new porn magazines, *For Women* and *Ludus;* the Virgin Books list of pornographic novels; nights out with the girls watching Chippendales strip; the safe-sex parties in which women learn to put a condom on a cucumber with their teeth; the Jack and Jill clubs in New York; the Kinky Gerlinkey drag balls in London; the escort agencies for women with disposable incomes; bondage wear; designer S/M; novels about telephone sex.

Dramatic changes have affected the family, too. Couples used to run along parallel tracks for a common purpose, the wife in her sphere, her emotional life centered on her children and the home, the husband in his, fulfilled by work, the bar, and other men. These tracks have crossed and recrossed each other. The necessity for women to contribute to the family finances has transformed women's expectations. Easier divorce has placed additional responsibility on them as heads of households and caused speculation that the future family may well be of a matrilineal structure. The universal availability of reliable (if unsafe) contraception has brought power over family size into the hands of women. Sex has stopped being "men's business," a burden periodically imposed on wives. There is the possibility of pleasure. The enormous popularity of Alex Comfort's *The Joy of Sex* has indeed brought elite delights out from the gentleman's library and onto the bedside table. When housewives organize sex-aids gatherings modeled along the lines of Tupperware parties, when magazines are full of "contact" ads for "reader's wives," one should be wary of declaring that the sexual revolution is something one sees only on TV. George Bush lost the 1992 election by appealing for a return to family values, a concept that bewildered electors until they understood that Bush meant a kind of family that barely existed in America anymore. Instead, confounding early predictions, they voted for a sexy adulterer.

The book you are reading is a personal story, though most of it will not seem that way. I am a product of the sexual revolution. For my generation, the one that read underground magazines like *Oz* and *International Times* and *Rolling Stone,* sex was not only an act of coition. It was a political gesture, a molotov cocktail to throw at the Establishment, blowing up censors and fundamentalists, the comically dressed bogeymen, the wretched hypocrites that were the paper tigers of the sexual revolution.

I went to university two years after the 1970 Oxford Women's Conference, when feminist organizations were forming all over Britain. There was one time when a group of us was sitting around talking about sex and someone said, "I'm not sure if I've ever *had* an orgasm." Our exhaled breath hung about in the air. It occurred to me then that an individual problem, what I thought of as my own neurosis, could be collective, a failure not of the self but a social condition to be studied and solved in a collective manner. It was the birth of political consciousness. There were wars in Vietnam and Nigeria, British miners were on strike—I could have found something else to politicize me, but this was what did it.

The book that deeply impressed me then was Anaïs Nin's *A Spy in the House of Love.* Its heroine, Sabine, was a woman of masks and fragments who prowled the city in her psychic disguises. She meant something different to each of her lovers; she had a different sexual persona for everyone. She picks up a man on the beach and later goes back to his apartment. For the first time she climaxes, and in that moment of erotic autonomy she opens her eyes "to contemplate the piercing joy of her liberation: she was free, free as a man was, to enjoy without love. . . . And then she remembered what she had heard men say: 'Then I wanted to leave.' . . . She wanted to become swiftly and cleanly detached from him, to disentangle and unmingle what had been fused for a moment, their breaths, skins, exhalations, and bodies' essences." She slips out of bed and tiptoes to the bathroom, where on a shelf she finds face powder, comb, lipstick in shell-rose wrappings. She smiles at them and wonders if they belong to his wife or his mistress: "How good it was to contemplate these objects without the slightest tremor of regret, envy or jealousy. That was the meaning of freedom."[22] I tried this myself. It worked. I could have as many one-night stands as I wanted, with no pain. I scorned relationships, engagement, marriage.

After I left university, gripped by wanderlust, dreaming of the road, I went to America, and hitched around the country. At one point I was holed up in Colorado with a man called Don Blood, a criminal who took me up the mountains and had me mind his gun when we were stopped by the police, who were checking whether his car was stolen (it was). These were the kinds of exploits that men boast of, and it interests me that until now I've never even mentioned them. Even in the liberated circles in which I move, no woman can afford to admit to the numbers of men she has slept with.

I wound up in graduate school in Canada, where I stayed for several years and became involved with a group of people older than myself, activists from the civil-rights and antiwar movements. We believed that the personal was political. We wanted to break down monogamy. On the whole, this scheme was a total disaster. We tried to smash monogamy, but it was ourselves who crashed, to slink off to coupledom and middle age. My boyfriend and I decided to have an "open relationship." We were an item but we could sleep with others from time to time, particularly ex-lovers who were now friends. My boyfriend had an exhaustive supply of feisty, attractive, intelligent feminists to choose from, each radiating the glamour he had once had himself when, as a draft dodger from the South, he had been Canada's student leader, burning his American passport outside the embassy. I, on the other hand, had greater difficulty in finding stocks of men to fulfil my side of the bargain. My ex-lovers were in another country and the available men seemed no more than another version of what I had already: aging, becoming bitter as they began to understand that the future was slipping away from them, a future which they had expected to be a playground of revolutionary ideas turned into action.

I returned to Britain on the last day of 1984, in the cold winter of another miners' strike. I was to have an affair so damaging that it would nearly cost me my life. When I was a human being again, I was in my late thirties. Lovers had always come along, in a convoy after a long wait, sometimes, but I had sexual confidence. I saw myself with lovers stretching to the end of my life. At thirty I had sat on a roof and realized that I was a member of the first generation of women for whom motherhood was a choice. I could choose to have sex and not children, and that is what

I did. I valued this freedom intensely. Now the men I met were divorced or separated, and their opening words were always, "The most important thing in my life is my children." They had all the emotional engagement they needed without having to take on the responsibility and risk of an equal and adult relationship. My friends were placing ads in personal columns, trying to find something they could love in the inadequate men they met through them, prepared to share the most intimate part of their lives with people they would not have had the time of day for in any other arena. It was enough that these men were solvent, unattached, disease-free, and had the right bit between the legs. The ones who bravely left husbands or partners, or were left by them, spoke of "not wanting to get involved with anyone else too quickly" and discovered that, when they were ready, there was no one to get involved with. In midlife, when women were feeling the greatest control over their sexuality, they were sexless.

So *has* there been a sexual revolution? It would be contemptuous nonsense to suggest there has not. But as the women I spoke to sensed, its potential for wholesale transformation has been only partially met. The mistrust that many women feel, the great groundswell of a withdrawal that began in the seventies, when feminism exposed the sexual revolution as a philanderer's paradise, is in itself the product of a flawed understanding. We have witnessed and defined the sexual revolution as essentially male, the indulgences of a gender in rebellion against a monolithic fixed morality. Men had been waiting millennia for a shift in women's behavior. One great technological advance, the Pill, swept away women's traditional justification for their own chastity. In the sixties, women briefly lost the power to say no, regained it because of the confidence that feminism gave them, and are only now learning a constructive yes.

I think it would be wrong to believe that my own generation of women, though perhaps the most profoundly affected by the sexual revolution and the first to have been confronted with the complex paradoxes of its choices, could be the one to *make* a sexual revolution. Younger readers and older ones will have no idea of how naive and underconfident we really were, we so-called liberated girls of Swinging London or hippy San Francisco. A new generation of women is not constructing its sexuality in terms of polar opposites, as men defined theirs against the repression of the fifties and second-wave feminists against that same male reaction. Hence the brave attempts to reclaim and feminize pornography. The mapping of the female sexual psyche by women for women is the next great subject, though not the only one with which this book is concerned.

My subject is history. What might have been forgotten in the current vogue for celebrating sexuality as somehow definitively "natural" is how sexual freedom was facilitated by a technological device, hormonal contraception. If anything is the symbol of the failure, but also of the sense of possibility that the sexual revolution gave us, it is the Pill. This book began as an attempt to chart a social history of the Pill and became a personal quest to find out what had happened to myself and a generation. If I had been born ten years earlier, my life would have been so different that it is hard to contemplate how I could in any sense have been the same person. I want to show that the sexual revolution was the product not just of mindless hedonism but of ideas. That the intellectual roots of the politics of desire were formed in Europe before the colonization of America.

Why bother to write about sexuality when, as we reach the end of our millennium, our most elementary destiny, our capacity to survive at all, is in doubt? Because until women find their own sexuality, what we will have is a single, hegemonic definition of pleasure, male sexuality: pornography, rape, the pursuit of younger and younger women, trophy wives, male fantasies structuring female consciousness and female libido. Because for twenty years—between the invention of the Pill and the beginning of the AIDS epidemic—there was a moment that had never occurred in history before, a time when sex was free from the threats of both pregnancy and disease. What, if anything, were the lasting effects of that window onto the light? How did we get where we are from there?

In fact two sexual revolutions took place simultaneously. The legalization of homosexuality and the assertion of gay pride after Stonewall have had an enduring impact on heterosexual culture and have produced a wealth of literature as gays and lesbians reclaim their history and map their future. Heterosexuals have been lazier, as if taking their new freedom as a right. There has been no real attempt to analyze the impact of the sexual revolution beyond partisan debates between the Left and Right. That is changing, and the change is taking on odd forms. For Camille Paglia,

"Eroticism is a realm stalked by ghosts. It is the place beyond the pale, both cursed and enchanted." She argues that, in trying to engineer progress, feminists and others have set themselves against nature, against sex as an atavistic force, against power. "Sexual freedom, sexual liberation. A modern delusion. We are hierarchical animals. Sweep one hierarchy away, and another will take its place. . . ."[23] The sexual pessimism of the Catholic Church, the theory that erotic passion is man's shortcut to death, has been revived. To Lawrence Osborne, as he writes in *The Poisoned Embrace,* "our sense of the erotic is indissolubly tied up with sexual pessimism. When we become sexual optimists . . . guilt-free Reichian stallions, healthy orgasmatherapists, we turn into . . . drab sexual aphids."[24] In its attempt to "exterminate temptation," sexual pessimism "succeeds only in intensifying its glamour. . . . And once its complex legacy is annulled, an eerie silence falls."

This book is called *Sexing the Millennium* not merely because we are close to the end of a thousand-year cycle. There have been two main strands in the history of ideas about sexual freedom. Paglia and Osborne reflect one only, libertinage, sex as transgression, sex as violation, freedom for the sake of rebellion rather than rebellion for the sake of freedom. Libertinage drives sex down into the dark places of the psychic imagination; it is antisocial, an existential stance. As one who frequently has to walk home in the dark, I am less enthralled by the glamour of sex as what Osborne calls a "destructive, dangerous adventure, a disequilibrium but also . . . something sacred."[25] Much of the male sexual revolution was only libertinage by another name, and rightly it degenerated into the seediness of swinging and the disintegration of group marriages. The second strand, millenarianism, is an invention of social optimism (which, ironically, we so conclusively lack at this fin de siècle). Personal freedom is indissolubly linked with a vision of transformation, of a world purged of misery and inequality. Feminism and socialism were the inventions of social optimism, of the *idea* of the future. Both Marxists and the builders of religious communes in pioneer America were united in the fervent belief in the possibility of change. The sexual revolution, I will show, has its origins in the struggles of those who fought not to explore the crevices of their own desires, but to change the world.

The term "postmodernism" is an over-flexible friend. In architecture it refers to the past as an attic stuffed with styles that can be raided to form a hip, ironic present tense. In culture, postmodernism regards all art, "high" or popular, as equal forms of discourse, narratives about reality. This is borne out in the field of political science and international relations, where the old Eurocentric liberal views of the Enlightenment are regarded as a futile attempt to arrive at universal definitions. They are discarded in favor of notions of diversity. In gender politics, diversity has proved a powerful weapon with which to argue against the centrality of the nuclear family and heterosexuality. Yet if postmodernism is right—all discourses being equal, each diversity being as good as the next—there is no chance of utopia, of the universal place of the imagination.

As we approach the end of the millennium, millenarians are, of course, irredeemably un-hip. In the new world order, we wander a broken landscape of failed visions, both social and economic. But there was a great moral adventure once, hopes that returned again and again to lighten our dreams. It is with these that we will begin.

2

The Sexual Heresy

She speaks highly in commendation of those husbands that give liberty to their wives, and will freely give consent that she should associate herself with any other of her fellow creatures, which she shall make choice of; she commends the Organ, Viol, Symbal and Tonges in Charterhouse-Lane to be heavenly musick [;] she tosseth her glasses freely, and concludeth there is no heaven but the pleasures she injoyeth on earth, she is very familiar at the first sight, and danceth the Canaries at the sound of a hornpipe.

A Ranter woman

By 1649 the military episode of the English Revolution was over and the troops were at leisure to debate the new world order. Cromwell's New Model Army had acted as an agent of mass communication, bringing together Dissenters from isolated villages. In those days, in town and country, men and women still believed in magic and witches, fairies and charms, in God and the Devil taking a personal interest in their daily lives. But the politically progressive followers of the millenarian sects disputed the existence of this spirit world. Their faith was in the future, and they trusted prophecy, the revelations of Merlin, Mother Shipton, Nostradamus, and Paracelsus. They expected that three important events would take place in the next decade: the fall of the Antichrist, the second coming, and the millennium.[1] According to the Book of Revelations, an angel had come down from heaven, holding in his hands a great chain and the key to a bottomless pit in which he had bound the Devil for a thousand years. When his time was up, Satan, the Antichrist, would be "loosed a little season" to deceive nations until he was cast into a lake of fire and brimstone. The true Christ would reign from a great white throne, the book of life would be opened, the land and the sea would give up their dead, and everyone would be judged. At the millennium, the faithful would enjoy collective salvation on earth rather than in heaven. Life would be transformed and the new dispensation would be no mere improvement on the present, but perfection itself.[2]

With Utopia imminent and established order in chaos, men were driven mad with excitement. Everything was up for debate. There was no law but natural law, and what exactly was that? It was possible to shed one's most atavistic desires in the pursuit of a lived truth, a personal becoming, both political and religious. The idea of mediators in the form of clergy was rejected. Sin was a human invention. If the Bible were approached in a spirit of scientific enquiry, it would prove to liberate men from the blind forces of Fate. Each individual had the right to a personal interpretation of his destiny.

Given this unprecedented freedom of choice in religious matters, people passed through all kinds of sects. They met in taverns and drank alcohol and smoked tobacco to heighten their spiritual vision, which acted like a drug culture to expand their consciousness. The wildest of them all were the Ranters, a short-lived anarcho-erotic movement that briefly disrupted English life for four or five years until the restoration of order, when Cromwell established his Commonwealth and instituted bourgeois stability. They were called Ranters because they were noisy—they cursed, laughed, shouted, clapped their hands, and were generally brazen, impulsive, and given to having a good time. Though they were spread throughout the country, there were said to be many thousands in London, where they inspired the writing of disapproving tracts by people who claimed to be eyewitnesses, the same sport of prurient reporting that one finds in the tabloid press today. A Puritan enemy expresses a barely concealed envy of their hedonism: ". . . they are the merriest of all devils for extempore lascivious songs . . . for healths, music, downright bawdry and dancing."[3] Their ideas were a scandal. Swearing they held as an act of defiance against bourgeois society and the imposition of Puritan middle-class standards. They were said to have discussed a good means of not working for a living—borrowing money and not paying it back. They mocked the pious moralists by lighting a candle in broad daylight to look, ironically, for their sins. They were pacifists and opposed to taxation to finance war: "Not by sword; we (holily) scorn to fight for anything; we had as lief be dead drunk every day of the week, and lie with whores i'th marketplace; and account them as good actions as taking the poor abused enslaved ploughman's money from him . . . for killing of men,"[4] one member wrote. Faced with persecution, they adopted a secret language; throughout the land during this most uncertain of times, the righteous must have felt that a fifth column of sybaritic blasphemers had invaded the soul of the nation.

At first sight the Ranters seem little more than a Dionysian cult, a demonic antisocial force. But at the heart of the Ranters' beliefs was the notion of sexual freedom as a liberating agent that brought them nearer to God. And in this they were not the first. It is possible that they had inherited ideas that had echoed down from the thirteenth century, from adherents of the Heresy of the Free Spirit, who claimed they had achieved a perfection so absolute they were incapable of sin. The Heresy was promiscuous on principle: emerging from a study of their creed "is an entirely convincing picture of an eroticism which, far from springing from a carefree sensuality, possessed above all a symbolic value as a sign of spiritual emancipation . . ."[5] writes Norman Cohn, the historian of the millenarian sects, whose study *The Pursuit of the Millennium* itself became a cult book in the 1960s. Women were particularly drawn to the Heresy: successive wars and the celibacy of a very large proportion of the male population meant that the numbers of women always exceeded the numbers of available potential husbands. To women born in the aristocracy and in the prosperous merchant class, there was no alternative role to marriage. They formed a movement of women with a passionate desire for intense mystical experience, and it acted as a kind of counter-culture for the Middle Ages, "an invisible empire, held together by the emotional bonds—which were of course often erotic bonds—between men and women."[6] To the men, just as cattle were created for the use of human beings, so a woman was born to be possessed by the Brethren. With each intimacy, she would become chaster. One of the surest marks of the "subtle in spirit" was the ability to be promiscuous without guilt. Adultery was a symbolic affirmation of emancipation. Ritual nakedness was common. One cult leader practised a special form of sexual intercourse that, he claimed, was how Adam and Eve had made love in the Garden of Eden before the Fall.

But the Heresy of the Free Spirit existed in sharp contradiction to the mainstream of society, to the great, hierarchical chain of being that descended from God to the beasts and in which every man knew his place. The rigid ordering of medieval life prohibited any earthly signs, at least in England, of the imminence of the millennium. The Ranters, however, like other sects, believed that the execution of Charles I was a prelude to greater international events, in fact a clearing of the way for the rightful sovereign, King Jesus. Very little is known of the Ranters except through writings about them, most often by their sworn enemies. Their rediscovery in the fifties and sixties, by the Marxist historians Christopher Hill and Norman Cohn, was timely, and the Ranter ideology mirrored the sexual revolution that was then going on in the universities at which Hill and Cohn taught: "Sexual promiscuity broke the peace of families and led to idleness, to a Hippie-like existence for which others had to pay by labour,"[7] Hill wrote. And, in defense of his own scholarship: "Each generation . . . rescues a new area from what its predecessors arrogantly and snobbishly dismissed as 'the lunatic fringe.' "[8]

The Ranters' leader, or chief ideologist, was Abiezer Coppe. The sect was undoubtedly a youth cult. Coppe was only thirty in 1649, the annus mirabilis of the brief Ranter years, when Charles I was executed, and other prominent Ranters were still in their twenties. His writings are reminiscent of a later anarcho-erotic poet, Allen Ginsberg: "Howl, Howl, ye nobles, howl honourable, howl ye rich men for the miseries that are coming on you . . . The true communion amongst men is to have all things in common and to call nothing one hath one's own."[9] At the height of his fame Coppe suffered from a pathological impulse to swear, probably the result of a severely repressed childhood. He would preach in the nude and pick up groupies from the crowd whom he would take to bed that night. His book, *A Fiery Flying Roll,* was condemned by Parliament to be publicly burnt as blasphemous and its author was committed to Newgate, where he managed to make a number of converts—he must have been a cheerful presence for bored prisoners. In 1651 he issued a partial recantation—the Ranters had little interest in martyrdom—though rather spoiled it by allegedly flinging nutshells about the court. He changed his name, became a doctor, died in 1672, and is buried in Barnes, West London.

Sexual freedom for women in the Ranter sect was another matter. But it is only in Ranter literature that we catch a glimpse of women's sexuality freed momentarily from the pious conventions of marriage and religion. In 1652, a woman stripped naked during a church service, crying "Welcome to the resurrection." This was common enough at Ranter meetings but rather less so at a chapel in Whitehall.[10] A Puritan divine wrote of "a Matron of great Note for Godliness and Sobriety, being perverted by them, turned so shameless a Whore, that she was Carted in the streets of London."[11] Mary Cary noted "The time is coming when not only men but women shall prophesy."[12] But while the Ranters afforded women the possibilities of openly expressing lust, in practice sexual freedom tended to work more in the favor of men than women. William Franklin joined the Ranters because a life of bourgeois respectability had let him down. In the 1640s his family was stricken by the plague and he became afflicted by some sort of mental illness that led him to believe he was God. He recovered, but something about his condition, he must have reasoned, could be exploited. Under the influence of the Ranters, he left his wife and began to live with other women. One of them was Mary Gadbury.

She was ten years younger than Franklin and earned a living in London selling trinkets to gentlewomen. Mary herself began to have visions and hear voices that assured her the monarchy and the lords were to be overthrown and replaced by the Kingdom of Christ—not a completely inaccurate prophecy, as it turned out. Her own special role in the wholesale dismantling of the state was to be privileged to see Christ face-to-face. In this condition she met Franklin, who persuaded her that he himself was the man she had been waiting for. Franklin pointed out that since God had destroyed his former body, he could no longer properly be married to his wife or even be the father of his children. A fresh start awaited them. Mary sold up everything to embrace voluntary poverty and received a divine commandment to go to Hampshire on a mission. There the couple acquired some disciples and took over the house of a local minister, as they believed was only their due, being a god and goddess. The minister's wife became discontented when Mary demanded white linen to make robes for herself; the pair was denounced to the authorities, arrested, and tried at Winchester. For a god and goddess this was only a minor setback, but, threatened with a long prison sentence, Franklin recanted, leaving Mary in the lurch. She was sent to Bridewell and whipped for several weeks. Similar events, of course, were to take place in our own century, when young women put their faith in various charismatic leaders of dubious religions.[13]

Many Ranters were itinerants, which would have been an attractive option for men who believed in sexual liberty but not its reproductive consequences. Gerald Winstanley was the leader of a rival sect, the Diggers, an early form of back-to-the-land socialism. His experience with the Ranters led him to envisage his own utopian community buttressed by structural supports including punishments for the unruly. He deplored the "excessive community of women called Ranters" and exposed the flaw in their theories of sexual liberation:

> The mother and child begotten in this manner is like to have the worst of it, for the man will be gone and leave them, and regard them no more than any other woman . . . after he hath had his pleasure. Therefore you women beware, for this ranting practice is not the restoring but the destroying power of creation . . . By seeking their own freedom they embondage others.[14]

Christopher Hill, however, points out that the Ranters' beliefs were not in themselves unsound: "Unfortunately Ranter theology leapt ahead of the technical possibilities of their society; equal sexual freedom for both sexes had to wait for cheap and effective means of birth control."[15]

The general clampdown on hedonism during the Puritan Commonwealth was absolute. The closure of the theaters, those palaces of fantasy, deception, and desire, is well known. On May 10, 1650, almost as soon as the Puritans assumed power, they introduced the Commonwealth Act, "for suppressing the detestable sins of incest, adultery and fornication."[16] The first two transgressions became felonies, carrying the sentence of death without benefit of clergy. Fornicators (married men who had sex with unmarried women) received three months in prison. Adultery was made a woman's offense, imposing and legislating the double standard. Brothel keepers were to be whipped, pilloried, branded, and gaoled for three years. A second offense was punishable by death. The Act proved impossible to enforce (a fifth of all brides were pregnant when they married and regarded a marriage contract as an expensive luxury) and in 1660 it collapsed and was not renewed.[17] After the decade-long closing down of the libido, the court of Charles II restored upper-class decadence in which licentiousness was permitted, and in which women of the lower orders could rise into court circles as gilded prostitutes and the aristocracy lusted after rough trade. Barbara Palmer, who bore the king five illegitimate children, also had liaisons with the Earl of St. Albans, a Miss Hobart, a rope dancer in his booth at St. Bartholomew's Fair, and an anonymous footman in her bath.

The poor, meanwhile, still had sex, but it was no longer linked to a revolutionary vision of the future, at least not in England. Although the Ranters, like all anarchist organizations, failed because of a lack of structure and because the vitality of their beliefs burst the bonds of a cohesive movement, their vision of a sexual revolution did not entirely die out. There had been a Ranter wing among the Quakers, and a series of splits produced the Proud Quakers, who swore and earned a living as footballers and wrestlers. Later, however, the Quakers decided to adopt a program of discipline, organization, and common sense, dropping such well-known Quaker habits like going naked as a sign of their being without sin. But throughout the century erotic freedom continued to preoccupy writers: in *The Isle of Pines* (1668), Francis Osborne suggested polygamy and marriage by renewable contract. John Hall argued that nudism was preferable for women because their naked bodies were less provocative than their clothes, a point with which the Puritan poet John Bunyan agreed.[18] Others discussed group marriage.

The millennium never came. But the nonconformist, dissenting tradition in English religious life was the backbone of the reforming movements down to our own century: pacificism and the campaigns for the liberalization of laws on contraception, divorce, abortion, and homosexuality were all rooted in the freethinking tradition that held that the state had no business legislating what should be matters of personal conscience.

Some of the millenarians realized that if God would not create his kingdom on earth, perhaps man could create it for him. The newly discovered America gave territory to the idea of Utopia, a land fit for millenarians to live in. The broadside ballad "The World Turned Upside Down," the anthem of the Digger movement, was said to have been played by the American revolutionaries when General Cornwallis surrendered to them in 1781. The phrase was also common among the Shakers, a sect that emigrated to the New World from Lancashire in 1774. Their membership was drawn from artisans, laborers, and servants, and they believed then that "they had actually risen with Christ and could live without sin; they danced, sang and smoked at their meetings."[19] The Puritan immigrants assumed that they were the chosen people, the pioneers of a perfectible future, harbingers of the new life with a capacity to wipe the slate clean. All immigrants that followed them, whether from the ghettos of Eastern Europe, the barrios of Latin America, or the cathouses of Saigon, shared this millenarian vision.

America was made for dissenters and for the possibility of establishing alternative societies. The Oneida community, which existed for twenty-five years in the middle of the nineteenth century in New York State, was established by John Humphrey Noyes, a renegade preacher who asserted that the Bible advocated communal love. His followers practiced "complex marriage," in which groups of men and women lived, worked, and made love to one another, limiting birth to a number that the community could financially support by means of coitus interruptus. When teenage boys were considered old enough to lose their virginity, adult women would initiate them—which had the double advantage, Noyes considered, of letting middle-aged women at some smooth-skinned young studs at their sexual peak, while giving the boys the opportunity to learn technique from an experienced female at *her* sexual zenith. The women were taught not to regard childrearing as their main role in life. They bobbed their hair, wore short skirts, and worked in the factories.[20]

Oneida was not the first utopian sexual community in America. The French aristocrat Charles Fourier conceived the idea of "phalansteries," living and working units of around 1,600 people that guaranteed sexual fulfilment to all, even to the most unattractive, by the intervention of erotic saints, commune members who would take care of minimum sexual needs in private suites set aside for the purpose. Monogamy and the nuclear family were outlawed because they promoted possessiveness and a narrowness of view that blinkered the grander vision. During the 1840s, dozens of experiments inspired by Fourier were established, even as far west as Texas, by advocates of free love.[21] Their members were escaping an increasingly bureaucratic state, and the Frontier was both a physical boundary to be crossed and a mental bolt-hole. There would be no millennium unless they built it themselves.

Europeans never had much chance of setting up Utopia outside society. In America dreams could be fulfilled alongside one another: a city chained to capitalism here, a commune dedicated to sexual freedom there. There was space. In Europe, however, society is all there is. There is no physical room for anything else and no hope of freedom outside culture. For several centuries, the classes remained trapped in separate sexual worlds. The aristocracy was permitted erotic freedoms and retained the old idea of marriage as powerbrokering conducted to fulfil certain financial or dynastic needs; they were unions to which no one was bound sexually, an arrangement that neither Princess Diana nor the tabloid press seems to have fully understood in our own day. The bourgeoisie, with its stress on the individual, conceived companionate marriage in which couples would invest their hopes for happiness, building a small private domain in which the emotional and the economic were tied into a protective unit of family life.

The working class continued to try to evade the legislating of its morality, not out of a commitment to social and sexual change but because sex was fun and it was free, a major attraction for the poor. Occasionally workers would have holidays, not just from their lathes and looms, but from the morality imposed by cramped homes and shared bedrooms. When the railways came they went away to seaside resorts. By the 1930s, Blackpool was known as the sin city of Britain. Researchers from Mass

Observation sent there in 1937 for an anthropological study of the proletariat at play, tabulated the pickups, the necking, the mutual masturbation,
the fucking. Between 1935 and 1938 one young man, then in his early
twenties, spent most summer Saturdays cruising:

> There was no thought of courting or marrying these girls. No, I think I
> was quite mercenary about it, I wanted sex, I wanted a one-night stand and
> a lot of the girls wanted the same thing, they knew what they were doing.
> You'd go prepared, go to the barber's and get a Durex. But that was done
> to protect you not them. I was scared of getting VD . . . You'd lie down
> [under the pier], and there'd be quite a lot of kissing and cuddling and the
> sex side of it was generally over quite quickly. I'm not saying I had what
> I wanted every time, perhaps it would be once a month, three out of every
> four attempts. Then after it was over I didn't waste any time, stand up,
> brush myself down, brush her down, we'd have a little chat. "Where are
> you staying?" If she wasn't staying any further away than the station I'd
> walk her to the steps of the boarding house. And that was it. I wouldn't
> see her again.[22]

The "sexual holiday" seems to be an unbroken tradition from the time of
the anarchic apprentice days that temporarily overturned normal relations
between master and servant, led by young lords of misrule, to the two-
week sex, sand, sun, and booze invasions of the Spanish Costas. They
represent nothing more than a defiant escape from regulation, a very brief
hiatus from the quotidian routine into the pleasure principle.

There was another group, however, not a class but the nucleus of a
movement that carried within it the seeds of the old millenarian links
between utopia and sexual freedom. Our view of the end of the nineteenth
century is formed from visual images of fin de siècle decadence. Desire as
disease—a sickly iris with a suffocating stench, lust paralyzed with fear,
genitals swollen with syphilitic sores—was the metaphor for a morally
corrupt and bankrupt culture. This was the France of the Dreyfus scandal,
a society to be blown up and cleansed by cloak-wearing anarchists with
bombs like Christmas puddings under their arms, like the antihero of
Conrad's *The Secret Agent*.[23] In those decades of sexual anarchy the first

wave of feminism made its appearance. In 1888 a novelist wrote a series of columns for the *Daily Telegraph* asking whether marriage was a failure; over 27,000 readers wrote in, mostly expressing strong approval of the idea.[24]

But as well as economic and social freedom, men and women—bohemians, the avant-garde—explored sexual freedom. In the late nineteenth century, sexual revolutionaries believed that they were the architects of a new future, not only for themselves but for the working class. In *The Origin of the Family, Private Property and the State* (1884), Engels had written of relations between the sexes that were characterized by personal freedom, not economic or reproductive necessity. Socialists believed in a new moral order; the socialist-feminist historian Sheila Rowbotham writes of their aspirations: "They were preoccupied with sexual pleasure, with how to live communally, how to live equally without fear of authority, how to love one another in a loveless world, how to create beauty democratically in the midst of ugliness and competition."[25] They were socialists when socialism had not been tried and so had not yet failed. Anything was possible. They were millenarians inasmuch as they believed in the innate goodness of humanity, in the capacity of society to be transformed, not by divine intervention but by ideas harnessed to human action. They thought paradise could be regained, often by such simple expedients as reverting to a plainer lifestyle. Their simple wooden tables and home-baked bread, their reverence for peasant customs and clothes, their admiration for the common working man (often concealing naked desire) rejected the glamour and the artifice of the fin de siècle.

The movement they founded was known as the New Life. One leader, Edward Carpenter, saw all civilization as oppressive and became interested in Eastern mysticism that challenged the order of a mechanistic universe.[26] He became infatuated with George Merrill, a working man with whom he established a household, and they built a considerable following around them in Sheffield, reaching into the heart of working-class communities with Carpenter's ideas about the breakdown of labor between classes and sexes.[27] They had less impact on the wives, who must have viewed with deep suspicion the sudden interest effete bohemians took in their husbands. For Carpenter, "working-class women remained symbols of an ideal of motherhood, nurture, suffering, labour, strength and earthiness,"[28] as Sheila Rowbotham points out. The women, with rather less enthusiasm for a return to practical peasant dress, and a longing for finery beyond the capacity of their purses to pay for, must have regarded with wild derision the New Lifers' claims that sandals should be worn at all times since boots imprisoned the feet. Our stale contemporary stereotype of the nut-cutlet-eating, sandal-wearing, bearded crank is a portrait of Edward Carpenter. He did, however, indirectly influence one important convert among the working classes. In Eastwood, Nottinghamshire, there was a group of socialists and feminists to whom Carpenter came to speak, which included one woman called Alice Dax who tried to live out the New Life. She had an affair with the young D. H. Lawrence, a fellow member, who depicted her as Clara in *Sons and Lovers*. Carpenter's book, *Love's Coming of Age*, was published in America and had a profound effect on the bohemians of Greenwich Village, where its ideas hung around long enough to influence the men and women who headed out west to found Californian communes later in the century.

The First World War, the sunrise of modernism, spawned a new breed of marginal men and women, part of an early club culture that Marek Kohn has described in his study of drug-taking during the period. With a shortage of men on the home front, a disruptive moment of Dionysian disorder slipped through the patriotic rhetoric. Lady Diana Cooper had a story of a couple of women arriving in a Rolls-Royce at a music hall, and giving the commissionaire a sovereign if he could produce a couple of guardsmen for them to entertain. "The air," she wrote, "is electric with this current of abnormal sexuality." Kohn describes a "carnival of female uncontainability and dominance" in a London in which the rigid distinction between prostitute and respectable woman was eroding.[29] In Daphne du Maurier's novel *Rebecca*, the marriage of Maxim de Winter to the eponymous villainess took place around the time of the Great War. Max's rationale for his murder of his first wife is her revelation of her life in London: "She sat there, laughing, her black hair blowing in the wind; she told me about herself, told me things I shall never repeat to a living soul. I knew then what I had done, what I had married."[30] What Rebecca might have got up to is described by two scholars, writing of the period from the vantage point of the thirties, almost too shocked to describe the Ranteresque orgies that took place while the men died in the mud on the other side of the Channel:

> Frequently parties were organized, consisting of a number of women and only one or two men, and generally only after prolonged bouts of drinking combined with drug-taking the worst sexual orgies took place. Cocaine addicts, losing all self-control and all moral sense, would practise every variant of "group love" which sometimes took such disgusting forms that it would be impossible to describe them even in a scientific work.[31]

Among intellectuals and political bohemians, the inherited ideals of the New Life movement and a rejection of the old sexual order after women had played their part in the war led to a new confidence and determination to live out the adage that the personal is political. Dora Black, who was to marry the philosopher, freethinker, and aristocrat Bertrand Russell, deliberately lost her virginity on a liner crossing to New York during the First World War. Her code placed at its pinnacle love, an airy idea to which many of her contemporaries were breathlessly addicted, infusing it with impossible nobility and grafting it onto the most hopelessly naive kind of idealism: "I held that one entered into a sexual relationship for love which was given and received freely; this might last long, it could also be very brief. No other motive but such love, which must involve awareness and acceptance of the other's personality, was to be tolerated,"[32] she wrote in her autobiography. Dora wanted to be a sexually fulfilled single woman when the only available sexual role for an unmarried woman was the kept mistress, whose job was seduction and whose pay was flats, clothes, and jewels. These were women who knew no other work and when they were abandoned they sank into poverty and starvation. The novels of Jean Rhys are full of them, always waiting in a flat for a letter with a check so they can buy a dress in which to go out to a café to nurse a drink and wait for another man to come along who will give them a check. If they were not skilled businesswomen, shrewd at managing their investments, they met sordid ends.

When Dora became pregnant Russell pressured her to marry him, which she regarded as a hypocritical move to legitimize an heir who would, after all, inherit his title. Dora objected to everything connected with bourgeois marriage and its property rights that extended to the possession of persons, its criminalizing of adultery encouraging jealousy and suspicion:

> The claim of Bloomsbury to shaping the future lay as much in its views on sex, the marriage laws and women's life in this aspect, as in political power and economics. . . . The efforts of men and women of my generation to strive for these ideals in human relations and for women's emancipation brought conflict and even tragedy into our private lives. But this has been the burden of the story, not only in this country, but wherever in the world the battle for women's liberation has been fought.[33]

Bertie's motives in his pursuit of sexual freedom were rooted less in political idealism than the symptoms of a severely repressed Victorian childhood that he claimed had made him impotent, except when carried away by sudden sexual passion. His desire didn't last for the duration. Nor did the Russell marriage survive the couple's experiments with free love. At her club in London one day, Dora was handed a scrawled note from Hannah, her Irish cook, telling her she must return home to Cornwall at once. There she found Hannah mounting guard over the two children and refusing to let their governess come near them because she was sleeping with the master. Dora was having an affair of her own, with a young man in town, but she "could not help feeling upset: an affair in one's own home with someone in charge of one's children is especially wounding."[34] The cook, however, had to go; in the Russell moral universe, adultery was one thing, a working-class woman imposing conventional morality on impressionable infants was another.

Armed with this dubious understanding of class, Dora traveled to the Soviet Union, where the commissar Alexandra Kollontai, a real sexual revolutionary, was mapping the moral framework of the new communist state. There were stringent assaults on prostitution (backed by Trotsky, who wrote on the subject); divorce by mutual consent; a father's maintenance of his children was mandatory; in a childless marriage an earning wife was obliged, upon divorce, to help her ex-husband financially for the first six months; abortion was fully legal. It was the most advanced program for women's emancipation that has ever existed, and it was enshrined in the Soviet constitution; by 1930, thirteen years after the revolution, Stalin had got rid of it, replacing it with a Soviet version of the Fascist view of women tied to *kinder und kirche*, the church replaced here by the Party meeting. In 1929, Dora also attended the World Congress of the League for Sexual Reform, where papers were delivered by George Bernard Shaw ("The Need for Expert Opinion on Sexual Reform"), by Vera Brittain ("The Failure of Monogamy"), by Marie Stopes (on birth control), by the novelist Naomi Mitchison ("Intelligent Use of Contraceptives"), and by Russell ("The Taboo on Sex Knowledge").[35]

In the end, Bertie left Dora for a younger woman after years of Dora's idealism sank into maternal nurturing: caring for her children, her school, her husband, and an ailing lover. But the ideas of the Bloomsbury group, which included the extraordinary marriage of Vita Sackville-West and Harold Nicolson, both homosexual, and Virginia Woolf, whose novels were outspoken in their defense of women's rights, began to be seen not as a lunatic fringe of upper-class cranks but a genuine alternative to middle-class moral virtue. It attracted the young modernists, readers of the suppressed texts of D. H. Lawrence, Henry Miller, and James Joyce; admirers of abstract painting, free verse, Corbusier armchairs, and houses with plain walls and no ceiling roses, seekers after honesty and authentic experience. In his autobiography, the travel writer Norman Lewis, then a young man still living with his parents in Enfield, North London, wrote of his alliance with the exotic and flamboyant daughter of a Sicilian businessman. Both were desperate to be free from the restraints of respectability:

It was to be a marriage with a difference, a bold experiment undertaken with open eyes, a step in a new direction. Society—in this case represented by Ernestina's father and mother—would demand a signed legal paper, and they should have it. Thereafter concessions would stop. We agreed that a working partnership between a man and a woman could be a valuable arrangement, but there were to be no ties or sanctions. Ernestina would keep her own name, and we declared ourselves free to come and go as we pleased, and to part—if it ever came to that—without claim on each other. Needless to say we were both earnest students of Bertrand Russell, and much as we agreed with his views on the subject of free love, we proposed to go a step further. This, we agreed, was not a love match. Romantic love was dismissed at best as an invention of Victorian novelists, at worst a psychotic interlude. It was an arrangement inconceivable in any period outside the thirties when revaluation of old customs could take extreme forms, and it was destined not to work as well as we thought it would.[36]

When war came, any thoughts of progressive and experimental relationships disappeared, but sex erupted under the protective cover of the blackout. Joan Wyndham points out that the postwar generation seems to think that its parents were too busy "thinking noble thoughts, doing war work, and lurking in shelters. How naïve and presumptuous!" Clambering over the ruins of a bombed house at the age of seventeen, she heard her friend cry out to her: " 'Come down! You can't die a virgin.' These words made a tremendous impression on me, and apparently on young girls all over London, because soon my convent friends were telling me: 'Oh Joan, I've done it at last, and it's *marvellous!* You don't know what you're missing!' " A month later, during a particularly bad air raid, Joan succumbed: "I didn't enjoy it very much, but I hadn't expected to. It was a rite of passage." Later she joined the WAAF. "A WAAF could have sex without guilt," she wrote. "She was only doing her bit for England and its brave boys." Unusually, Joan Wyndham carried the memory of the war years through the fifties and marriage until the sixties, when she got herself a boy-toy, dropped acid in Ibiza, and became a fifty-year-old hippie.[37] Sexual revolutionaries sat out the fifties but they were still there. In a decade that ruthlessly imposed the nuclear family as the building block of the new mass-consumerist economy, there were some, like the biologist Alex Comfort, who joined anarchist organizations and wrote futuristic novels; he would eventually publish *The Joy of Sex*. They bided their time and finally the sixties came around.

*   *   *

The millenarian tradition was not the only culture to inform the politics of sexuality. There were also the libertines, so suited to our own postmodernist times, who believed progress to be a delusion. The libertines had style. They exhausted the taxonomy of desire. They turned their attention away from society inward to the body, which they regarded as a pleasure machine or unmapped territory whose erotic geography they wanted to explore, discovering every conceivable site of sensation. In the century after Britain's civil war, the libertines would deconstruct the moral order by demonstrating that virtue brings no rewards, as the sexual torments of Justine, de Sade's creation, were designed to teach her; sex equaled power and the capacity to control others' lives. A handful of female libertines made fortunes as brothel keepers. To George Steiner, de Sade's perversions prefigured the Industrial Revolution, flesh as raw material, as parts "torn or twisted in turn with the impartial, cold frenzy of the piston, the steam-hammer and the pneumatic drill."[38] To de Sade himself, his brothels and torture chambers were laboratories. His fictional victims learn that goodness is merely a means of social control and that love transforms nothing. There is no hope of a release from suffering unless it is through death. But at the end of the road is no liberation, as Angela Carter so dramatically proved in her brilliant critique of de Sade:

> The pleasure of the libertine philosophers derives in a great part from the knowledge they have overcome their initial disgust. By the exercise of the will, they have overcome repugnance and so, in one sense, are liberated from the intransigence of reality. This liberation from reality is their notion of freedom; the way to freedom lies through the privy. But the conquest of morality and aesthetics, of shame, disgust and fear, the pursuit of greater and greater sexual sophistication in terms of private sensation lead them directly to the satisfactions of the child; transgression becomes regression and, like a baby, they play with their own excrement.[39]

Libertinage is the antithesis of millenarianism. For its acolytes, there is nothing ahead but darkness, silence, despair. Only through the body's pleasure can we feel, experience, and be. Libertines know there is no self, only a collection of masks, the flesh itself becoming a series of costumes.

Sadist and masochist, switching roles, test the limits of identity. Human relationships are a charade. Sex is the ritual playing out of power, parodying the political. The eighteenth-century libertines had been prepared to cross every known sexual frontier out of a kind of existentialism, an egotism that made them believe they were separate from the rest of humanity. Libertinage is an erotic politics for the end of a millennium, when you believe that there will not be another thousand years. It is safe sex for a crowded planet about to be annihilated by nuclear war or environmental disaster. It reflects the pain it witnesses all around it. It leads to death; why not? Everything else does.

Millenarians, to our age, are naive, idealistic, earnest, and wrong. They deserve the contempt they get from the fashionable; they are ridiculously enthusiastic and make notoriously unreliable predictions. They dream of a world that can never be, for utopia is impossible. In gilded masks with powdered beauty spots—the very picture of a degenerate Venetian nobleman—or leather masks and Lycra all-in-ones, libertines never date. We love them for their decadence, their style, their honest depiction of sex and death. But let us not be too scornful about the millenarians. After all, what did the libertines ever give us apart from syphilis? It is to the millenarians, however, and their half-baked ideas that we owe the sexual revolution. Millenarians rejected church and state control over personal relations; their philosophy is a refusal of official notions of "sin," an invention by the ruling class to suppress the poor. Libertines never went on protest marches to legalize abortion or homosexuality or engaged in protracted and bothersome committee work to prepare the legislation. But sexual freedom for the millenarians had reached an impasse by the beginning of this century. For the moment they began to extend erotic liberty to women they returned to the problem Gerald Winstanley had identified: the need for a technology that would free sex from reproduction.

3

The All-American
Offshore Population Laboratory

Take Spain and move it to a tropical island. Hire a cast of thousands to play friendly, welcoming people who speak at least some English. Set design is strictly Cecil B. DeMille: graceful Old World buildings, Gothic cathedrals, flower-filled plazas. When you are looking for exotic locations, miles and miles of white sand beaches, plus an unbelievable rainforest and mountains, you come to Puerto Rico.

Puerto Rico Tourist Board brochure

This old maternity dress I've got is going in the garbage
The clothes I'm wearin' from now on won't take up so much yardage
Miniskirts and hot pants with a few little fancy frills
Yeah I'm making up for all those years, since I've got the Pill.

"The Pill," country-and-western song from the
coalfields of Tennessee

Nora Ephron, American screenplay writer and journalist, moved to New York in 1962 having just graduated from Wellesley, the Ivy League women's college. She was starting a new life, so she knew she had to do something about birth control. *The Group*, Mary McCarthy's novel of a gang of Vassar girls' sexual progress through the thirties, had just been published and a famous scene from it, in which a leading character has a diaphragm fitted, led Nora Ephron to the Margaret Sanger clinic in a brownstone on Sixteenth Street, at the edge of Greenwich Village. Intimidated by her welcome there, she untruthfully announced that she was engaged. She sat in a room with eight or ten other women until a nurse came in with an attaché case that opened out to reveal a rubber relief of a woman's internal reproductive organs. The nurse demonstrated three contraceptive methods: she rubbed the model with contraceptive cream; she inserted a diaphragm into it; finally she shot it up with an IUD. Given the examples on offer, Nora Ephron chose the Pill. All she knew about it was "that it had been tested on several thousand Puerto Rican women and not one of them had had a child in years." Later she recognized that

> They contained a larger dose of estrogen than they do now, and they were also larger pills. Nobody was sure if they caused blood clots or prevented them, or if they caused breast cancer or prevented it . . . But it began a long and happy relationship between me and my birth control pills.
>
> When I first started with the pill, I would stop taking them every time I broke up with someone. I had a problem making a commitment to sex; I guess it was a hangover from the whole fifties virgin thing. The first man I went to bed with, I was in love with and wanted to marry. The second one I was in love with, but didn't have to marry him. With the third one I thought I *might* fall in love. It was impossible for me to think that I might be a person who "had sex," so whenever I had no boyfriend it was always a terrible emotional mess. I couldn't start sleeping with someone until I could begin the pill's cycle again. It was awful. Finally, my new gynecologist explained it all to me: "Dahlink, who knows what's coming around the corner?"[1]

Puerto Rico. Thirty years later a foreigner could go into a bookstore in any major American city, including Cambridge, Massachusetts, home of the most important and powerful university in the world, ask for a book on Puerto Rico, and perhaps be directed to the Latin America section. Puerto Rico, a Caribbean island and American colony since 1898, was a vacation destination. And the naive foreigner would be told in all seriousness that for an insight into Puerto Ricans, their customs and culture, one could do no better than to make a close study of the musical *West Side Story*. Puerto Rico produced, it seemed from these bookstore conversations, nothing but Hispanics who loved to divide themselves into gangs and conduct warfare against other ethnic minorities, preferably from the drivers' seats of vehicles customized to reflect their style and taste, emitting carefully coded sexual messages to young women who might be enticed into the passenger seat. What no one seemed to know was that there would have been no sexual revolution without Puerto Rico, land of stereotypes, an island that in this century became the world's most important test site in the search for safe, effective contraception.

For millennia women had tried to regulate childbirth by the application of various unpleasant messes. The Egyptians recommended plugs of honey, gum, acacia, and crocodile dung. The Greeks had a specific term for contraception, *atokion,* and the Romans a vaguer one, *venenum,* which meant poison.[2] A second-century physician argued that if a woman did not have an orgasm during intercourse she would prevent the semen from reaching her uterus; she should then get up, sneeze, and drink something cold. There were reports from Byzantium of the efficacy of the right testicle of a wolf wrapped in oil-soaked wool. In ancient China women were advised to swallow twenty-four live tadpoles in the early spring to ensure five years free of conception. Alfred the Great amended this to substitute bees for tadpoles, a considerably more painful form of protection. And lest men should escape these nasty remedies, a sixth-century Roman suggested that reluctant fathers should drink a draft consisting of the burnt testicles of a mule mixed with a decoction of willow.[3] But until the invention of the condom, contraception was a woman's secret, literally the stuff of old wives' tales, for who better to transmit information to young brides than experienced older women?

In 1564, Gabriello Fallopio (who discovered and had named after him the fallopian tubes) described a small sheath made of linen that could protect the penis and guard against syphilis.[4] During the First World War condoms were distributed semi-officially to the troops and were to be equated forever, in the minds of older generations, with disease rather than birth control, making condoms particularly unpalatable to wives who considered them part of the professional apparatus of prostitutes. They were purchased in England by mail, or you could go for a haircut and when back and sides were red-raw and trim, the barber would euphemistically ask, "Will there be anything for the weekend, sir?" In America, a federal court decision in 1930 had permitted the shipping and advertising of condoms, and by mid-decade they were selling at drugstores, gas stations, and newsstands. As a young man, Malcolm X supplemented his earnings from shining shoes at a Boston dance hall by selling rubbers.[5] Although they were legally available to women, only a prostitute would buy one.

At the beginning of the nineteenth century, America and western Europe became uneasily aware of a different kind of millennium. Where feudal societies had struggled against disease and infant mortality to keep up adequate numbers to maintain agricultural settlements, the new science of demography warned that childbirth must no longer remain a private subject for women but was now a matter of national significance with possibly traumatic economic effects. Thomas Malthus, in his *Essay on Population* published in 1798, argued that large families put a strain on available resources and that social improvement could be attained only if the lower classes exercised moral restraint, which was to be achieved by postponing marriage.[6] But it was the middle classes who enthusiastically embraced birth control, particularly during the economic recession of the 1880s. The trial of William Bradlaugh and Annie Besant in 1877, accused of disseminating "obscene" literature about birth control, only served to make known to the working class that "something" was available.

To the socialists, communists, and revolutionaries of the early twentieth century, birth control was a most central demand for liberation. In 1910, Emma Goldman, the anarchist, made a historic link between contraception and women's rights and won to her cause Margaret Sanger, a tiny, charismatic redhead and New York housewife who had been born in 1879. Sanger soon broke with Goldman's radicalism, but a trip to France in 1913 astonished her with its revelation of the sexual sophistication of French wives. Back in America she dropped the old term that had been used for contraception up to then—"neo-Malthusianism"—and coined "birth control." At the same time in England, Marie Stopes, one year younger than Sanger, had discovered in 1912 that something was wrong with her year-old marriage to a Canadian botanist. It slowly dawned on the university-educated daughter of an enlightened upper-class family, with a doctorate in paleobotany, that the union had not been consummated. She filed for an annulment and began a four-year study of sex that was to result in her book *Married Love,* for decades the sex manual of middle-class English women.[7]

The lives of these two egocentric women were to run more or less parallel courses. Both reversed the belief that sex was repugnant to women. Now sexual fulfilment became a marital duty and, supported by Freud, any reluctance or lack of interest was ascribed to frigidity. Both set up pioneering birth-control clinics that, until the state and doctors took over their work, provided the only contraceptive services available to the majority of women. In doing so, they removed contraception from the position it had occupied for centuries, down among the women, and medicalized it. They advocated various forms of female barrier methods that could only be fitted by a physician in an approved clinic. By winning over the medical establishment to their views, they gave birth control scientific respectability.[8] Both were opposed to contraception for unmarried women. Both were passionate eugenicists, believing that only by a drastic reduction in the birthrate of what they considered the lower orders and lesser races could society advance. Sanger and Stopes were deadly rivals, and in the end Sanger must have known that it was her own work that was to have the wider significance. For, in her eighties, she became one of the magic circle of men and women who were responsible for the development of the oral contraceptive.

The Pill was a cultural product as no other pharmaceutical has ever been. It was developed in a climate of passionate optimism in which it was believed that science was poised to solve all social and economic problems. After the Second World War, in the frantic redevelopment of industry, transport networks, and health care, people became mesmerized by growth, by the statistics of expansion, with the city as the metaphor for that sense of acceleration. In those postwar years, the idea of the future, until then a concept limited to the political vocabulary of radicals and the avant-garde, took hold in the mass imagination. The World's Fair just before the war, with its futuristic pavilions of the city of 1960; the space race; the sudden availability of consumer goods (particularly commodities like vacuum cleaners and washing machines, which mechanized the home and liberated women from the worst drudgery of domestic labor); what Harold Wilson was to call the "white heat of the technological revolution": all of this combined to convince people on both sides of the Atlantic that everyday life was subject to scientific perfectibility. In the Soviet Union, Stalin believed that communism could be hydraulically hoisted into place by training up a generation of engineers to control every aspect of Soviet life through Five-Year Plans. In the west, industry that had been destroyed by bombing or geared to producing instruments of destruction retooled to build a consumer paradise on earth. By the 1960s conservatives and radicals were briefly linked intellectually by a shining image of Utopia. It is this more than anything else that divides those born before and after 1960. On the earlier side of that dividing line is a generation with a profound and millennial vision of the future.

But this bright certainty that a brave new world was imminent was darkened by another vision: of the planet crushed and shifted off its orbit by the weight of an equivalent amount of human flesh. It engendered a deep anxiety that was later fed by the identification of a new syndrome in 1965: "future shock," coined by Alvin Toffler to describe "the shattering stress and disorientation that we induce in individuals by subjecting them to too much change in too short a time."[9] Americans' lives in the stable fifties were full of fear: of communism as a kind of infection, often mythologized and reified in science-fiction literature as aliens silently insinuating themselves into small-town life. If the Russians were the invaders of the night, then the Chinese were a yellow tide that would swamp the world. Only American technology, it was thought, could correct the violent tendency toward the impoverishment and racial overwhelming of the western middle classes.

From the beginning of the century many had been seduced by the pseudoscience of eugenics, a quasi-Darwinian weeding out of "degenerates." In 1910, Winston Churchill had drawn up a scheme to sterilize criminals, paupers, unemployables, prostitutes, ne'er-do-wells, and the feeble-minded, and incarcerate others in forced-labor camps.[10] Even the Fabian writer of science fiction H. G. Wells was convinced by eugenics. But by 1945 the world had become aware that such a grand experiment had just been conducted in the Nazi death camps under the intellectual aegis of *Mein Kampf*, and eugenics suddenly declined in popularity. What replaced it was population control. Every aspect of reproduction, or the prevention of it, had to be taken out of the hands of women and given over to scientific and bureaucratic "experts" who would in future manage all aspects of birth. The last vestiges of moral doubt about contraception vanished.

This nightmare vision of the future, its paranoia and bogus scientism, is nowhere better communicated than by Margaret Sanger, by then about eighty-eight and a convinced and rabid racist:

> I consider that the world and almost all our civilization for the next twenty-five years is going to depend on a simple, cheap, safe contraceptive to be used in poverty-stricken slums and jungles, and among the most ignorant people. . . . I believe that now, immediately, there should be national sterilization for certain dysgenic types of our population who are being encouraged to breed and would die out were the government not feeding them.[11]

She was writing around 1951 to Katherine Dexter McCormick, who, since they first met in the twenties, had taken a keen interest in Sanger's work.

Katherine McCormick was born in 1875, one of those late-Victorian feminists whose intelligence, vitality, and determination resulted in major social changes in women's lives. In 1900 she entered the Massachusetts Institute of Technology as a science major. There she met her future husband, Stanley McCormick, heir to the fabulous wealth of the International Harvester Company, which had put the Midwest to the plough. In 1904 they married, but two years later Stanley went mad. Diagnosed as a schizophrenic, he became a recluse in their baronial mansion in Santa Barbara, California, where he was attended to for the rest of his life by a staff of forty gardeners and six musicians who played to him while he ate his solitary meals. What was the continuing nature of their relationship through those decades of madness? They remained married, but Katherine McCormick determined that they should have no children, for it was still believed that insanity was hereditary. After a long legal battle with Stanley's father, she managed to gain financial control over the estate and put it to work to fund her favorite causes. She joined the women's suffrage movement, occasionally contributing funds or the use of her château in

France to Sanger and the birth-control movement. She was six feet tall and for the rest of her life continued to wear the fashions that were in vogue at the time of her marriage.

A great deal of the money from the McCormick estate went into research for a cure for schizophrenia; she funded the Neuroendocrine Research Foundation in Worcester, Massachusetts, which undertook numerous unsuccessful attempts to treat the illness with adrenal steroids. After Stanley's death in 1947, Mrs. McCormick seemed to lose interest. Then, suddenly, sometime in the early fifties she developed a passion for a new project. In her seventies, she had become infected with the same terror of a population running out of control as everyone else. Reputedly, she burst into the office of the head of the Foundation to ask what he was going to do about it.

The person she needed to talk to was Gregory Pincus, commonly nicknamed Goody, born in New Jersey in 1904, the son of a Jewish immigrant farmer. Pincus went to Harvard and became an experimental biologist when both the educated and illiterate were demonized by fears of Jewish scientists out to discover and take control of the origin of life itself. Throughout the thirties, Pincus kept getting press coverage for his work on the parthenogenesis of rabbits, a contemporary "virgin birth" scandal. In 1936 he appeared in *Colliers* magazine as the controller of a Wellsian world; he was depicted with an untidy tangle of curly hair, a cigarette hanging from his mouth, holding a large white rabbit in "slender, almost effeminate hands." The rabbit, one was led to believe, would remain neither furry nor cutely snuffle-nosed after the sinister Semite with Dr. Frankenstein tendencies was finished with it. The reporter, J. D. Ratcliff, warned that Pincus's work would create a world in which "woman would be a dominant, self-sufficient entity, able to produce young without the aid of man . . . man's value would shrink. . . . The mythical land of the Amazons would then come to life. A world where woman would be self-sufficient; man's value precisely zero."[12] Pincus was married with two children and living in a conventional household. He did not regard himself as a sexual revolutionary. The sensational publicity combined with the anti-Semitism common in universities then lost him his chance of tenure at Harvard. Just before war broke out he found himself at Cambridge University, embittered because institutionalized racial prejudice at home had forced him into such close proximity to Hitler. Luckily, a donation from Lord Rothschild allowed him to move to Worcester, Massachusetts, to continue his research into fatherless rabbits throughout the war.

By 1951 he had begun testing the contraceptive value of steroids with a small grant of $3,100 from the Planned Parenthood Federation of America. In 1937, researchers at the University of Pennsylvania had shown that large injections of progesterone inhibited ovulation in rats by tricking the body into thinking it was pregnant. Progesterone, which occurs naturally in our own bodies, causes the lining of the uterus to thicken, ready for the implantation of the fertilized egg. The placenta then sends large amounts of progesterone through the bloodstream, putting out a message that the body is in a state of pregnancy. It had worked on rats. It worked on rabbits. Furthermore, a man called Russell Marker, more adventurer than scientist, had discovered that hormones could be synthesized from the roots of wild Mexican yams, so there were large supplies of artificial progesterone available.

Katherine McCormick wrote to Margaret Sanger to ask if there was anything she could do to help the population crisis. Sanger wrote in turn to Mrs. McCormick about Pincus's rabbits. In 1953, McCormick moved from Santa Barbara to Boston and met Pincus at the Worcester Foundation. She promised $10,000 a year immediately and subsequently gave between $150,000 and $180,000 a year to the Foundation and its contraceptive research team for the rest of her life. Another man was recruited to the team, John Rock, a gynecologist who was an expert in the application of discoveries by endocrinologists to clinical gynecology. Rock was a Catholic and a father of five. His goal was to find a method of birth control that would be acceptable to the Vatican. He believed that a hormonal method of interfering with the reproductive cycle very early on could not be regarded as a barrier to pregnancy, which, according to Catholic doctrine, the Bible quite specifically prohibited. Margaret Sanger had initially opposed bringing Rock into the Pill project, arguing that his Catholicism was incompatible with contraceptive research. She did not trust him. But in public-relations terms a team headed by a Jew could only benefit from association with a Catholic.

Other scientists were to play a crucial role in the development of the

Pill: Carl Djerassi at the Syntex Corporation in Mexico, who synthesized progesterone initially to regulate menstrual disorders, and Min-Chueh Chang, the biologist who tested it on rabbits. None of these fathers of the Pill had any idea what they were preparing. "I was not interested in liberating women," Rock told a journalist when he was ninety-three. "That's not why I was interested in the Pill. Women ought to stay at home and take care of their men and babies." Did Dr. Chang's wife or daughters take the Pill? "I never discussed it with [them]," he said in 1983. "My personal attitude is, if you can help it, don't take any pill, even aspirin."[13]

By 1954, Pincus had graduated from rabbits and was ready to carry out clinical trials on women. But Massachusetts, like many other states in America, had Comstock laws (named after the late-nineteenth-century anti-vice crusader) that made contraceptive research illegal. Katherine McCormick, using a metaphor borrowed from the lab, asked Sanger, "How can we get a 'cage' of ovulating females to experiment with?"[14] They did not need to look far. Right on their own doorstep was a Third-World population of second-class American citizens, members of America's only colony. They were poor and they were brown and there were, it was generally agreed, too many of them.

Puerto Rico, "The Shining Star of the Caribbean" according to its tourist board, is the last of a string of islands coming like a full stop after Cuba and the territory shared by Haiti and the Dominican Republic. When Columbus found it on his second voyage to the New World in 1493, it was populated by the Taino Indians who, like all the other indigenous people of the Caribbean, did not survive Spanish settlement. For the next 300 years it was ruled, from a distance, by Spain. In photographs taken as late as the 1940s, families of eight children appear with only the youngest staring into the camera's lens, for as soon as boys or girls were old enough to learn they would avert their eyes from their betters as a gesture of respect. In 1898, Puerto Rico became the object of a minor skirmish in the Spanish-American War; after a seventeen-day military campaign it was ceded to the U.S., which for some time had coveted a strategic outpost in the Antilles, as an American equivalent to Gibraltar.

Large tracts of the hundred-mile-long island are still under the control of the American military. The population was the usual genetic mixture of Spanish, African (from the slaves who were transported there), and native Indian. The economy consisted of three exportable products, what were called the "after-dinner commodities" of coffee, sugar, and tobacco. In Puerto Rico, however, they didn't have the dinner.[15] To the hygiene-obsessed American eye, Puerto Ricans were dirty, ignorant, and lazy, "the victims of a cultural lack of concern about time."[16] They were tubercular, they had no sanitation, they drank contaminated water, and four-fifths of them were illiterate. But after the Jones Act of 1917, they were American citizens.

By 1922, enlightened members of the Puerto Rican bourgeoisie had discovered Margaret Sanger: "Let us take [our island] out of poverty by reducing the number of mouths to be fed, the number of feet to be shod, the number of bodies to be clothed, the number of children to be educated. How? By following with due seriousness the doctrines held by Mrs. Sanger in the United States," wrote Luiz Manoz Marin, the son of one of Puerto Rico's most prominent politicians. And in a subsequent interview, he characterized the island as "a raft adrift with 1,300,000 victims who scratch, bite and kick to obtain the few supplies on board."[17] In 1928, Puerto Rico was hit by a hurricane that dramatically affected the island's agrarian economy and plunged the population into deeper poverty. The Brookings Institute conducted a survey that concluded that the rising population was the key impediment to economic growth.[18] Emigration was considered by the Americans to be the nightmare scenario. Rexford Tugwell, the fantastically named U.S. Assistant Secretary of Agriculture, wrote down his impressions while on a fact-finding mission to the island:

> I rather dislike to think that our falling fertility must be supplemented by these people. But that will probably happen. Our control of the tropics seems to me certain to increase immigration from here and the next wave of the lowly . . . succeeding the Irish, Italians and Slavs . . . will be these mulatto, Indian, Spanish people from the south of us. They make poor material for social organization but you are going to have to reckon with them.[19]

It was this xenophobic terror that made Puerto Rico, for the next thirty years, America's offshore experimental laboratory for birth control. For much of that time its research was funded by Clarence Gamble, heir to the Procter & Gamble fortune. The diaphragm was tested because, Gamble was informed, Puerto Rican women were constitutionally adapted for it, "due to the lithe figures of the women, their long fingers, lack of inhibitions in regard to sex and their teachability."[20] Researchers tried foam, sponges, powders and jellies. They got the cooperation of the sugar companies and opened clinics right on the plantations. The sugar interests were keen supporters of contraception at a time when they were introducing labor-saving technology that would replace the work force with machines.[21] In 1937 all final legal obstacles to the development of the population laboratory were cleared with the passing of two laws. Law 116 created a Eugenics Board to which applications for compulsory sterilization for medical or moral reasons could be referred. And Law 133 amended the penal code to remove the clause that made the dissemination of contraceptive information and practices a felony.[22] Puerto Rico now had the most advanced legal constitution on contraception in the United States.

Puerto Rico was a Catholic country in name only. The Church had always appeared to the people as a foreign presence. The Spanish at first imported their own priests; later they came from the Irish-American communities in the United States and, after the Castro revolution, from the disestablished churches of Cuba. At the turn of the century, more than half of all Puerto Rican marriages were not officially certified by the state, and women had children by more than one partner, giving them the luxury of support from several families. In the fifties, Adeline Pendleton Satterthwaite, who supervised the clinical trials of the Pill, would find two women side-by-side in hospital beds, each in labor with a child by the same man: "I asked these women, 'How do you feel about this?' And they would say, 'Men are too dynamic, they want too much, they tire us out.' They sometimes talked about their own sexual feelings, but not very often." As part of the early attempts at colonizing the island and Americanizing the population, evangelical Protestant missionaries and Pentecostal sects set up hospitals, promising the poorest and most economically disadvantaged millennial salvation through Christ. And so while the Catholic Church in the thirties, supported by American Catholic women's organizations, attempted to curb the influence of the birth controllers, the antisexual doctrines of Catholicism were simply not well enough internalized by the island people.

By the end of the war emigration to the mainland was getting out of control. Around 65,000 Puerto Ricans had served in the armed forces and many had been stationed in the U.S. Glimpsing life in America, they decided to stay and bring their families with them. In 1945 there were 13,500 Puerto Ricans in New York. By 1946 there were almost 40,000. When Leonard Bernstein originally proposed the idea of what was to become *West Side Story* in 1946, he imagined it as the Romeo-and-Juliet story of a feud between Jews and Catholics. By 1955 he was writing in his diary: "We're fired again by the Romeo notion; only now we have abandoned the whole Jewish-Catholic premise as not very fresh and have come up with what I think is going to be it: two teen-age gangs, one the warring Puerto Ricans, the other the self-styled 'Americans.' Suddenly it all springs to life."[23]

Confronted with mass exodus, the government of Puerto Rico decided to initiate an offensive that would drag the island into the twentieth century. It was called Operation Bootstrap, and its aim was to create an environment of "assured profitability for mainland venture capital"[24] through tax incentives, the creation of a technological infrastructure, and the training of a literate, motivated workforce. At the same time, a traditional agrarian economy would be converted into an industrialized one and the island would be promoted as a major Caribbean tourist destination. Slums would be razed and the downtrodden population, whose life expectancy was then forty-six years, would be turned into an army of smiling waiters and chambermaids.[25]

In 1956, Dr. Edris Rice-Wray, medical director of the Family Planning Association, wrote to Clarence Gamble to inform him that Pincus had perfected an oral contraceptive tablet and suggested that the Worcester Foundation be invited to test it on Puerto Rico's population of impoverished women. There is no doubt that Puerto Rican women were crying out for birth control, anything that would limit their families and reduce their poverty. Adeline Pendleton Satterthwaite arrived on the island in the summer of 1953 to work at the Ryder Memorial Hospital in Humacao, established in 1914 by the American Missionary Association, a Baptist organization "committed to the removal of caste wherever its sins were found."[26] Her husband, a Quaker, had died in China in 1949, only two years after they were married. Adeline had grown up in a family dedicated to notions of service and spent the rest of her life in furthering the cause of family planning in the Third World. "The women who came for pre-natal care all said they wanted to be operated on," she says. "This really threw me. I thought they wanted a caesarean section. And then they explained that what they wanted was a post-partum tubal ligation and they were doing a great deal of those at the hospital at that time, for anyone who had delivered a third living child. It was suggested to me that I should teach them how to use diaphragms, but I had a lot of trouble with that because they didn't want to touch themselves. Condoms were never popular in Puerto Rico because they were associated with prostitutes." In 1956, Clarence Gamble wrote to her and suggested that she turn her attention to the Pill studies that were then beginning.

It was one thing setting up Pill trials; it was another matter finding the subjects, as the correspondence between Pincus and his field-workers shows. They first tried to recruit medical students, but Dr. David Tyler, professor of pharmacology at the University of Puerto Rico School of Medicine, wrote a despairing letter to Pincus in Massachusetts on July 8, 1955, threatening punitive action against female medical students who were being lax in their service to research:

> Among these samples are a number of 24-hour, instead of 48-hour collections. From the variations in volume it appears to me that little attention is being paid in the matter of supervisions. This I have pointed out a number of times. I have also told Garcia that if any medical student exhibited irresponsibility of this sort, I would hold it against her when considering grades.[27]

At the beginning of the following year Pincus received another dispiriting communication, this time from the director of the Cytology Center, who despite menacing coercion had failed to find any candidates for his field work:

> First of all the idea of using student nurses from the San Juan City Hospital failed completely . . . not a single student nurse volunteered for the study. I had practically the same results with my private cases. As far as the medical students are concerned, the only one that volunteered soon dropped out from the study. . . . The only remaining source of subjects were the female prisoners. . . . We explained to the Director [of the Industrial School for Women] the details of the project and she seemed very interested and co-operative. After this interview and a survey of the facilities at the prison we were very optimistic. . . . At this point things started to go wrong. . . . There seems to be some resentment among some of the prisoners about the project, even among the ones that have volunteered, disrupting the discipline of the prison.[28]

Edris Rice-Wray and Adeline Pendleton Satterthwaite, the two women on the ground in Puerto Rico, had a blinding advantage that the university professors did not: their family-planning work gave them invaluable contacts with local women. Dr. Rice-Wray eventually chose a site in a slum-clearance area and recruited a hundred women. But the initial trials were not promising, as her letter to Pincus of June 11 shows: "We have had some trouble with patients stopping the tablet. A few cases have had nausea, dizziness, headaches and vomiting. These few refused to go on with the program. Two were sterilized. One husband hung himself because of desperation over poverty."[29] Thirty of the original one hundred dropped out. Nine months after the trials began, Edris Rice-Wray handed in her resignation, tabulating her results: 221 women had taken the Pill; the dropout rate exceeded 50 percent; 17 percent had experienced negative side effects. The most frequently mentioned symptoms were dizziness, nausea, and headaches. Dr. Rice-Wray's conclusion was that while the oral contraceptive seemed to give 100 percent protection it was unsafe.[30]

Six months later, in June 1957, the Pill was released for sale by Searle, the Chicago-based drug company that had developed the first American treatment for syphilis in the 1920s. It was called Enovid and was marketed for miscarriages and menstrual disorders; what doctors prescribed it for was another matter.

That year, an eighteen-year-old student in Pietermaritzburg, South Africa, went to her doctor to try to get contraception because she was having an affair with her professor. She was one of the first women in the world, outside Puerto Rico, to be put on the Pill:

"My GP said, 'there's this new thing, it's just come out and what we prescribe it for is regularizing periods, so if anybody finds out about it you just say that you have it for that. But it's a foolproof contraceptive.' He said that about regularizing periods to cover himself. They were massive doses and I used to feel nauseous but that was the price I was prepared to pay for this mad affair.

"One was so green. I wouldn't have asked about clinical trials, so naive was I. I didn't even know what they were. I didn't in the same way that women in Third World countries didn't know about how they were being used for Depo Provera later. I feel now that I was part of a human guinea-pig system and it wouldn't surprise me if that GP was offered a financial reward for prescribing it. In South Africa in the late fifties there must have been plenty of doctors willing to try it out on a young powerless girl who was incredibly frightened of getting pregnant and knew she was doing something that was socially forbidden and that there was no such thing as abortion. So when I was offered Enovid I didn't even think about it, I said thank you very much. It was only later that I realized what the Pill was for, when I saw how terrified the whites were of the exploding black population."

Only days after Enovid began to appear on doctors' prescription pads, Pincus received a letter from a thirty-five-year-old Panamanian working for the Americans in the Canal Zone. It was one of his first pieces of fan mail:

Dear Dr. Gregory Pincus
I have been reading in my home town about the Wonderful PILL TO PREVENT PREGNANCY. I am very happy to Hear of such Great things which Men in you Standing can able to Help out Poor Families like myself . . . I have 2 children and my Wife is expecting another

one . . . and I am afraid to have any more at the Present kind of Life
we are having to care for the 2 we have and expecting another so soon
they are 3 years and 2 years old Boy & girl I am asking you to
PLEASE ADVICE ME HOW I CAN GET THIS PILL FOR MY
Wife so as TO PROTECT HER FROM having any more children
for the present time . . . I will appreciate to know of ANY DRUG
STORE IN THE UNITED STATES WHICH I COULD ABLE to
buy this Pill on your RECOMMENDATION. Please do your best to
help me out.[31]

A year later, on April 15, 1958, Pincus received an airogram from
England:

Dear Sir
Having just read the most heartening news I have ever seen in a
newspaper ever—that is an article in the Daily Mail on your research
into anti-pregnancy pills. May I offer heartfelt and grateful
thanks—I'm sure on behalf of millions of women in this country too,
for your work.
    To one who has suffered unbelievable mental and physical agony on
account of unwanted pregnancy, I speak with deep personal gratitude
on your work. I'm sure it will add immeasurably to the happiness of
women on earth. May God bless your efforts.
    Yours faithfully,
    Miss ——— ————[32]

Pincus's papers in the Library of Congress are filled with hundreds of
letters like these from all parts of the world, many containing moving
accounts of poverty and hunger; of dying children and agonizing childbirth; of marriages blighted by sexual frustration because of the terror of
more mouths that could not be fed. They came from the illiterate and they
came from the educated. They hailed him as a god; the writers believed
that science could at last liberate them from the chains their desires had
forged. They knew little or nothing of the extent of the clinical trials in
Puerto Rico. They were desperate for the Pill and they begged their
doctors, often successfully, to prescribe Enovid as an oral contraceptive.

Sometimes they suggested other avenues of research with a sinister faith in the extent of the social problems science could "solve," as in this letter of 1966:

> Dear Doctor Pincus
> Could I suggest another project for you in keeping with your background and abilities?
> It seems to me that a pill or treatment could be devised which could affect the pigmentation of the skin, enabling negroes to remove an important part of their stigma and be judged as equals.
> It could also remove a crutch that some negroes have been using extensively to compensate for their lack of effort.
> The solutions to the world's problems has come from your laboratories and the solution to a second problem, however expedient a solution, could also come from there.[33]

For the rest of the fifties the field work continued under the direction of Adeline Pendleton Satterthwaite. At another slum-clearance project only fifty-six out of a total of 175 women approached, less than a third, agreed to be Pill guinea pigs and even those who did had difficulty in following the directions. The shantytown was soon razed by developers and the women disappeared. The next study, in Humacao, found high rates of breakthrough bleeding and marked changes in the cervixes of the women who had been on the Pill for six months or more. The women on whom the Pill were tested were illiterate, not always capable of following complicated directions that had to be committed to memory, and often displaced in the massive slum-clearance programs of Operation Bootstrap, making follow-up awkward or impossible. In 1960, after the poorest-conducted, most cursory trials of any pharmaceutical ever licensed by the Food and Drug Administration, Enovid was approved as a contraceptive. It had been tested on thousands of women but only 123 had taken it for twelve months or longer. Two years later it was approved for use in Britain. By the end of 1967, six million American women a year were popping ninety million dollars' worth of birth control pills. Searle had a 40 percent share of the market.[34] By the end of the decade, the Pill had been nominated as the most popular item for inclusion in a time capsule to be buried in Osaka, Japan, in 1970. One reader of the *Observer Magazine* even wrote a poem to accompany its interment wrapped in a miniskirt:

> *The 'permissive society', they sneered with a sigh.*
> *But true freedom's much more than a glimpse of a thigh.*
> *Technological progress, advances by strides*
> *Count for nothing compared with the freedom of brides.*[35]

Adeline Pendleton Satterthwaite worked in the Third World until she retired. Puerto Rico remained the test site for all new contraceptives throughout the sixties. Jack Lippes brought his Lippes Loop IUD to try out. Depo Provera was tested there. Trials were done on reduced dosages of the Pill. Some women on Enovid died under mysterious circumstances and autopsies were not conducted. The Ortho Pharmaceutical Company, lured to Puerto Rico by Operation Bootstrap, fell victim to employee lawsuits when workers in the oral-contraceptive plant found their bodies showing sexual changes as a result of occupational exposure to estrogen in atmospheric dust. None of this has had much effect on Puerto Rico's birthrate, and in this the dreams of the population controllers were cruelly dashed. Science did not save them from the specter of overpopulation nor the Hispanicizing of their cities. Puerto Ricans continued to migrate to the mainland. White scientists bearing contraceptives are no longer welcome. Sterilization is now the single most popular contraceptive measure in Puerto Rico.

Margaret Sanger, Katherine McCormick, and Gregory Pincus all died in the mid-1960s, never witnessing the brave new world they had called into being. John Rock survived into the 1980s, embittered by the promiscuity he had helped to bring about. Carl Djerassi writes novels and is still a scientist, at the University of California; in his book *The Politics of Contraception* he ventured: "I do wish to emphasize that on safety grounds the diaphragm is clearly the best contraceptive."[36] When Adeline Pendleton Satterthwaite returned to America in 1990, she was astonished by what she saw and heard:

I went to a meeting of the American Health Association last October and I went to a session on women's health and I was amazed to discover they only wanted what the women could do themselves. The Pill, no. Injections, no. Norplant, no. Sterilization, no. Depo Provera has been very much condemned by the feminist movement and it's most discouraging because it's easier to administer, though granted it's not as good as Norplant which can remain effective for up to five years. But it's working very well in Bangladesh. I was abroad all that time and I didn't see what was happening but coming back I had a tremendous shock seeing the change in the patterns of women delaying their first birth until they are thirty-five or forty and the congenital problems that causes, making obstetrics very different, although in a sense it's positive. It's great for women to fulfil themselves.

In 1982, after years of damaging reports about the Pill's side effects, a family-planning expert would point out: "The Pill has fallen from its pedestal to take its place among the other contraceptives, each with its flaws and its assets. But without the advent of the Pill and the freedom it promised, our present age would clearly be very different and so would our vision of the future."[37] The Pill was to become one of the most potent symbols of the sixties' faith in progress, an iconic representation, like the inner-city tower block, of the failure of technology to fulfil our dreams.

But like the internal combustion engine, it transformed the fabric of society, radically restructuring social and economic roles. Dilys Cossey, chairwoman of the Family Planning Association from 1987 to 1993, said:

The concept was too much to grasp, that women could just put something in their mouths and were safe. It profoundly challenged men because if you have an independent, sexual being she can behave in any way she wants to without being controlled. People always think that big new developments like a man on the moon are the answer to all their troubles; they are not, because new problems start asserting themselves. The Pill was hailed as an answer to a maiden's prayer (or a non-maiden's prayer), but there were all sorts of hidden problems; one was that sexuality threw up as many problems for women as for men; another that having the power to choose is not the same as being happy. But it forced women to grow up. It doesn't mean you'll have an easy life, but it gave women the power to plan their lives.

It is worth remembering, briefly, the world into which the Pill came. Until 1966 it was virtually impossible for an unmarried woman in Britain to obtain contraception. According to a report by the Family Planning Association, in 1963 the British birth-control movement "was pioneered by women, medical and lay, rather than men; and was conducted as a crusade partly to rescue women from male selfishness, partly to rescue lower-class families from the ignorance and unhappiness perpetrated on them by the prejudices of their betters."[38] Clinics had initially been set up, in the thirties, as women's welfare centers, restricted to working-class families. The doctors there were usually wives and mothers between the ages of forty and fifty who were not able, while their children were young, to resume a full-time career. The report discussed "sexual activity amongst the unmarried" as a series of "specific social problems" that included prostitution, divorce, and the immigration from the Caribbean of women in common-law marriages.[39] The report concluded that the Association's primary function was to "advise on fertility regulation *within the context of marriage. . . .* A voluntary body much in the public eye and seeking official support cannot afford to expose itself to the suspicion of 'encouraging immorality.' "[40] Not until 1966, when Lady Helen Brook opened the clinics for young (and unmarried) people that bore her name, was contraception widely available outside the family. Even then, initially there were only two places in Britain, London and Birmingham, that would prescribe the Pill to the unmarried. Students at that time remember hitchhiking from their universities every three months to get their supplies.

The novelist Margaret Drabble was at Cambridge between 1957 and 1960. In 1965 she wrote *The Millstone,* a novel that shocked Britain, about a postgraduate student who has a baby after a one-night stand. Yet even educated, intelligent women sympathetic to the earliest ideas of feminism were naive innocents compared to women of only a few years later:

The books I'd read included Simone de Beauvoir's *The Second Sex,* which made me realize that there were other, grown-up ways of looking at things that involved sex before marriage or without children, but because I was trapped in a British culture it was a dream to have free love. People at Cambridge then were terrified of sex, they were terrified of pregnancy and they were terrified of contraception because it was messy, unreliable and not easily available. A lot of men were virgins too and they were also frightened, frightened of getting a girl into trouble and having to stick with her for the rest of their lives. I admired those people who knew how to get it organized, but I didn't. There was very little literature to read, fiction or nonfiction. You had to go and see the university-recommended doctor and he would give you advice but it was a very bold step to take. I waited until I got married and got pregnant immediately. I know that if it hadn't been for the Pill I would have had a child a year because all other contraceptive methods had failed for me. I was incredibly fertile. After three children, luckily they invented the Pill. It saved my life. From a woman's point of view there were two great inventions, the tampon and the Pill. When people say they weren't, they're talking revisionist rubbish. I remember what it felt like. I would have rather died than have another child. I thought, I don't mind if I die of side effects in twenty years. I'd rather live now. But I'm very glad to have these children. I can't imagine a happy life without them. That's the paradox.

Could the sexual revolution have taken place without the Pill? Probably not. The diaphragm or cap was never a popular method, particularly in Britain. It was difficult to insert and required expert supervision to teach women how to use it. It was a good contraceptive for marriage, when a woman could prepare herself two or three hours in advance for the Saturday night bump and grind in the marital bed. It was less suited for the one-night stand. The Pill scored highly on what has been called the "daintiness factor": "When they were little girls most 'nice' American women were taught that it was naughty to insert their fingers—or anything else—into their vaginas," points out Barbara Seaman, one of the Pill's main critics in the seventies.[41] The Pill was the first reliable, effective contraceptive method over which women had complete control, putting the power of reproduction back into their own domain. It freed them from the burden of large families to have careers, the goal that the most progressive family planners had always secretly pursued. In the film *Educating Rita*, the heroine, who is taking an Open University course in English literature, keeps her supply of the Pill hidden under the floorboards, away from the eyes of her laborer husband, who wants her to give up her useless pursuit of education and advancement in order to have children. The Pill put an end to the sight of worn-out women, old before their time, who sagged in the waiting rooms of doctors' surgeries with their disheveled, impoverished children.

And as we shall see, it liberated women's desires, turning them into sexual beings. The impact of female sexuality would have its most profound effect on social institutions, particularly the Church. No one predicted it, least of all the poor women of Puerto Rico who helped the scientists open Pandora's box.

4

The Country Run by Men in Dresses

John Rock beat the Pope.
Father Andrew Greeley

Conservatives dream of a world in which the sexual revolution never took place. What would such a country look like? In Ireland abortion, homosexuality, and divorce are, at the time of writing, illegal. Contraception can be obtained by married couples from the handful of family-planning clinics that struggle on with no state support. You can buy a packet of condoms in Dublin but not in the villages, where the pharmacist, the doctor, the priest, and the policeman all watch out vigilantly for the well-being of their neighbors' souls. There was no sex in Ireland, an Irish politician remarked, until the television sets could begin to receive the BBC. Nonetheless, Kevin McNamara, Archbishop of Dublin, used the new technology in the mid-eighties to predict to a captive national audience that contraception would result in "moral decline, the growth of veneral disease, and a sharp increase in the number of teenage pregnancies, illegitimate births and abortions."[1] But in 1984, Ireland discovered its own underworld, a secret country that lay beneath the sentimental vision of rural Eire for which Eamon de Valera, the first president, had written the legal constitution. De Valera had dreamed of athletic young men playing Gaelic sports, uncontaminated by heathen soccer, tended by comely maidens, like commercials for Irish creamery butter. In the other Ireland lived Anne Lovett, a fifteen-year-old girl who was found dead in a grotto by the statue of the Virgin Mary near her hometown of Granard, County Longford, her newly born baby beside her also dead, still attached by the umbilical cord. The next year, in Cahirciveen, County Kerry, Joanne Hayes, then twenty-five, was arrested for infanticide, charged with stabbing her newborn baby twenty-two times and throwing it off the cliffs at Slea Head, Ireland's last landfall before the Atlantic reaches America. Joanne, who had been having an affair with a married man, had become pregnant by him three times in just under two years. Her defense was that she had indeed borne a child that had died immediately and she had buried it on the family farm.

Who was the baby found washed up on the beach in an empty fertilizer bag? The police came up with an ingenious identification. Joanne, they said, had been pregnant with not one but two babies. She had tossed one off the cliffs at Slea Head and buried the other. Unfortunately the autopsy demolished that idea. Genetic testing proved that the children could not have been twins. The police went back to the drawing board. This time they surmised that Joanne had had two lovers and, by a one-in-a-million chance, each of her ovaries had released an egg that each man had fertilized, a medical syndrome known as superfecundation. The Garda was prepared to swallow such an awkward and indigestible lump of a theory because the alternative was an even more unpalatable truth; that the countryside was littered with dead, unwanted infants, killed by unmarried mothers with no recourse to contraception or abortion.

During her trial Joanne was consigned to a mental hospital in Limerick. In the same ward was a woman who had sat down on the toilet to relieve her pressured kidneys and had delivered herself of a baby that died in the bowl, its head smashed on the porcelain. Another had given birth through an incestuous relationship with her father who, after her mother's death, had taken her to his bed when she was twelve.[2] Joanne Hayes's cousin Mary Shanahan was a witness at the "Kerry Babies" trial. She said that the night before the miscarriage, Joanne's sister Kathleen had come over to the house and they'd watched *Hill Street Blues* together.[3] In Ireland, you could live in a world where infanticide was the only form of birth control available, as if you'd blundered into the pages of Walter Scott's *Heart of Midlothian*, a novel that turns on an eighteenth-century Scottish law holding that the punishment for concealing a birth was the death penalty.

Then you could step right out of it through the TV screen to crack dealers and pastrami sandwiches and rap. Through the cases of Anne Lovett and Joanne Hayes, Ireland discovered that despite its laws it had had a sexual revolution. "We live in a promiscuous society," said a detective who worked on the Hayes prosecution (and who carried with him during his investigation a copy of Germaine Greer's critique of reproductive technology, *Sex and Destiny*). "There have been umpteen cases of neighbors getting pregnant by their next-door neighbor. It is happening, has happened, and continues to happen."[4]

For nearly a decade after Joanne Hayes's acquittal, Ireland went quiet, acquiescing in the fiction that there was no sex in the country. In 1983 there had been a traumatic referendum on abortion that resulted in the enshrining in the constitution of the equal right to life of mother and unborn child, as if a wife who had borne her husband a clutch of children, wiped their noses, got their teas, made his dinner, and mended his clothes was on the same physiological and spiritual plane as a cluster of cells. Wearily, campaigners for choice gave in and ran underground networks helping pregnant women to get abortions in Britain, the ex-colonial power to which Ireland now exported all its moral problems: the pregnant teenagers, the single mothers, the gays and lesbians.

But in February 1992 this warm, blanketing fug of moral self-satisfaction lifted again. An anonymous fourteen-year-old girl became pregnant. The child grew up in Tallagh, Ireland's future—a new bedroom town on the outskirts of Dublin, a mushroom development of a hundred thousand people around a two-street village. Tallagh swallowed up the country and the people who lived there and sent to be their neighbors the population of Dublin slum clearance. There were no buses, pubs, shops, or cinemas. Your recreation was joy riding. The girl was quite innocent, but she had been menstruating since the age of eleven and her mother noticed that she had missed two periods. The girl said that she had been sexually molested by the father of a friend and penetrated twice. The girl's parents talked to the Garda before taking their daughter to England for an abortion. They wanted advice on whether they should get a sample of tissue for DNA testing to help in the prosecution case against the rapist. When the Director of Public Prosecutions ordered the girl back to Ireland to prevent her from terminating the pregnancy, rumors went round that there had been no rapist, that she was pregnant by a boyfriend, an Iraqi student. A priest said on television that the case was a setup designed to challenge the constitution.

While the girl's abuse went on, Tallagh was changing. In the middle, like a castle surrounded by its subjects, they built the Square, a mall on a hill with a multiplex cinema, a McDonald's, a late-night, condom-selling chemist, all the English chain stores—everything you could want. Underneath the multiplex sign advertising the latest film was another attraction, now showing, the family-planning clinic. In it women relieved the privacy of their souls—of how they had not had penetrative sex with their husbands for ten years because they feared another child, but that last night they got carried away and let him.

Why are the Irish so hung up on sex when the French, the Italians, and the Spanish, all Catholics, have managed to separate church from state? It was not always the case. Until the Middle Ages, the country was regarded as a primitive backwater by the rest of Europe because divorce and remarriage were common and polygamy was practiced by the upper classes. Cut off from the Continent, Ireland was still influenced by the pre-Augustinian Christianity of the early missionaries that would only die out when England took a firm grip over its colony's government in the seventeenth century.[5] The critic J. Middleton Murry said of James Joyce's *Ulysses* that it described the "liberation of the suppressions of an adult man who has lived under the shadow of the Roman-Catholic Church in a country where that Church is at its least European, and is merely an immense reinforcement of Puritanism."[6] The Church was the unifying factor of the anticolonial consciousness. It sewed itself into the fabric of the emerging state. It was a religion of the oppressed, promising in the afterlife what couldn't be delivered during the traumas of the Famine.

The British never permitted in Ireland the nonconformist tradition that, from the seventeenth century, asserted the right of the individual to decide matters of his own conscience, the millenarian project that in this century was instrumental in setting up family-planning clinics and defeating the laws against homosexuality in Britain. Instead, the Irish proceeded by subterfuge and secrecy, saying one thing, doing another. Two months after the case of the fourteen-year-old girl, another scandal sank whatever hopes remained that Ireland could avoid the ingrained persistence of its own sexual desires. Annie Murphy, an American divorcée, produced a nineteen-year-old boy said to be the son of Eamonn Casey, Bishop of Galway, who immediately resigned amid allegations that he had paid out more than £100,000 in Church money to support the mother and child. The press was filled with rumors of a secret Vatican slush fund set aside to pay off women who became pregnant by priests. Annie went on the radio to talk about her love affair. She enthralled the country as no other Catholic sex scandal had done since an episode of *The Thorn Birds* in which the heroine and the priest finally make love overloaded the National Grid when the population went to make a cup of tea during the commercial break to calm themselves down.

The fall of the Church's privileged position as the power base of Irish life and guardian of the people's morals must have been viewed with deep despondency in Rome. For decades, according to the Irish journalist Peter Lennon, most citizens of the republic had accepted "with varying degrees of restlessness and rebellion the most grotesque relationships and most pitiless edicts of the hierarchy. The vast majority accept having their lives policed by people, often of low intelligence, wilfully rejecting normal relationships for themselves but imposing their bizarre and furtive understanding of sexual matters on others."[7] It is the sexual revolution rather than any other social or economic change that is transforming Ireland into a modern secular state.

A priest is no more than a man in a dress, and the priesthood a kind of sex-defying transvestite brotherhood, an élite tended by a second tier or female-servant class of nuns who, shrouded in the costume of the Middle Ages, take in laundry and attend to girls' education. A celibate brotherhood stands guard over the morals of the masses, attempting to enforce not only a biblical tyranny over desire, but a vast, antiquated, rusty, dusty, musty machine of control over people's erotic lives made up of the crankiest of half-baked theories. This medieval restraint mechanism jolted along through the twentieth century providing a jerky but secure ride for its passengers, the millions of faithful all over the world. But in 1968 it collided with a large obstacle, the invention of which it had never anticipated. It reacted toward it much as it had received Galileo's assertion that the earth revolved around the sun. After its smash-up against the Pill the Church would survive, but so battered, dented, and unroadworthy that large numbers of its riders would abandon it. Sex effectively derailed Catholicism, the religion so troubled by desire that its founder had even proscribed his own mother's sexual pleasure.[8]

One might argue that religion is the only area of life that represses men and women equally when it comes to sex. The Catholic Church has never permitted a double standard, as strands of fundamentalist Islam seem to do. The Catholic Church in Ireland recently urged women to vote against a referendum liberalizing divorce, arguing not only against a fatal weakening of the sanctity of marriage but appealing to a justifiable fear of abandonment, and, for those married to farmers whose houses were handed down through the male line, a terror of homelessness and economic hardship. Irish women had seen divorce in other countries and thought the old ways protected their interests. But within a religion in which the virgin mother looms large over the spiritual imagination, the relationship of women with an all-male priestly caste is particularly problematic; it is not surprising that such notorious lapsed Catholics as Madonna and Camille Paglia are obsessed with authority and transgression.

The Catholic Church inherited many of its doctrines from the ancient world, which feared and was repelled by the evidence of women's sexual nature. Menstrual blood was thought capable of contaminating semen, and intercourse with a woman who bled was a particular taboo.[9] (Catholic women active in the Church today have told me that they were forbidden by parish priests from touching the communion wafer or approaching the altar while menstruating.) Isidore of Seville, who died in A.D. 636, disseminated the popular belief that "after contact with it fruits cannot germinate, flowers wilt, grasses wither . . . iron rusts, bronze turns black, and dogs that partake of it develop rabies."[10] It was the early Christians who first laid down that the purpose of marriage was procreation, although there is ample evidence of widespread contraception in the ancient world, even the acceptance of infanticide as a natural method for weeding out unwanted or handicapped babies. The Jews were reviled in an anti-Semitic polemic by Tacitus for not killing their surplus children, and it seems to be from

Judaism that Christianity inherited a more narrow perspective on family planning.[11] In order to enforce this utilitarian view of the purpose of sexual desire, the early Church put forward the theory that women were at their most fertile when their libido was at its peak, and it followed that God had made lust for the sole purpose of effecting conception. There was one flaw in this argument. Scientific knowledge of the timing of ovulation was still uncertain, and it seemed that a woman's libido varied according to the current state of medical research. Hence priests were constantly having to go back to women to inform them that the height of their desires were at a different time of the month from what they had previously been told.[12]

The German feminist theologian Uta Ranke-Heinemann believes that the prohibition on sexual pleasure was accomplished by Augustine's wilful inversion of Manichaean doctrine. He was, she says, "the man responsible for welding Christianity and hostility to sexual pleasure into a systematic whole . . . the theological thinker who blazed a trail for the succeeding centuries—indeed for the ensuing millennium and a half."[13] Manichaeism, founded by a Persian called Manes, held that the earth was a realm of boundless darkness created by the Devil and procreation was "a diabolical act because every human being was a particle of light imprisoned in a body begotten by a demon."[14] The Manichaeans, therefore, advocated childless marriages, tolerating sexual pleasure but condemning procreation. It was this theory that Augustine was to turn upside down. He thought that before the Fall sex had existed without desire; that Adam had been able to achieve erection at will, as some men could wiggle their ears. The punishment for Eve's sin was for the body to refuse to obey the mind as a permanent *aide-mémoire* of that first disobedience.[15] Augustine's misogyny was so deep that he never conversed with a woman unless it was through a third party and never allowed one into his house, including relatives.[16] Sex was elevated above violence in the Church's penitential system. The Anglo-Saxon penitential of Pseudo-Egbert (*c.*800) imposed the following punishments: oral sex—seven years to life; anal sex—ten years; abortion—seven to ten years; murder—ten years. And there was a complex system of penances for minor offenses, like twenty days on bread and water for a man who had sex with his wife while she was pregnant.

It was not until 1827, when K. E. von Baer discovered the ovum, that science began to challenge the medieval view of sex. This had serious consequences for the ideal of the virgin birth, according to Uta Ranke-Heinemann: "To accept it . . . is to deny the sole agency of God and limit the Holy Ghost's participation to fifty percent," she points out.[17] The challenge to all religions of Darwin's discoveries in the nineteenth century created a paradoxical figure in the twentieth century, the Catholic scientist. In the thirties John Rock was fitting diaphragms in Massachusetts, a state in which contraception was illegal, and a group of Catholic doctors attempted to get him excommunicated.[18] He had first spoken out on the issue of contraception in 1931, in an article that argued that children were completely necessary to the maintenance of happy families. But he also considered himself a humanist for whom life's meaning derived from service to others. He believed that sexual fulfilment was vital to married life and that no man should be expected to sublimate it into what he called "sexual martyrdom."

By the end of the Second World War, Rock was convinced that undisciplined population growth was a threat to a well-ordered society and he became an advocate of the small family.[19] In the early fifties he started to use large doses of progesterone on the reproductive organs of sterile women. During the treatment, which lasted for three to five months, the women did not ovulate; but after the withdrawal of the progesterone, about 15 percent would become pregnant almost immediately in what became known as "the Rock Rebound Effect." In 1953, Gregory Pincus approached Rock to ask him if he would cooperate in a study on the use of progesterone as a contraceptive.

For several years between 1960, when the Pill became available by prescription in America, and the *Humanae Vitae* encyclical of 1968, it seemed quite possible that the Church would lift from Catholics the burden of large families and extend the hedonistic delight of the fathers in good food, drink, and precious art to the erotic pleasures. The Catholic Church was also worried about the population explosion; Pope Pius XII had even addressed delegates to the World Population Conference in Rome in 1953. The initial response to the Pill was cautious optimism. In 1962 Dutch bishops organized an opinion survey on marriage in the Netherlands; it found that most Catholics thought Church teaching on the subject wholly inadequate. Out of twenty theologians who took part eighteen believed that the Pill was acceptable, and priests were told to tell their parishioners that the Church was divided and the strictures against the Pill fell into the category of "doubtful law." Under Jesuit teaching, "a doubtful law does not oblige."

On April 19, 1964, *The Times* carried an article about Thomas d'Esterre Roberts, a Liverpudlian and Jesuit bishop of Bombay, a maverick who had marched with Bertrand Russell and the sex-book guru Alex Comfort on Ban the Bomb marches. Several years in Bombay had won Roberts over to the fashionable faith in population control, and he was quoted in *The Times* as saying: "The whole end of marriage is not to have as many children as possible, but as many as can be brought up to lead happy and useful lives. An Indian lives in a mud hut with his wife and several children, too poor to be able to afford any light, and forced to be with his wife every night for twelve hours in the dark, and having nothing else at all but her love." On May 7 there was a response from Cardinal Heenan, once a parish priest in Liverpool. Intercourse, he said, was unlawful and wicked where the conception of offspring was prevented. God's law could not be changed. That night the BBC asked for a comment from the Catholic MP Norman St. John-Stevas (later Lord St. John of Fawsley), who declared that Cardinal Heenan's comments were so categorical that the debate should end there.[20] St. John-Stevas was unused to public examination of Catholic doctrine, which he believed should be restricted to theological discussions in Catholic newspapers. But dissident Catholics were using secular newspapers, television, and radio as instruments of mass communication to debate religious issues and to reach far beyond the limited circle of scholars, theologians, and priests who would interpret those discussions to the masses.

The Pill broke the silence. It permitted debate not only on sexual life but on the very role of the Church in modern society. Cardinal Leo Josef Suenens of Mechlin and Brussels argued later that year:

We must say something about the very life of the human person, the inviolability of that life, its procreation, its extension in what is called the population explosion. The church must speak on social justice. What is the theological and practical duty of rich nations towards the Third World or the nations that suffer from hunger? The church must speak about bringing the Gospel to the poor and some of the conditions the church must meet to make that Gospel relevant to them. The church must speak about international peace and war in a way that can help enlighten the world.[21]

He was countered by Ernesto Ruffini, Cardinal Archbishop of Palermo, who implored: "Let us imitate Saint Augustine, who did not hesitate to say that if parents do not use marriage in a Christian way, they fall into debauchery and prostitution. Let us not fear to speak the truth."[22]

These contrasting views reflect two cultures. The Catholics of northern Europe were living in predominantly Protestant states in which were embedded the nonconformist traditions of the millenarians, with their emphasis on individual conscience and social engineering. Palermo, on the other hand, was the capital of a downtrodden island of peasants for whom social progress was an unreal idea; for Sicilians *omertà*, or clan loyalty, the long-held grievance against colonizing powers and the deep pessimism that life would never improve, were woven into their every response. But the Church was a worldwide movement trying to bind together under a central doctrine people of heterodox cultures. The Vatican decided to set up a study, the Pontifical Commission for the Study of Population and Birth. There were eight representatives from Belgium and France, seven from the United States, five Germans, five Italians, three from Spain, and a handful from the Third World. John Rock was not invited.

The commission took, however, a historic step. Among the American contingent were Patrick and Patty Crowley, who led an organization called the Christian Family Movement. Patty had had six pregnancies and four children and finally surgery performed to save her life, which sterilized her. It was the first time opinions had ever been sought from lay people.[23] They were told to keep the invitation secret. When they arrived in Rome they were told that the five women on the commission had been allocated accommodation at a convent. It did not seem to have occurred to the celibates at the Vatican that a married couple would want to sleep together. For the duration of the meeting they too became celibates.

Initially, the commission was cautiously favorable toward the Pill. The Crowleys testified that in their experience the rhythm method did not work. In their view, it turned spiritual and physical love into sexual relief. It made couples obsessed with sex and made marriage into a form of licensed prostitution.[24]

The commission concluded with a report based on a three-foot stack of documentation. It went far beyond simply addressing the matter of the Pill, but struck at the heart of medieval thought. It argued that Nature was not immutable, that truth was something that could be true "for the moment," that tradition should be open and forward-looking, and that behavior could not be dictated. It urged the pope not to solve the birth-control question, but to tell the faithful that it was theirs to solve. Like a cartoon character that runs off the edge of a cliff, its feet scrabbling in midair, the Church suddenly looked down and saw a chasm below it. The debate on birth control had led it into the most fundamental questions about the Church and its authority, and its solutions involved "a radical revision of the way Rome had exercised its authority for a century."[25]

The pope became confused. In October 1965 he gave what came to be known as the "no more war" speech at the UN. Afterward, he was interviewed by Alberto Cavallari of the Milan newspaper *Corriere della Sera:*

So many problems! How many problems there are and how many answers we have to give. We want to open up the world, and every day we have to make decisions that will have consequences for centuries to come. . . . Take birth control, for example. The world asks us what we think and we find ourselves trying to give an answer. But what answer? We can't keep silent. And yet to speak is a real problem. But what? The church has never in her history confronted such a problem. This is a strange subject for men of the church to be discussing. Even humanly embarrassing. . . . We have to say something. But what?[26]

Into the vacuum of the pontiff's uncertainty, the Right began to marshal its arguments. But even in doing so, it was led into hidden traps. Rightists wanted to argue, for example, that the love between man and woman was uniquely expressed through the conjugal act, but in doing so they found they had elevated sex into the central place of marriage. In the meantime the Crowleys had undertaken a survey of three thousand Catholics from eighteen countries. They confirmed that the rhythm method produced sexual frustration, irritability, and fear of pregnancy, placing a harmful degree of stress on the marriage relationship. What about menopause, when periods were irregular? Couples had never been heard from before in Rome, and their influence began to terrify the conservatives who suggested that their emergence from outside the pale of clerical life was dazzling the clergy into forgetting God.[27]

Until now the tide had seemed to be in favor of the reformers. The Crowleys were optimistic and in Britain Cardinal Heenan decided to prepare for the inevitable by drafting a pastoral letter in which he admitted that notions of right and wrong were subject to change. Catholics, particularly in the United States, were no longer waiting for the word from Rome. An auxiliary bishop was piloting a chartered Cessna 180 round Minnesota telling the faithful that the matter was resolved and they should use their own judgment.[28] John F. Kennedy had represented the new face of Catholicism—youthful, attractive, progressive, and humanitarian. To liberals, Kennedy seemed something like a major prophet who redefines and gives inspiration and new direction to an existing faith. His death may even have appeared as the martyrdom of a figure of such secular inspiration that it bordered on the holy.

But behind the scenes the conservatives were lobbying. Cardinal Alfredo Ottaviani, secretary of the Sacred Congregation of the Holy Office, took the pope aside. He told him that a sexual revolution was taking place throughout the West, that the licensing of birth control would open the door to a tide of hedonism, that governments would set up state-run family-planning clinics. The pope sent him away to draft a new report. It took six months to write *Humanae Vitae*. On July 29, 1968, the speculation was over. The encyclical did not even bother with the pros and cons. At its heart was one main point, contained in Paragraph 14:

> Every matrimonial act must remain open to the transmission of life. To destroy even only partially the significance of intercourse and its end is

contradictory to the plan of God and to His will. . . . Similarly excluded is any action, which either before, at the moment of or after sexual intercourse, is specifically intended to prevent procreation—whether as an end or as a means.[29]

The Church had repudiated sex as a hedonistic act, as pleasure or intimacy. It was to be the mechanical method by which life was to be created. The reaction was immediate, and today Catholic Americans regard the moment they heard the announcement of *Humanae Vitae* in the same way as they remember where they were when President Kennedy was shot.

Jim Brandes, a Texan priest, was having breakfast when one of his lay assistants brought in the newspaper with the announcement that the pope had banned birth control. "The first words out of my mouth were 'Oh shit,' " he told David Rice, an Irish ex-priest and author of *Shattered Vows*, an attack on clerical celibacy. "It was extraordinarily devastating. All my abdominal muscles knotted up and stayed that way for weeks," Brandes said. Weeks later, again sitting at the breakfast table, he decided to leave the priesthood.[30] More than 2,500 American scientists signed an open letter to the pope deploring the decision. Almost two dozen theologians from the Catholic University of America, joined by sixty others from around the U.S., accused the encyclical of paying "insufficient attention to the ethical import of modern science."[31]

In Britain, leading Catholic laypeople began to dissociate themselves from the Vatican. Auberon Waugh, father of four children and regular churchgoer, then working for *The Spectator,* was asked by *The Observer* in 1970 what he would do if he were pope: "I would certainly wriggle out of the contraception fuss," he replied. "I remember discussing the point with an eminent Jesuit—who shall be nameless—and we constructed between us an encyclical pointing out that our comprehension of the wisdom of God is an organic growth. With the world facing a population explosion of dangerous proportions, God in his wisdom has given us this rather useful way of controlling it." Shirley Williams, then Secretary of State at the Home Office, an MP who had voted against the 1967 Abortion Bill, urged a Fabian approach: "Firstly I would draw a sharp line between dogma and the whole of the rest of the administration of the church. The position on birth control, for instance, has never been an *ex cathedra* statement of doctrine. It is, I would have thought, one of the many similar issues that could safely be discussed fairly openly."[32]

America could not settle down to passive acceptance of Vatican doctrine. *Humanae Vitae* embodied Augustinian views of sexuality and a woman's duty to her children. But affluence and the emerging women's movement made American women dissatisfied with the limitations of motherhood. Even portions of the celibate priesthood regarded *Humanae Vitae* as a medieval pronouncement for a static world order. They felt themselves to be disenfranchised from the Church. They believed that Catholicism needed a second Reformation that would transform the faith rather than establish a new one. They called for a theology of dissent. On October 1, Bishop John Noonan spoke to the commission for the American contingent. He said that the pope's opinion was no more than that, an opinion. And it was these seemingly inoffensive words that shattered the glass of papal infallibility.

Father Andrew Greeley, America's best-known priest for his blockbuster novels of the social and sexual pressures on the modern priesthood and for his espousal of the theology of dissent has addressed the issue twice:

It was a peculiar historical thing. The Pill came along and the church hesitated and vacillated, while people were making up their own minds. Had the church acted more quickly, perhaps the outcome would have been different. But as it was, the people reacted by saying, you're wrong on the Pill, maybe you're wrong on a lot of things. . . .[33]

Catholics gave the church's positions serious consideration and they said no. The whole thing is really sex. The papal decision is that you can stop having children, but you can't have sex. Well this may be a decision that some superannuated bureaucrats in the Roman Curia would push who probably don't know the meaning of sexual desires of any kind, but it isn't the position that most parish priests would push . . . They've simply blown their credibility on sexual matters sky high. They've done it on pre-marital sex, on abortion, on everything else . . . John Rock beat the Pope.[34]

Other religions, other institutions, were affected by the Pill and by the sexual revolution, but none so profoundly as Catholicism. In no other religion did sex eat away at the fabric of faith. In 1977 a conservative German Catholic journal precisely located the Church's decline in John Rock's invention:

> The Pill will undoubtedly stunt the growth of the church in the next ten or twenty years, with all the consequent effects on recruitment to the priesthood and religious orders and on church tax revenues. No new churches will be required. . . . The results will precisely . . . accord with [our] warnings about the propagation of "the Pill," namely: an ominous decline in the birth rate, the demoralization of society, the sexualization of public life, overt propaganda on behalf of pornography and nudism . . . public contempt for chastity leading to a decline in the social standing of the priesthood . . . all in all, spiritual environmental pollution on an unprecedented scale.[35]

By and large these predictions came true, though not in the way the writer intended. Nearly a hundred thousand priests left the ministry to marry. For some, telling women they could not use effective birth control was the shame that drove them out.

As a young Dominican in Kilkenny, Ireland, David Rice was asked if she could go on the Pill by a woman whose husband would beat her up if she would not sleep with him. And if she still refused, he would do it with the dog.[36] Ireland had its sexual revolution. Silently, the Pill has been smuggled across the border by women's groups whose Pill Train brought contraception to Irish women. A member of the Irish Family Planning Association was stopped by customs with a parcel of two hundred diaphragms. When challenged, she thought quickly and said they were jam-jar lids. The page of *Cosmopolitan* that in Britain would contain advertisements for abortion clinics is blanked out in Ireland by the censorship board. But the phone numbers are inscribed on the inside doors of the ladies' lavatories in the pubs of Dublin, replacing the usual graffiti.

Could Ireland have held out longer? De Valera's dream was always of a rural state as well as a religious one. He did not share the futuristic vision of the two countries across the water, Britain and America. But Ireland was unable to resist technology and its offspring, mass communications. Images of a different life were relayed from the BBC's service in Northern Ireland and later the satellite channels came too. Ireland picked up "Dallas" and "Dynasty." Even the films censored by the film board came in on video. John Rock had beaten the pope and sex beat the Irish government. In one real way, the ideology of the colonizing nation had defeated Ireland's attempts at self-determination. The nonconformist religious tradition of the seventeenth century, which rejected intervention of church and state in private morality, caught up with Ireland four hundred years later. Catholicism would have its revenge in a postmodern doctrine of libertine sexuality interpreted by Camille Paglia and Madonna, both Italian Catholics. But twenty-five years and a sexual revolution would intervene before that happened.

Witness

Anatomy of a Dolly-Bird

I must have been about eleven when the Profumo scandal happened. My mum bought me this black-and-white PVC mac and when I was walking down the road in it someone said, "There's Christine Keeler," and I thought, "That's good." All I knew was that she was a bit notorious. Scandal was on last night. The first time I saw that I couldn't talk to any men afterwards. I went to a party and I walked home on my own. I identified with Christine Keeler. She was normal. Women behave that way and most men can't hack it. She didn't really know what was going on. She just acted from her desires and she got conned by all those awful men. She was persecuted when she was just being herself, she was conned by bourgeois society, by everything. I felt that happened to me. I just really enjoyed sex.

I was a rocker first when we lived in Leicester, then I became a Mod when we moved to Manchester. That's when it all started. I had the Mary Quant hairstyle, the white lipstick. We were a bit androgynous really, flat-chested with trousers and short hair. It got serious when they brought skid-lids in for scooters, which flattened my hair that I'd spent hours puffing up. Eventually it evolved into this style which I never used to wash for three weeks. I'd put lacquer on it and it set rock-solid. Once I left two rollers in and they'd got buried. I don't know how long they'd been there when I found them. When I went out in the rain it went frizzy, so I used to part it down the middle, Sellotape it down and put one roller in the top to lift it up and then I'd back-comb it. I used to have to cycle to the station and if it was raining I had a waterproof scarf and I'd clip my hair to it. I had to cycle with my hand holding my fringe. I went into the back of a car once and came off my bike.

And the platform shoes later. I had six-inch heels and I couldn't walk in *them, so I had two people on either side of me supporting me as I walked down the cobbled stones to get down to this club. I used to go away to Abersoch with all the hairpieces and the platform shoes, in a tent. It was an absolute scream. Never went out without makeup, I virtually stopped going to college because you had to walk up this big hill and it was all wet and windy and my hair would be all over the place. Everything was looks, looks, looks. I had a real hangup about my weight. This was in the sixties when you had to be like Twiggy. My friends used to go on about that, they'd make comments about my legs. I'd thump anyone who said anything like that now. This bloke used to go on and on about my weight and about my sex drive. I'd go out in a little white miniskirt, a white jacket, a big bow in my hair and stand there. That miniskirt was guaranteed to pull. I decided when I was thirteen that I wasn't going to get married and that sex had nothing to do with love. I think I may have been born that way. I'm very masculine in my attitude to sex. I was born at exactly the right time. I didn't want to lose my virginity in any sort of relationship. I went to a party. I was in the bathroom, he didn't think I was a virgin. I had loads of makeup on and he must have thought I was older anyway. I can't remember who it was, I was just pleased that it was out of the way. I knew I never wanted to get conned into falling in love with somebody.*

Until I was seventeen I'd not used contraception, well a couple of them had used Durex. I knew I wouldn't get pregnant. When I met this guy I went on the Pill. We split up after that. I was in such a state about him I went off the rails, failed my A-levels, well I got one, I got English. I went completely promiscuous for three years. Then I met a similar type again. It was like this self-punishment, I had to punish myself for having such a highly charged sex drive. It really did my head in because of this slaggy association. I was totally, completely judged by a double standard. They wanted a fantastically experienced female but I never had any serious relationships.

By the time I was seventeen I'd had sex with about seven blokes. We used to hitchhike up to this pub and spend all night trying to get a lift home and of course you'd get quite pissed as well. There was a price you had to pay for that. There were two girls I knew who were having a race up to the first hundred men. In the sixties you could do that, you never caught anything. I never got any diseases. I never even got thrush. I've got a theory about people who get those things, I think it's guilt that's causing the body to react in that way, the same with getting pregnant as well.

As soon as I started having sex I had orgasms. I used to read Cosmopolitan *and think, what's the hassle? If I'd been born ten years earlier I'd have had to get married because there wasn't the contraception available. That would have been me written off really, stuck with children. The most fundamental thing that happened was the Pill. It was the most wonderfully liberating thing that ever happened to femalekind because it meant you could behave like a man if you wanted to and I'm eternally grateful for that. I stayed on the Pill all the way through. I've come off it now, which is hell, it's really ruined my skin, I've got spots again. I hate not being on it, it's awful, awful. The best thing that ever happened to me was going on the Pill. Apart from freeing me up sexually, it did wonders for my boobs, which fortunately I've not lost. My skin was fantastic and it gave me complete freedom, I could do what I wanted. But don't forget this is pre-AIDS.*

When I got into my mid-twenties I got really fed up with this swine I was living with. I used to have affairs on the side that he knew nothing about. I loved it because I could control and manipulate all these men because I had all this sexual experience. It was wonderful, wicked stuff. When I was thirty we split up and I reverted to how I'd been when I was a teenager. I looked much younger and I'd go out dressed up as a dolly-bird. I used to play them at their own game, which was really childish but it was great fun. It's a very difficult one to get off. I think it's all about power, using sex in the way men use sex. Then I met a guy who used to run the company I work for. He was like a god, he was a lot older than me and I completely fell in love with him, he's still quite powerful in the City and he appreciated my sex drive, he thought it was great. And I suddenly thought, I'm okay really. I tried to work out once with my husband how many men I've slept with. Since I left the man I was living with until I was thirty there must be about twelve. But through that promiscuous phase I don't know, it could be anywhere between fifty and a hundred, I've no idea.

I loved the sixties, hated the seventies, loved the eighties because I was free again. Music was pretty crap in the seventies. Even Tamla Motown went off. My whole world was going to clubs. I still do really. In the seventies I was trapped with someone who thought he was an old man at twenty-eight and I had to go the dinner party route. I never even went to a club when all that stuff was going on in Manchester.

I didn't want to know about politics. I thought the Labour Party was the absolute pits. I would have shot all the unions down. All I cared about was going out and having a good time. Then during the Falklands War I was unemployed, my parents had become pensioners, I saw inequality—I'd never even been aware of it before. So I voted Labour for the first time in 1983. I don't really like the middle classes, I feel as if I stand apart and that's why the sixties fitted me so well because of the breakdown of class. I never had many female friends. I find it difficult in large groups of females. I'm not really feminist in a feminist sense, I'm more feminist in a me sense, I'm just as important as a man and I was always treated that way at home. Fortunately, not having any brothers helped.

I met my husband in a writing group and he went out with a friend of mine but we met again three years later. He's very intelligent and I had always found before that I was brighter than all the men I went out with. He doesn't possess me at all. When I first started seeing him, I'd go out with my girlfriends and snog these men. It was part of my vanity that I had to attract them. Then I'd come home and tell him. I don't think I'd do that now. I don't honestly think I could sleep with anyone else. I'm not saying that it's particularly easy, but because I've had so much sexual experience I could fancy somebody and go through the whole sexual scenario in my mind and know that it's a waste of time if it puts our relationship in danger. We've talked about how we would feel if we had other lovers and neither of us would be very happy about it. I couldn't handle it at all. I'm not possessive, but I am jealous. He's only slept with about a dozen women because he's had long-term relationships. I don't seem to be as interested in sex as I used to be which isn't a bad thing. I'm not a great initiator because I'm used to people chasing after me. I wouldn't say to a man, how about it? I'd put myself in a situation where he seduced me.

I'd never wanted children. I didn't like them very much and I hadn't met anyone I wanted to have children with until I met my husband. I do think that having a child is a massive responsibility that I never wanted to take on. I've only just got cats and I wouldn't have got those if I'd still been on my own. Now there's so much between us it's like a physical manifestation. Plus the fact that I've got to the stage where I've been through all the career stuff and I'm just not interested anymore. I'd be quite happy to stay at home. Although that's not going to be possible because of money. I could never have had a child before, I just wasn't grown up enough. I will have children, next year. I'm having a son. I think I know. I'd find it difficult with a daughter, I don't know what I'd do. Assuming AIDS is out of the way I'd teach them to detach sex from love and have a healthy attitude towards it. Keep your dignity and self-respect, do what you want to do and don't get pregnant.

The women I wanted to look like were Julie Christie, Susan Sarandon and Diane Keaton. They're women in their own right who get on with what they want to do but still retain that feminine mystique or glamour which is important to me. I never related to traditional women's lib types with no makeup. I don't wear that much now, it sits in the cracks as you get older, but when I was young I used to pile it on. I used to like men wearing makeup as well, I do like effeminate men, pretty; very sixties that. I think I'm a very sixties person. I don't think I've changed that much since the sixties. I took in all that side of it, the style. I saw the film Darling *with Julie Christie, where she went to meet Dirk Bogarde with a fur coat over her nightie and I thought that was really good. I met one of my lovers with a coat on over my underwear once.*

5

Our Age Buys a Fun Fur

Let us be on the side of those who want people to be free to live their own lives, to make their own mistakes, and to decide, in an adult way and provided they do not infringe on the rights of others, the code by which they want to live; and on the side too of experiment and brightness, of better buildings and better food, of better music (jazz as well as Bach) and better books, of fuller lives and greater freedom. In the long run those things will be more important than even the most perfect of economic policies.

Roy Jenkins, *The Labour Case* (1959)

The first bite of the apple brought the knowledge of good and evil. Now, a hundred million pips later, that knowledge embraces atomic energy and birth control. The Act no longer results necessarily—or even probably—in a baby, and so to bear children is no longer women's inescapable lot; she has achieved choice and with it the responsibility which before was the monopoly of the gods.

Catherine Storr, "Why Have Babies?" *Nova*, May 1967

There were only three years between Profumo and Swinging London. In 1963, John Profumo, Minister of Defence in Harold Macmillan's Tory government, had an affair with a call girl who was also sleeping with a Soviet defense attaché. Profumo lied to the House of Commons and was later forced to resign. Stephen Ward, the society osteopath who introduced Christine Keeler to Profumo and others, was charged with pimping and committed suicide during his trial. I was a child when all this happened, staying in London at the Cumberland Hotel at Marble Arch with my parents. While evidence was being given against Ward, Christine Keeler was put up in a flat in Cumberland Place. Our hotel room was opposite her bolt-hole and I would look out of the window at the door-stepping press corps. On the news, it was announced that Ward had killed himself and there was a cutaway shot of the Cumberland Place mansion block. I could turn one way, out of the window and see the flat and then turn back to the screen to see it again. I asked my mother, as I had so many times, "But what has Christine Keeler *done*, Mummy?" I was never to get a reply.

Children live in years of fog when everyone else knows that something momentous is happening in public life, yet *we* can't see it. We just hear the muffled commotion and glimpse shapes in the mist. That is what the Profumo years were like for me. Three years later I knew about sex. I understood Swinging London better than my parents, though not as well as I do now. During the Ward trial, the Labour Party's lead in the opinion polls reached twenty points, the highest that had been recorded since polls began. The *Financial Times* index dropped seven points. At the October Labour Party conference in Scarborough, the leader, Harold Wilson, would speak of his message for the sixties—a socialist-inspired scientific and technological revolution releasing energy on an enormous scale. Labour was willing itself into the future, into the new utopianism of ruthless competition, research, investment, youth, classlessness—a Britain of motorways and monorails, tower blocks and spaghetti junctions. Macmillan, in his velvet-collared Edwardian overcoat, seemed to preside over a government of inertia, corruption, secrecy, aristocratic privilege, and depravity, as if one had turned over a fallen branch to find it crawling with maggots. A year later the Tories were gone.

What Christine Keeler did was to legitimize sex as a subject for dinner-party chatter. But more profoundly she came to represent the shame of sex. Before the sexual revolution, it seemed to me as a teenager, there was a prurient world of furtive encounters, a work force of working-class girls who turned a trick for the nobs. Sex was the only territory on which the classes met: the tart and the cabinet minister, the marquis and the rough trade. One of Christine Keeler's lovers, for whom she did it for free, was Lucky Gordon, a Notting Hill dope dealer from the West Indies. Sex was like a knife which cut through the cake of English society and showed how the layers were connected. There were silent and unspeakable perversions, mainly carried out, it appeared, by the aristocracy and judiciary. At one of Ward's parties, it was rumored, a man in a leather mask served guests with printed instructions that if he did not give satisfaction, he should be beaten. The Profumo affair familiarized the public for the first time with "kinky sex," that old libertine refrain, and "kinky boots" became all the rage. The word for sex in the fifties and early sixties (the kind of sex that did not take place between married couples neatly positioned one above the other, penis in the right place, lips in their right places) was "Vice." The Profumo affair came to stand for the corruption and hypocrisy of postwar Conservatism, its libertine grandees reserving sex for themselves while denying it to the working class. Keeler's subsequent decline was rapid. In the space of time required for me to move from prepubescence to adolescence, there were miniskirted dolly-birds who were giving it away. She became an anachronistic figure in Swinging London, a city that knew nothing of Vice.

Three years after the Profumo affair, *Time* magazine commissioned its Swinging London cover edition of April 13, 1966. It was the staff at the New York bureau of *Time* who appended the word "swinging" to London, a term that was beginning to gain currency as a description of the parties taking place in America's sexual underground. Britain, *Time* argued, was "in the middle of a bloodless revolution"[1] under the leadership of the youngest prime minister of the century, Harold Wilson, then a mere fab fifty. New York was staid, Paris had calcified. London, like Barcelona three decades later, epitomized classlessness, verve, style, irreverence, and above all, the New York bureau of *Time* hoped, sex. Andrea Adam worked on the Swinging London *Time* and later edited the British edition of *Oui*, Hugh Hefner's class porn magazine:

We were all riveted by London. London was special, it had a kind of mystique. But what prompted the bloody cover story was not a fascination with a socio-cultural phenomenon, it was the fascination among the senior editors for mini-skirts. There was no more depth of emotion than that. They were the randiest bunch of pseudo-intellectuals you could ever have the misfortune to meet. Any opportunity to put legs, tits or bums in the magazine and they would do it. . . . That's what made that cover a reality. We knew that there actually was a phenomenon going on in London which kind of differed from what was going on in the States. I don't think we understood it. We felt that the way in which England adopted these new mores was based on some kind of cultural maturity, England, after all, being an older culture, whereas in the States it was yet another crazy fling. We felt that it had a kind of legitimacy in London that we were uncertain about in the States. . . . At that time in New York everything English had cachet.[2]

A decade earlier, this view of England could barely have been imagined by the young men and women who were to become the stars of a classless society. The eighties advertising fantasy of the fifties—of ponytails and bops, of James Dean and flareless Levis, Ruth Ellis sultry in her nightclub, all red lips and revolver—was later unrecognizable to the young meteors, as they were dubbed, who had shared a bag of chips in the rain and fought over rationed nylons. Margaret Forster, author of *Georgy Girl*, which was to become one of the quintessential films of Swinging London and the changing sexual climate, first came to London in 1960 from Carlisle, in the north of England, with her husband, the journalist Hunter Davies, later a friend of the Beatles. They had married because it was impossible then for unwed couples to rent a flat:

> The 1950s were horrible. We were a very starved generation in our teens. The fifties were particularly awful for girls. It was grim and in a place like Carlisle it was grimmer still. We were so starved we queued six deep for all the Hollywood pictures, the glamour, the life we wanted, which you could only see in the pictures. We had so little, it was so austere, even compared with our parents who had known pre-rationing and were always going on about what beautiful Easter eggs they had before the war. Your one aim in life was to be greedy, we were greedy for cultural things, greedy for materialistic things, we were fueled by greed.

A number of factors were responsible for the brief resurgence of Britain: the affluence of the period from the mid-fifties onward; technological change and the expansion of mass communications that brought television to a majority of British homes by the early sixties; the erosion of the class system and the possibility of a meritocracy. The classes were to rub shoulders in Swinging London as they had not done before and probably have not since, for there was a deliberate courting of the working class in the figures of such rough trade as John Lennon, Joe Orton, and David Bailey. The sexual aspirations of the lower classes were already in evidence by the mid-fifties, Christopher Booker, historian of the sixties points out, emblematic in the figure of Alison, the ironing wife in *Look Back in Anger:* "Osborne's elevation of the figure of Alison, so central to the play, into a kind of all-purpose order image, symbolizing upper-class society . . . was revealing . . . [because] this pattern, of lower-class boy dominating upper-class girl, was to become familiar in the fantasy projections of lower-class writers in these years."[3] In Kingsley Amis's *Lucky Jim,* John Braine's *Room at the Top,* and D. H. Lawrence's *Lady Chatterley's Lover,* working-class men fucked the ruling class, and took possession of it through its women. Britain was in a process of disintegration and reconstruction. A decade after *Look Back in Anger,* her colonial possessions had gone and any pretense at being an imperial power, sober, responsible, authoritarian, was finished. Britain was anyone's for the taking.

In the aftermath of the Profumo affair there was an obsession with kinky sex: "Never before had London been a town so fashionably obsessed with kinks, with sexual abnormality and make-believe violence,"[4] Christopher Booker argued from the vantage point of 1970. Throughout the sixties Britain's cult television series was "The Avengers," in which an emancipated woman, Cathy Gale, played by Honor Blackman, and later Emma Peel portrayed by Diana Rigg, exhibited male toughness combined with the exotic sexiness of a woman. The part had originally been written for a man. The producers deliberately had custom-made the black leather cat suits which they knew were the uniform of the Miss Whiplashes of Soho. In one episode, "A Touch of Brimstone," which was banned by ABC in the U.S., Diana Rigg infiltrated the eighteenth-century Hellfire Club as the Queen of Sin; she appeared in a spiked collar and was whipped four times by a Regency buck played by Peter Wyngarde.[5] The bowler hat of John Steed, the leather all-in-one and the saucers of champagne that ended the successful conclusion of each episode's adventure summed up Swinging London's engineering of class, affluence, and forbidden sex into an erotic, potent, and eminently marketable replacement for the drabness of fifties Britain.

Christopher Booker believes that the sixties' erotic preoccupation had less to do with the reality of sex than "the idea of sex, the image of sex; the written image, the visual image, the image that was promulgated in advertisements, in increasingly, 'daring' films, in 'controversial' newspaper articles and 'frank' novels; the image purveyed by the striptease clubs and pornographic bookshops that were springing up in the back streets of Soho and provincial cities; and the image that, mixed with that of violence, was responsible for the enormous boom in the sales of Ian Fleming's James Bond stories."[6]

This notion of sex as idea and image was exemplified when the first topless dresses appeared in the streets of London. Alexander Plunkett Greene, Mary Quant's husband and business manager, remarked: "They've been taken in, poor things. No one was actually intended to wear a topless dress . . . it's simply a caricatured symbol of the fact that busts are in."[7] Later his wife was to shave her pubic hair into the shape of a heart and dye it pink. A vox-pop interview by a tabloid found that the majority of teenage girls found pubic hair ugly.

Topless dresses, miniskirts, hipster trousers, edible panties, see-through blouses, nudity on stage, streakers, the word "fuck" first heard on British television—all the ephemeral images of Swinging London said that Britain had abandoned conventional morality and replaced it with the most frivolous forms of hedonism. The culture of fun cohered in the single icon of the dolly-bird. She symbolized everything that was new, liberated, daring, sexually abandoned, independent, and free. Yet the dolly-bird is a deeply ambiguous figure. She was best epitomized by Twiggy—the unisex body, the curtains of blond hair, the huge blank eyes fringed by false lashes top and bottom, and pale denuded lips. She was the complete antithesis of the elegant, worldly models of the fifties who were twenty-three and looked thirty-two. It was a look essentially created by Mary Quant, who had rebelled against growing up, against the oppressively formal conventions of couture.

In her op-art dress, round-toed shoes, and painted-on lower eyelashes the dolly-bird seemed completely modern, but to people in their sixties she was merely a second pressing of a prototype of forty years earlier, the flapper. In the 1920s youth had been fashionable as a reaction against the old men who had led a generation to their deaths in the trenches. The class hierarchy, with the rich middle-aged woman at its social pinnacle, had crumbled. Fashion minimized the breasts with their association with motherhood and emphasized the long, shapely legs of adolescence. "A woman wearing twenties dress was much more *touchable* than a woman in Victorian or Edwardian dress," says Valerie Steele, historian of fashion and the erotic. "Clothing weighed a fraction of what it had previously and little underwear was worn."[8] The miniskirt and the flat chest in the sixties were a walking advertisement for the Pill, which was all about sex and nothing about maternity. The cult of youth in the twenties and in the sixties was to place enormous demands on the body. Its emphasis on "naturalness" not only reduced women to sex objects but gave them no role to play in manipulating their attractiveness and eroticism through artifice or fetishes. Requiring women to be as near as possible to simplicity and a state of nature, the new fashions in the twenties and the sixties generated both massive booms in dieting and the creation of the beauty industry.[9]

Enthralled by the dolly-bird, America continued to be complicit in constructing the mythology of Swinging London. In 1968, Vance Packard, the American sociologist who had woken the world to the subliminal messages of advertising with *The Hidden Persuaders,* published a 557-page study called *The Sexual Wilderness.* Packard disputed that there had been a sexual revolution. He argued that the scene he surveyed was "too chaotic and varied to describe yet as a revolution," which implied, he thought, "a clear movement in an understood and generally supported direction." He preferred the phrase "sexual wilderness" to describe the terrain of a lost generation.[10] Packard based his assumptions on research in trends in "pre-marital intimacy" among 2,259 college students, including 806 from Britain, Germany, Canada, and Norway. Of those, 245 were English. The main surprise of the research sample, Packard wrote, "was the extreme freedom of behavior and permissiveness of attitudes reported by the English students, both male and female. They headed the list in virtually all cross-national comparisons. Our findings lend support to the statement of the English political commentator Henry Fairlie in 1966, the same year we did our sampling, that 'Britain, at least in its public behavior and public exhibitions, is now the most immoral country in the West.' "[11]

Yet if one examines the youth subcultures of the period that Packard was studying and of which *Time* wrote, they seem curiously asexual. The Mods, who flourished from the early sixties on, were a form of male bonding, an asexual reaction *against* any kind of relationship culture, as punk would be over a decade later. The boys were neat and precise; they wore little suits, shirts with round collars, desert boots, knitted ties, clip-on braces, and, as outerwear for use on their scooters, parkas—army surplus anoraks with a ratty bit of fox fur around the hood. You can see the look in early photographs of The Who and Pete Townshend who wrote the Mod anthem, "My Generation." In 1967, when Mods were pretty much finished, Nik Cohn, rock journalist and son of the author of *The Pursuit of the Millennium*, chronicled their demise in the *Observer Magazine*. He interviewed Geoff McGill, a seventeen-year-old living in Shepherd's Bush:

I go up West every Friday night. I go to a club and stay until it closes. Then I go to some more clubs until it gets light out. Then I go home. Then I go back the next night and do the whole thing again.

I don't have a steady girl but I've dated for up to a month at a time and I always have to finish because the girls get boring. I don't mind girls but men are more intelligent and I think they're meant to be set above.

I'd like to meet a girl who wasn't a slag. I'd still try to pull her but I'd have more respect for her if she was a virgin and wouldn't let me. I think that would be nice.

I don't have enough drive—I would like to get somewhere and be famous but I don't know what to do and, anyhow, I get bored before I've even started. Mostly I don't want to get old. I have a strong dislike for all old people over the age of 30 and I'd say that they were all pathetic.[12]

If these were Mod boys, the prospect for the sexually liberated Mod girl was dispiriting. There were female Mods, Cohn noticed: "Their girls, meanwhile, camp followers, wore long fake-leather coats, suede shoes and had cropped hair and, traipsing around the boys, were ignored. They looked extremely miserable."[13]

Either the Mods were mainly asexual, or they were gay. They denied the latter, but gay men who came out with Gay Liberation in the early seventies had found Mods an extremely convenient subculture to be a part of. It was male, and there was simply no pressure to have a girlfriend. Cohn speculated that it was girls' new self-assurance as earners in their own right and equal spenders and fashion setters that had caused a defensive male reaction, a retreat into a *Boys Own* world.[14] They "were curiously self-contained. They tended not to be interested in girls, nor in anyone else. In clubs they danced by themselves, lost in narcissistic dreams and, wherever there was a mirror, they formed queues. Often, they would wear make-up—eye-liner and mascara—but that didn't mean that they were queer, or not necessarily; it was just a symbol of strangeness."[15] As well as creating the dolly-bird out of male wish-fulfilment, the sixties deconstructed the male in ways we have forgotten. For the first time since the eighteenth century, men were transforming their dress, a change of plumage that came to be called the Peacock Revolution after the bird that has the most spectacular male sexual display. To the fashion historian James Laver, in 1964, the reasons were obvious: "Women can now afford to choose as husbands men who attract them as men, not providers."[16]

Sometime in 1965, my mother bought my father a pink shirt from Marks & Spencer. My father was horrified. He couldn't wear that, he said. Only *nancy boys* wore pink shirts. My mother and I protested. We knew nothing of nancy boys. We did know that pink shirts were all the rage and my father must discard his white ones and become youthful. My father, as it happened, was right. Up until the early sixties, only homosexuals had worn pink shirts. What had happened was that the coding of a sexual subculture had emerged from the underground into the mainstream. Its epicenter was Carnaby Street, on the outer edges of Soho.

Before there was Carnaby Street there was Bill Green, a photographer with a deep interest in muscle men. After the war he began to design briefs and trousers that he sold by mail order from a shop off Carnaby Street. The catalogue would have been immensely popular in those days when homosexuality was illegal, with married men able to ogle the handsome young models, and it probably acted as a licit form of mild pornography. But the clothes were important too. Pre-Green, if you wanted style there was Cecil Gee and nothing else. Gee suits were Italian, elegant, tight, with narrow trousers, and that fashion lasted for years. Green's clothes were not particularly original, but they were bright and bold and colorful: "I always put the emphasis on impact, not make," he told Nik Cohn in the early seventies. "I used materials that had never been used before—lots of velvets and silks, trousers made of bed-ticking, and I was the first with pre-faded denims."[17] And pink shirts. Almost all of Green's customers were gay men. Like Polari, the secret gay language, certain clothes contained coded messages. Only the most socially comfortable or bohemian heterosexual could dare get away with them: Lord Snowdon was rumored to have ordered his entire trousseau from Green. But it was one thing for a few in people to share an in joke, quite another for an entire country to be turned on to it. Green was in his fifties when the sixties began, out of touch with what young people wanted. It was down to one of his shop assistants to transform the sartorial conventions of a subculture into the beginnings of the Peacock Revolution.

The second men's shop on Carnaby Street was opened in 1957 by John Stephen, a working-class Glaswegian who came down to London after a few miserable years working in a metalwork factory. Still barely out of his teens when he opened his first shop, Stephen, unlike Green, knew what the kids wanted. Stephen's shops—eventually he would own several on Carnaby Street, in New York, and in Europe—were the first real boutiques in London, shops like amusement arcades, Cohn thought, "records blaring as loud as they would go, kaleidoscopic window displays, garments hung around the open doorways and spilling out across pavements, in imitation of St. Tropez."[18] Stephen parlayed the camp style of fifties gay men into *the* clothes conventions of Swinging London. In 1962 he secured a coup: he persuaded the British boxer Billy Walker to model his clothes. Walker was then the great white hope of boxing, not a limp-wristed queen but a man in full butch blossom. Blowup posters of Walker wearing pink denims appeared in the windows of Stephen's shops. Beatlemania the following year turned Carnaby Street into a worldwide cult, the place to which a generation of American teenagers made (and still perplexingly continue to make) a pilgrimage to buy their clothes, often dragging their embarrassed parents with them. "I just don't know when I'm going to wear these lamé pajamas," a balding American clutching a John Stephen bag told a *Daily Mail* reporter in 1968, while next to him a young man in a pale-blue, see-through organdie shirt and blue satin taffeta tie asserted his manhood: "You wouldn't find me wearing a mini-kilt, ducky."[19]

Stephen's real interest, one suspects, was less fashion than business. He was a man with an eye for the main chance and the ambition to be a retail giant, as George Davies of Next became in the eighties. Judging by contemporary photographs, his own look was more a turned-on Jermyn Street than the brash disposable gear he sold. It was the next major menswear designer who had the greatest political consciousness of the revolutionary potential for clothes in deconstructing gender. And as Stephen had briefly worked for Green, so Michael Fish, the man who invented the kipper tie, served his time as a managing director with Stephen. Fish, born in 1940, grew up in Wood Green, North London, and was probably destined for the same sort of life as John Stephen, in a factory, until a great-uncle "who had some sort of involvement with the royal family—he used to go and listen to Chopin recitals with somebody at the turn of the century and talked about the Chelsea Flower Show a lot" took him to the south of France when he was fifteen. "And suddenly I saw clear bright colors and dazzling white for the first time. He wouldn't have taken me if I had not been gay and had he not seen something in me that was in his youth." On their return, the great-uncle's connections secured him a job at Collett's, a haberdashers on Shaftesbury Avenue. In those days Soho was gangland—Albert Dimes and Jack Spot having their knife fight there, Neatawear where the prostitutes went to buy their panties and Fish selling stiff collars to old farts, wearing a plastic one himself, which he scrubbed with Vim in the evenings after he had sat and made eyes over a frothy coffee or a proper drink in a proper club: "The men stood in their stiff collars, with their G-and-Ts, stiff as ramrods in their suits, their stiff necks turning to see who was available for thirty bob," he remembers.

As he moved through the buttoned-up world of Jermyn Street shirtmaking, Fish developed a political consciousness: "Men would come in for a navy-blue tie with white dots on it and we had sixteen sizes of dots and they would complain that if they bought *that* one daddy would cut them off without a penny. I had a black lover and I was going Aldermaston marching and worrying about the so-called race riots in Notting Hill and someone was saying they couldn't possibly wear that tie because the spots were too big. Suddenly I thought, oh God, I'm rather tired of all this." Fish wanted to start up on his own and with the financial support of Barry Sainsbury, of the supermarket family, he opened his shop, with its camp label, "Peculiar to Mister Fish," in 1966. Like the impact of Vivienne Westwood a decade later, only the true fashion victim wore his wildest follies like minikilts, but his roll-necked silk shirts and leather maxicoats were soon standards in the high street. Fish became a young meteor: "It was interesting to be courted by the upper classes when I was a common boy," he says. "In a book by Jilly Cooper someone says it's extraordinary that people invite their shirtmaker to dinner these days, meaning me." Fashion for Michael Fish became a form of anarchy, a revolt against the class system. He designed a dressing gown for Muhammad Ali to wear in the ring (now it's in the Smithsonian); some of the clothes for the film *Performance;* and the famous dress worn by Mick Jagger at the Hyde Park concert a few days after Brian Jones's death. (The dress was originally designed for the photographer Patrick Lichfield to wear at a fashion show in aid of Biafra held at the Planetarium and organized by Arabella Church-ill; Lichfield backed out, deciding he looked too girlish in it.) The shop, as seen by Nik Cohn, "was a holocaust of see-through voiles, brocades and spangles, and mini-skirts for men, blinding silks, flower-printed hats. . . . He coincided perfectly with the first eruptions, grew up alongside UFO and Flower Power, and he caught the mood. It was a time when the young rich wished, above all, to be wild and exhibitionist and foolish, and he was all of these things in abundance."[20] Fish didn't care that much about success, although he enjoyed it. He was mainly motivated by ideas and in this, again, he resembles Vivienne Westwood: "I don't care about taste," he told Cohn. "I think taste is a word like love; it should be forgotten for fifty years. I don't even know what it means. Actually, I always think I'm very vulgar. Revolutionaries have to be."[21]

* * *

You do not need to be an archaeologist to excavate the images of sixties sexuality; endlessly recycled, they still inform our own culture. What lay behind them is more puzzling. Although they seem at first sight to be postmodern in their jokiness (the pop-art icon of Barbarella, the pneumatic cartoon girl), there is something genuinely earnest and endearingly simple about the sexual values of the period. We can isolate those images from history, but the models, the rock stars, and the photographers lived through their own times. And much as it may seem that the dolly-bird with her packet of Pills, ready for a night out at the Marquee Club, embodied that freedom, it could not have occurred without a major adjustment to the legislation of morality in Britain. The dolly-birds had no control over this. They couldn't even vote. Freeing sex would require government intervention and the consensus of those with power, particularly the educated middle classes. It needed men like Professor George Carstairs, who delivered the 1962 Reith Lectures called *This Island Now,* and remarked: "The popular morality is now a wasteland. It is littered with the debris of broken convictions. A new concept is emerging, of sexual relationships as a source of pleasure."[22] This is where the millenarian ideas that had resurfaced in the thirties put in a third appearance in the twentieth century.

The men and women with the power to hedonize Britain in the sixties have been dubbed by Lord Annan as members of "Our Age," the generation at university in the thirties and forties, which had come back from the war to vote in the most radical, reforming government of our century. The end of the war offered a watershed in British society: for a hopeful nation a glimpse of a future socialist Utopia—a welfare state, a national health service, the expansion of higher education. Those of Annan's generation "were driven by a laudable ambition. They wanted to call a truce in the class war. That was why they put such a premium on full employment and the provision of generous social benefits without a means test."[23] At Oxford or Cambridge they had read Russell: "He hated and distrusted authority: the enemy of teachers, the police, civil servants and the whole 'insolent aristocracy of jacks in office . . .' " Annan writes. "He denounced 'the system' which demands we show loyalty to our country, impose discipline on children and repress our sexual drive."[24]

The retooling of morality in the sixties has been depicted as a kind of anarchy, a violent overthrow of established customs and traditions, or even as a form of sociopathy, an obsession with the new that Christopher Booker, in his study of the same name, was to call "neophilia." But the influences on Annan's contemporaries urged a reordering rather than a detonation. Russell believed that "politics should be governed by the same principles as govern relations between decent human beings and rejected the syndicalism and class war of Labour politics."[25] It was an attractive doctrine for the liberal middle classes. Annan's generation—in Parliament, in the judiciary, governing the universities and the teacher-training colleges, sitting on Royal Commissions, and editing newspapers—heeded the closet homosexual E. M. Forster with his novels of personal relations: "Each novel was a tract," Annan writes. "Don't lie about your feelings: trust your sexual desire, even if you are a well-bred young girl overwhelmed with the advice of well-bred ladies, says *A Room With a View*. . . . Think clearly not conventionally and act out your feelings: no passion can be wrong nor thought dangerous if it is honest. Renounce religion, dogmatic atheism, class, respectability and you will be saved: you will never experience Agape, spiritual love, unless you have first satisfied Eros, sexual desire."[26] Bloomsbury, ascendant in the twenties and thirties, made Our Age, and its members studied the intricate sexual networks of the Bloomsbury set, itself influenced by the sexual socialism of Edward Carpenter. They were less drawn to the search for sexual authenticity that characterized the American modernists—who would go to hell for a good fuck—than to the proper regulation of new models of sexual arrangement. "My generation was taught by Bloomsbury that the conquest of jealousy was the mark of civilized behaviour," Annan says.[27]

The men and women of Our Age believed not in licentiousness but in tolerance: "Why stop a minority from doing what they want? There is enough suffering in private life; why not diminish it? When a marriage has run on the rocks, why try to identify one guilty party? Why pretend hanging deters murderers when statistics show otherwise and you run the risk of hanging the wrong person? Tolerance, in particular of homosexuals: was it not the mark of totalitarian states to treat such men harshly?"[28] The novelist and journalist Brigid Brophy spoke out in an article titled "The Immorality of Marriage" in the *Sunday Times Magazine* in 1965:

To any rational view, any increase in the *voluntariness* of our behaviour is an advance in civilization. It is the mark of a peasant that he is tied to the land, of a civilized man that he chooses—and he may, of course, choose to go 'back to the land'. Equally, modern married people are free to choose to go back to the 'natural' division of roles between the sexes—provided they can discern what on earth that is; for what distinguishes the human from other species is that our instincts impose no single pattern on our marriages or our societies, and the one thing which is consistently natural for humans is to try by intelligence and imagination to improve on society.[29]

I have never heard Brigid Brophy speak, but when I read this I hear the self-confident tones of the English middle classes of that period; and when she talks of going back to the land, I don't think of hippies in their communes but an early *gîte* in the Dordogne, a stripped pine table and *boeuf en daube* for dinner.

You might say that this desire for tolerance and civilization is watery gruel and compares poorly with the thick soupy passions of the anarcho-erotic sects of three hundred years earlier, with their ecstatic, visionary sense of tomorrow, their mystical belief in the imminence of perfection. In a millennial utopia, sin was a black giant with knotted muscles to be wrestled from the garden. There was riot and excess. In the place of that, Our Age substituted compassion, a judgment from the heart, the impotent, syrupy, Jesus-ridden "loving kindness" of postwar Anglicanism, the fight gone out of it. Compassion preserved the status quo and kept people in their places as victims allowed a little leeway. It lacked the political element of justice, the communist vein that seemed, to Annan's generation in power in the sixties, to run like a disastrous fault line through the thirties. Yet what would Abiezer Coppe have given for the freedoms that Our Age brought about: the Family Planning Act of 1967, which enabled local authorities to set up or support birth-control clinics and to make no distinction between married and unmarried women; the legalization in the same year of abortion up to twenty-eight weeks' gestation; the partial decriminalization of homosexuality in 1968, which permitted sex between consenting male adults in private (though kissing or holding hands in the street continues to be illegal); the abolition of the office of the Lord

Chamberlain that year, putting an end to state intervention into the censorship of the theater; the Divorce Act of 1971, which permitted divorce on the grounds of irretrievable breakdown after two years?

Our Age went to Oxford, to Cambridge, or to the London School of Economics. At Oxbridge, until the seventies, only a fraction of the places were for women. And those who got them quickly married. The men legislated, the wives lobbied. "We were very bourgeois. We were supported by our husbands," says Dilys Cossey, secretary to the Abortion Law Reform Society throughout the sixties, at the time of the passing of the 1967 Abortion Act. "Middle-class women were key movers in social reform; for example, they ran the family-planning clinics as volunteers, because they were not in paid work." In every campaign there were women: filling envelopes, editing newsletters, learning hesitantly to knock on doors and buttonhole politicians, speaking at public meetings, getting seconded onto committees, being made chairpersons of things, receiving honors, a few even entering Parliament and finally wondering if they should no longer consider themselves to be "just a housewife." These liberal, middle-class women, now in their fifties, sixties, and seventies, were the footsoldiers of the sexual revolution.

Dilys Cossey came to London in 1957 after reading French at Manchester University. Her parents were progressive, Welsh nonconformists and Labour Party activists in the rock-solid Conservative constituency of Cirencester and Tewkesbury, where it was said that a broomstick could get elected as a Tory member of Parliament. Yet despite a political education at home, she was typical of thousands of educated, middle-class women who changed jobs frequently, looking for some challenge and fulfilment:

We didn't talk about sex very much. We really were all rather naïve and ill-educated, but we all thought that if we slept with our boyfriends we were being progressive. I had a couple of relationships before I got married. It took me a lot of thinking. I'd not yet actually slept with a bloke and I can remember standing in the room with him and saying, yes, I'll do it. I was twenty-three, for God's sake.

The year I married I did a postgraduate certificate in education, but my expectation was that we would start a family fairly soon so I had no sense of purpose. I had two sets of qualifications—I was a fully trained teacher and I was a fully trained secretary and I was not using either properly. I think that no young woman with the education and training I had would today have got married at twenty-six, got a part-time job with the Abortion Law Reform Society earning the princely sum of two pounds a week, and have her husband subsidize her. Women now do not assume that marriage is for life and they don't assume that marriage is a meal ticket.

By the early sixties this generation of women was married. Although the Pill had liberated them within marriage, it came too late to extend their single life. They were intelligent, and their intelligence was going to waste. They had inherited the social and intellectual assumptions of an earlier generation but without the vision. They grew up into postwar affluence and the gradual decline of Britain as an imperial power. They were bored stiff and undervalued. They were also part of a social trend. Since the twenties, women had been buying the same magazines—*Women's Realm, Woman's Own, Woman, Good Housekeeping*—magazines that created their circulation out of the post–World War One shortage of servants. They helped new wives to learn to cook and sew and bring up their children. They were practical and they were aimed, universally, at housewives. But by the early sixties there was an uneasy feeling among magazine publishers that the market was changing. Women were better-educated and better-paid, better-housed and better-traveled. They put down their housewife's magazine and watched television, opening into a world not only of light entertainment but documentary and news.

In 1964, the publishing conglomerate IPC became convinced that there was a new woman. It commissioned Dr. Ernest Dichter of the New York Institute of Motivational Research to undertake a study on the future of *Woman's Own*. He produced a massive report that spotted a new social and sexual revolution in women's lives that the magazine industry would have to reflect in order to survive. Dichter's study became the publishing Bible. Age and class should stop being the basis of readership classification; there needed to be a revolution in women's magazines.[30] In March 1965, Newnes launched *Nova*, which was billed on its masthead as "A New Kind of Magazine for a New Kind of Woman." *Nova* was sensational. It was a maverick, outrageous, insolent, and stylish challenge to the Establishment. It broke every rule of women's magazine journalism by propelling women out of their traditional roles and forcing them to question every aspect of their lives and their values. It was a model for the Sunday color supplements and it trained the best of British journalists and photographers today.

But *Nova* went far beyond its influence in publishing, where its memory is still regarded with reverence. As we shall see, it was crucial in both formulating the image of this new woman and reflecting the world she lived in; but more significantly, *Nova* had a profound influence over another magazine, the American *Cosmopolitan*. And *Cosmopolitan* was to be one of the most important expressions of women's new sexual freedom.

The origins of *Nova* are obscure. Everyone involved in its early success claims responsibility, and it is probably true that the idea was circulating throughout the magazine industry in various, broadly comparable forms. Certainly one of its progenitors was Alma Birk, a woman of Our Age, without professional magazine experience but embodying the post-Bloomsbury, Labour politics that were reshaping the decade. If she was a little old to be the typical *Nova* reader (who was between twenty-five and thirty-five), she expressed the zeitgeist of the new woman—educated, married young, financially supported by her husband, yet intelligent, restless, and bold in her examination of conventional morality.

Alma Birk's whole upbringing, in a newly affluent family, had hammered into her the need for education in order to achieve economic stability and social advancement. She had been born in London in the twenties to a Jewish immigrant who had come from the Ukraine, first selling sheet music in Ireland, then Woodbine cigarettes for a penny each in London, finally building up a greetings card business. "He was very ambitious and determined to educate himself. He went to night school and read voraciously," she wrote of her childhood in 1965. "Education was always his great love, and he wanted us to have all he had missed. He never ceased instilling in me not only its necessity but its beauty. To him education and a career were not the monopoly of boys, but also the right of girls."[31]

But her father died of cancer at forty-six and her mother, rejecting school advice that Birk should try for Oxford, insisted on a conventional education at secretarial college. Secretly she enrolled in a degree course at the London School of Economics. By twenty-two she was married and quickly had two children. She joined the Labour Party, stood three times for Parliament, sat on Finchley Council from 1950 to 1953, became a justice of the peace and a prison visitor, and by the early sixties was writing a column in the *Daily Herald*. Her husband, Ellis Birk, a lawyer, was a director of IPC and the couple had extensive connections in publishing. Alma, a *New Statesman* and *Spectator* reader, had little experience of women's magazines, which she found cloying. Asked to work out a proposal for a new house magazine for L'Oréal, the hairdressing-products manufacturer, she came up with a concept that an executive was to decide was too good for the house magazine sector and was to become an early blueprint for *Nova*. What she had realized was that between the agony columns of *Woman* and the fashion pages of *Vogue* were thousands of women in desperate straits, for whom marriage was not working out as a story with a happy ending. They were educated women stuck at home, and they were women who had never realized they had any potential at all. In her own mind, it was to these readers that *Nova* was dedicated.

"I wasn't interested in the role of editor, getting in advertising and having rows with printers and so on," she says, nor did she have the crucial production experience needed to do the job. Her name appeared on the masthead as "editorial consultant." After a false start with a launch editor, Harry Fieldhouse, Dennis Hackett was brought in. Hackett was a flamboyant character, the enfant terrible of the magazine world. He was a practicing Catholic who was prepared to confront moral issues to which he may well have been personally opposed. But his brilliance was in getting the magazine off the newsstand and into the hands of the reader by the use of provocative and startling cover lines, a strategy that was to last well beyond his own departure after five years as editor. Because the magazine had no obvious niche market, it had to be an impulse buy. The covers were fantastically diverse. One, timed to coincide with the introduction of the Homosexual Practices Reform Bill in February 1967, depicted a pair of Dutch gay men and disappeared off the shelves in two days, despite an advertising ban by every national newspaper apart from *The Guardian* and *The Observer*. But the regular readers boycotted it. The rationales the staff used to get the covers past management were highly duplicitous: "The managing editor called Dennis Hackett in and Dennis came rushing over and asked me what he was going to tell him," Alma Birk remembers. "I said, say that so many women have homosexual hairdressers and dressmakers and that they find them very *sympatique*. Tell him we wouldn't dream of doing it with lesbians. He said, why not? I said, all I'm saying is what you tell him this afternoon, now."

The covers ranged across every issue of the sixties—racism, childbirth (depicting a baby emerging from its mother's womb), adultery, the crisis in the Catholic Church, the Vietnam War, homelessness, living in sin, swearing, immigrants. In one year, 1968, Hackett blazed through the months captivating and antagonizing his readers. In February 1968: PRIN-CESS PIGNATELLI PLUCKS EACH HAIR OFF HER LEGS WITH TWEEZERS. WITH THAT DEDICATION AND £5,348 TO SPARE, YOU TOO MIGHT MAKE NINTH IN THE BEST-DRESSED LISTS. SHARE THE AGONY—PAGE 60. In May 1968, beneath a picture of three Biba-eyed aggressive beauties, their black-leather fists chained to the railings of the Houses of Parliament: 50 YEARS AFTER THE VOTE: ONLY THE CHAINS HAVE CHANGED. In August 1968, above a portrait of two couples and their children: MICHAEL HALSEY AND GEOF-FREY HULL THINK THEIR WIVES HAVE SUFFERED ENOUGH ANXIETY ABOUT BIRTH CONTROL. SO THEY'VE DONE SOMETHING POSITIVE ABOUT IT. THEY'VE HAD THEMSELVES STERILISED. In October 1968, below a line drawing of Twiggy shaving her armpits: PRIVATE FACES. TWIGGY, THE QUEEN, PRINCE PHILIP, THE POPE, FROST ETC—PAGE 60. In December of that year there appeared a scene of a middle-aged couple watching television, photo-graphed through the miniskirted legs of their daughter, with the caption: "What makes children revolt, take pot, drop out, love in and not under-stand their parents." And in that one breathless year, the September cover summed up the fracturing of the conventions of women's lives in the sixties:

I have taken the pill.
I have hoisted

my skirts to my thighs,
dropped them
to my ankles,
rebelled at university,
abused the
American Embassy,
lived with two men,
married one,
earned my keep,
kept my identity
and frankly . . .
I'm lost
Find yourself on Page 38.

It was possible to sustain this controversy only when buoyed up by heavy advertising to supplement falling revenues whenever a cover offended. *Nova* was an adman's dream, "an art director's show place, a walking, breathing, dossier of their artwork which would amuse and impress their artistic friends in NW2 and perhaps advance their careers,"[32] according to Brian Braithwaite, a magazine executive who began his career in the sixties. There was an advertising South Sea Bubble in progress, spearheaded by the massive color campaigns for synthetic fibers like Bri-Nylon, Terylene, Dacron, and Acrilan. A war broke out between the synthetics and the natural fibers of the International Wool Secretariat and the Cotton Board. The synthetics stood for modernism, for pop art, Perspex jewelry, PVC macs, Courrèges white plastic boots, the surface texture of technology. By March 1967, the petroleum products were beginning to look dated, fashion was replacing the vertigo of futurism with hippie style, and Courtaulds countered with a campaign for a fiber called Vincel by plagiarizing *Nova*'s assertion of the revolution in women's lives:

WOMEN ARE REVOLTING . . . against the geometrical state of op and pop. Against too-far-out pacemakers, over-imitated trend-setters. Down with the Establishment of Fashionable Kinkiness! Up with a new standard of feminine fancies! Fabrics as soft as a snowflake or as crisp as a misty dawn.

In colours that gleam and glow. Women have one invincible ally. Vincel.
Vive la Revolution!

Compared with the Sunday color supplements, with their endless serial-
izations of books about Churchill and Stalin, their obsession with Henry
VIII and the roots of Englishness, *Nova* was excavating the foundations
for a radical restructuring of the lives of middle-class women. Alma Birk
was anxious not to allow the brain of a married woman to disintegrate into
mush. In the first few months of the magazine's life she dreamed up a series
called "The Intelligent Woman's Guide to Isms": Freudianism, Marxism,
Logical Positivism, Existentialism among them. Under the guidance of the
literary editor, the young A. S. Byatt, there were articles on "the Saigon
of the sex war" conducted by London's "rich crop of articulate, witty
women novelists." It was noted that: "A taboo seems to be growing up
around the phrase 'I love you' as delivered from the lips of woman to man.
It could be that this declaration is the ultimate in identity-submergence,
and therefore unreal, a bestowal of total responsibility on another human
being, and not in keeping with the new feminine strength and ability to
go it alone."[33]

The emergence of a new man was detected to accompany the "Quant-
dressed, Sassoon-cut, Courrèges-booted, Oliver Goldsmith–spectacled
girl . . . custom built, coolly functional." It may be, it was speculated, that
a new set of attitudes was coming into being, "in which efficiency and
convenience are more to be desired than the pain and the passion and give
and take of the sex war as we knew it. There are no causes left to fight
for, and the land we are marching forward to build must be one fit for
computers. Why shouldn't it be the same with personal relationships, and
the new ideal a kind of third sex, dispassionate, invulnerable and effi-
cient."[34] Two months later, Alma Birk took on the stereotype of the
widow and her sexual deprivation: "I had heartbreaking letters from
women who felt so guilty that they were betraying their dead husbands.
Cruse [the organization for widows] wrote and said how disgusted they
were and how it had upset all sorts of people. It wasn't hard for me to have
the courage of those sorts of convictions."

In October 1966, Irma Kurtz looked far beyond the sixties to identify a new class of women that education and the Pill were in the process of creating. She called the article "The New Spinsters," and it was perhaps to be the last time that such a word would be used of single women:

> Maiden aunts who don't drink, don't smoke, rarely earn their own bread and who, if not virgins, have filed the memory of defloration under "ugly" or "true love" are becoming fictional characters. We modern young spinsters are real and resemble our maiden aunts only superficially: our Sunday papers are read in order, some of us empty ashtrays and our flats, that ten years ago had a slapdash charm, are beginning to absorb as much furniture polish as the houses of our married sisters. . . . Of course we go to bed with other people's husbands. Infidelity provides us with most of our lovers and although they solve the problem of an escort only to darker restaurants, unfaithful husbands keep us from one sort of frustration. . . . Most of us have learned to make love without fuss and embarrassment, a business meeting with the man whose tea we brewed that morning. . . . No matter how we felt in our teens and our twenties, the longer we're spinsters, the less we want to stop. . . . Forced to do better than just survive in the big man's world, we became self-sufficient and pretty tough; these are called masculine attributes. Not many of us are lesbians, although that label is attached to us by men whose advances we have rejected as the only explanation for our single lives. . . . We didn't start out to be spinsters. We made the same first steps as other women, but one of them took us over the threshold of the mirror, where we found ourselves on an unexpected path, walking away from what we used to want.[35]

Throughout these early *Nova* articles there is the recurrent emphasis on efficiency in relationships, the streamlined lover and her no-nonsense attitude to the sexual act. The "civilized" behavior of "decent" people, embodied by Russell and his acolytes, had undergone a technological revolution for the computer age of the sixties Labour government. By 1968, however, Catherine Storr, in an article ominously titled "LOST" was questioning the capacity of society to socially engineer women's lives. "Where in hell has Modern Woman got to?" she asked. "For it is no longer just the archetypal suburbanite who is looking for a way out. If the vote was just a beginning, the pill was by no means the end of her road to a new life. Does the new freedom imply, after all, just a new and more sophisticated suffering?" By the late sixties, the women who had voted in the postwar Labour government and campaigned for progressive social legislation were beginning to fear that planned morality was getting out of hand. "It isn't surprising that we're a floundering, hesitating, bewildered, distracted sex just now. It's one thing to be told you're emancipated, it's quite another to know that inside yourself you are truly free," Catherine Storr thought. The scientific model was failing:

> The trouble about our new freedom is that it's too theoretical, it's too competitive, it's expressed in terms which are too absolute. Its theoretical nature is dangerous because, in the flush of a successful scientific age, we incline to believe that we can solve all our problems by subjecting them to the techniques of the science laboratory. We forget that the validity of result of a laboratory experiment relies on the deliberate exclusion of as many extraneous factors as possible, and that in ordinary living you can't do this—and a very impoverished life you'd have if you could—so the conclusions reached by the experimenters aren't necessarily true for any situation outside the lab.[36]

From the late sixties onward, *Nova* lost some confidence and gained some wisdom, but by this time some of its lessons had been absorbed elsewhere. Dennis Hackett was promoted to editorial director of all Newnes titles, to which he applied the *Nova* treatment. *Nova* was no longer as distinctively different as it had once been.[37] In the early sixties, every Aunt Sally was there to be knocked over. But once a mass-circulation magazine had done the unthinkable and put homosexuals on the cover, once it had provided chatter for an hour or two at dinner parties on the subject, it needed to move on. It had already provided more than most readers wanted to know about homosexuals or abortion or swearing or the sex lives of widows. *Nova* ran out of subjects. It never lost its radical vision, but it became more serious. Still committed to social change, it was left to do the drudgery needed to improve the position of women. In the early seventies, *Nova* had got beyond the stage of saying the outrageous, the unsayable. It investigated the new issues of vaginal politics, self-help, breast cancer, pornography. In the newspaper and magazine world, there is one word that spells death to a feature idea and it is "worthy," in the sense of, 'I know this is important but I'd rather think about something else.' This is what *Nova* became, an early prototype of *Ms*, if only it had had the energy of the American women's movement behind it. But *Nova* had never been just a women's magazine. Male journalists fought to work on it, men edited it, men were seen reading it as they read *Vanity Fair* today.

Management had never been fully behind *Nova*. "It was a struggle all the time because there weren't enough people at the company who really believed in it," Alma Birk says. She and other members of the staff were constantly undermined by the supposed opinions of directors' wives: "The managing director would say to me, my wife says this, and that was hell. If you're an engineer or a doctor no one tells you their wives' opinions. It was as if running a magazine didn't need any particular skills at all and any old amateur could knock it and that would be given equal weight with everything else. I got really fed up with what people's wives thought of *Nova*. Years later, they apologized and told me, well, you were ahead of your time."

In 1967, Harold Wilson was trying to bring a new generation of young peers into the House of Lords, particularly women. One of them was Alma Birk, created a baroness. She continued to write for *Nova* and before she left for the Lords she originated the idea for a new service aimed at putting married women back to work, trying to overcome the frustration, lack of training, and sparse work experience of those who had married too young: "There is a part of her still unfulfilled, a part not entirely covered by the functions of wife and mother, and that part is silently screaming to be satisfied. In other words, she wants to do something beyond her domestic, marital and maternal routine," she wrote.[38] Under the direction of Carolyn Faulder, the service aimed to target national and local institutions that could redirect married women back into the work force. It promised to campaign, lobby government departments, and influence policy. In 1969, Alma Birk became chairman of the Health Education Council and commissioned the young Saatchi brothers to produce the campaign that inaugurated their career—the poster of a pregnant man, his hand on his arched-in back, asking, "How would you like it if you were pregnant?" Richard Crossman, the Labour Minister, rang her up and told her he didn't like it. "I told him, you're not supposed to hang it up in your drawing room." It was a classic *Nova* cover. Dennis Hackett has remained, for his whole career, a troubleshooting editor. Alma Birk sat on committees, and in the seventies was a minister at the Department of the Environment, responsible for national heritage. Now in her sixties, she is still a front-bench spokesman.

In the second issue there had been an editorial on the magazine's title. A nova's brightness fades quickly. The riposte was that in the universe, time is relative. It wasn't just the flash of brilliance *Nova* was named for: "It's *Nova* because all over the world the name means new—and that seemed a good enough reason. Besides, we like it. Don't you? It's just an encouraging coincidence that the name of the space project that is to take over lunar exploration where the current Saturn rocket leaves off is— you've guessed it, Nova."[39]

The economic recession of the early seventies, the oil crisis, and the three-day week burst the consumer boom of the sixties. Throughout magazine publishing, advertising revenue plummeted. Circulation, which had once been over 120,000, reached an all-time low of 86,000 (still considerably higher than magazines today like *Esquire* and *Tatler* or the British circulation of *Vanity Fair*). IPC, which had taken over Newnes some years earlier, reduced the page size from thirteen by ten to ten by eight inches. Its last edition, in October 1975, featured on the cover the light-comedy pair of Morecambe and Wise to illustrate a feature on baldness. Another cover line asked: "Will your doggy have a white wedding?" It looked rather like a slightly larger version of the American *TV Guide*. It was an ignominious burnout for a dazzling star.

But it was not just the economy that killed *Nova*. It was a magazine of its era, dazzling, impudent, restless, propelling itself into a marvelous future of machine surfaces that never dulled, decayed, or grew old. The age changed. Huddled round a coal fire, if you could find one, during the three-day week with its government-instituted evening power cuts, London ceased to swing. The next city to be claimed as the capital of erotica would be San Francisco. Having bequeathed the vision of sexual freedom to America, London reverted to the dreary provincial city it is today. In April 1972, another magazine was launched in Britain. And it was that which in the end killed off *Nova*—though, very curiously indeed, before it did so it had effortlessly cannibalized the politics of Our Age.

6

Fun, Fun, Fun

I should confess that half my life ago, I was a willing supplicant to the Cosmo zeitgeist . . . I was quite smug when I scored highest of all my friends on "How Sensuous Are You?," which gauged sensuality through such revealing factors as how you eat ice-cream cones. In the narcissistic pit of my adolescent ego, I believe I was convinced that with the right make-up, lighting and fab designer gown, I too could be one of those Scavullo-shot models pouting from the covers, or (as the come-ons of those rip-off modeling agencies put it) "just look like one." Yes! I was, to quote one of Helen Gurley Brown's early gushatorials, "a grown-up girl, interested in whatever can give you a richer, more exciting, fun-filled, friend-filled, man-loved kind of life."

Moira Farr

I have considered myself a devout feminist from the beginning.

Helen Gurley Brown

While Alma Birk was pursuing legislative change for a Labour Britain, Helen Gurley Brown was pursuing, and getting, her man. What are Helen Gurley Brown's politics? Who knows? In England, Alma Birk could knock herself against substantial things—class, education, title, the mahogany furniture of state that in the sixties used to be called the Establishment. America is a big country. Helen Gurley Brown was the little girl from Little Rock, Arkansas, who lit out for the city at the end of the Depression, a rootless wanderer in a society where anything was possible and your class could be shed like your old cloth coat when your success demanded a mink. She was the iconic aspirant, the undiluted essence of the girl-on-the-make, the tits, teeth, and eyelashes with attitude that were to become the *Cosmo* Girl.

The *Cosmo* Girl was guys' fantasy of the liberated woman, all legs and edible panties, with her own job and own studio apartment, adept at giving great head and getting great breakfast. Financially independent, nominally feminist, she scorned those dated old presents—minks, diamond bracelets. She lived in a throwaway culture and was happy with the occasional Perspex bangle. You had sex with her because she was hot, she wanted it, she was insatiable. Her folks were half a continent away. In the city, you might never see her again.

Cosmo was liberation with the politics sucked out of it. It was quizzes and how-to sex guides and pop psychology and gee whizz, the world is an interesting place. It was fun, fun, fun. In the mid-eighties, the British edition of *Cosmo* started to take issues other than sex seriously and for a while it became an important manual for the working woman, taking on campaigns about workplace issues and career development. But the editor, Linda Kelsey, moved on to another magazine, *She,* which had as its niche market "women who juggle their lives," the working mothers that the *Cosmo* Girl would become. And British *Cosmo,* under the editorship of Marcelle d'Argy Smith, demonstrated that, despite AIDS, sex still sells, with cover lines like "The best SEX TIPS ever (We're still recovering)" combined with "Ask him to marry you (The worst he can do is to say yes)." Yet *Cosmo* is unabashedly feminist, in its way, as it reveals in articles by journalists such as Melissa Benn, more familiarly seen in the pages of *The Guardian* and *New Statesman,* warning us to brace ourselves for the backlash: "Finally women are achieving!" the "sell" read. "We're really getting somewhere at work and gaining independence at home. But some men feel we're too close for comfort. If we believe the hype, equality is bad for us and freedom makes us unhappy. Only by recognizing the propaganda can we fight it and then move forward."[1]

How real is *Cosmo* feminism? Real enough for millions of women who have glimpsed in its pages the possibility of another life. *Cosmo* has always told its readers to go for it. It has encouraged them to fulfil their own needs. It is the philosophy of the old Virginia Slims slogan—"You've come a long way, baby." It *is* feminism, but of a kind most committed feminists have long moved on from.

As some species of animals alive today represent an early phase of evolution, stubbornly and anachronistically surviving from a primeval age, the *Cosmo* Girl harks back to the earliest years of second-wave feminism. But if she is an anachronistic holdover, she is, of course, an astonishingly successful one, as if evolution had run ahead of itself in the other species. The *Cosmo* Girl was what happened to single women once they got hold of the Pill. Later, of course, early *Cosmo* contributors like Gloria Steinem would realize that the power relations between men and women were more complex than had earlier been thought. That sexual freedom was a minor gain in the main engagement for equal rights and a restructuring of society to reflect gender difference. But sexual liberation, the eroticization of women's lives by and for themselves, was profound and important. Unleashing the power of women's sexuality has never had minor effects. And *Cosmopolitan* as much as anything else encouraged women to free their desires, if not their souls. The *Cosmo* Girl was not born, like Athena, ready-made out of the brain of some godlike male. Nor was she bolted together from the sole imagination of Helen Gurley Brown, a Dr. Frankenstein of women's lives. The *Cosmo* Girl had a genesis and that, unlikely as it seemed, included the influence of the European sexual pioneers.

Helen Gurley, as she was then, moved to Los Angeles during the war, to a series of secretarial jobs from which she was successively fired, always hanging about the bright lights. She was one of those aging girls, still girly, who always live in hope. And at thirty-one she entered a contest in *Glamour* magazine called "Ten Girls with Taste." She won. Well, she won the competition but not the war; she was still single. There were men in her life, of course; one was married, another was a shit. On the strength of the competition she got a job as a copywriter in advertising and worked on the Max Factor account. She was sending money back to her ill and impoverished family in Little Rock and still she saved. By 1958 she had enough money to walk into a Beverly Hills Mercedes dealer and buy a used blue-gray convertible with a cloud-gray leather interior for $5,000 cash. It was a fantastically reckless thing to do, but it was bait. It caught a whopper.

David Brown was a vice president at Twentieth Century–Fox, handsome, charming, rich, ambitious, and forty-two. He fell for the wrong kind of woman, the kind who would leave him. Helen Gurley was thirty-seven and needed to close a deal now. The car did it. Here was a woman who was a sticker, who bought and paid for her own vehicle. In cash. Reader, she got him. They were married in 1959 and she moved into a Mediterranean-style house overlooking the Pacific—plus a hundred acres of virgin forest near San Francisco, two Mercedeses, a full-time maid, and the good life. She brought with her a few trinkets from her old single days: six-pound dumbbells, a slant board, an electronic device for erasing wrinkles, several pounds of soy lecithin, powdered calcium and yeast-liver concentrate for Serenity Cocktails, "and enough high-powered vitamins to generate life in a statue."[2] But that was not the end of the fairy tale. Marriage had not fulfilled her every need. She and David were on their Sunday afternoon walk in Will Rogers State Park in Los Angeles when she confided to him that while she had been a career girl for twenty years, no one valued her. His solution was that she should write a book. He suggested a title like "How to Have an Affair." She wrote it under the hair dryer and at work and it was her own story.

Sex and the Single Girl was published in 1962 and it is one of the most important books of the sexual revolution. This is what was revolutionary about it:

The *Reader's Digest* once published an article about an unmarried woman who had Given In, suffered unspeakable guilt and humiliation, decided she could no longer face the degradation of the relationship and had moved to another city to Start Over. The *Digest* left little doubt that she'd done the only thing a single woman under such circumstances *could* do. . . .

A recent issue of the *Ladies' Home Journal* summed up its stand in that last paragraph of an article entitled "Is the Double Standard Out of Date?" by stating that a single woman confronted by a man who "insists" can do only one of two things. She can marry him or she can say "No."

I don't know about girls in Pleasantville and Philadelphia, where these magazines are published, but I do know that in Los Angeles, where I live, there is something else a girl can say and frequently does when a man "insists." And that is "Yes." As for moving to another city to Start Over, if all the unmarried girls having affairs in my city alone felt called upon to do that, there would be the biggest population scramble since the Exodus.

Nice, single girls do have affairs and they do not necessarily die of them! They suffer, sometimes, occasionally a great deal. However, quite a few "nice" single girls have affairs and do not suffer at all.[3]

In print, a married woman had revealed that she had had sex before marriage. Brown said more. That there was nothing particularly attractive about a thirty-four-year-old virgin.[4] That once in bed there was no point in faking inexperience and that aggressive advances might even be regarded by men as a turn-on. That not only could one have one lover, it was perfectly permissible to have two or more.[5] That sex would be better for the single girl and with her because it was not bound by duty. That marriage was the best insurance for the worst years of a woman's life, when she could no longer pull guys in by the dozen. That the single woman was emerging as the new glamour girl of the age, a winner, not a loser. She had time and money to spend on her looks and because she worked in a man's world (albeit as his secretary) she understood men. She spoke their language, the language of retailing, advertising, exporting, and motion pictures, while a wife spoke the language of the PTA, Dr. Spock, and the jammed clothes dryer.[6]

A vast propaganda exercise had been conducted in America for the whole of the century. Its aim had been to obliterate the sexuality of the unmarried woman. Its theme was that nice girls don't, that sex out of wedlock could only end in despair, diseases, exile, and death. As a young teenager, I learned about sex from the *True Confessions* stable of magazines imported from America, with their stories of small-town life, moral fables of the expulsion from a clapboard Eden by a right-thinking populace of the girl with no ring and a maternity dress. Sex before marriage brought a specific retribution: pregnancy and shame. Throughout the sixties, *True Confessions* would struggle to restructure its moral worldview to account for the technological revolution in the garden that had removed the wages of sin from sex.

Did the sexual revolution change anything? Yes. It brought about a definitive change in the sexual lives of women. As Barbara Ehrenreich,

Elizabeth Hess, and Gloria Jacobs have argued in *Remaking Love: The Feminization of Sex,* the story that has been told of the sexual revolution has been for the most part that of a male sexual marketplace: "In fact, if either sex has gone through a change of sexual attitudes and behavior that deserves to be called revolutionary, it is women and not men at all,"[7] they write. Before the sexual revolution men slept with a few women—prostitutes, girls who were easy, their fiancées—then married. They boasted of their conquests, if they had any, and liked to give the impression that their adventures continued outside the nuptial bed. Women were under tremendous pressure to be virgins until they married. Sex was a dirty thing, a contamination. Speaking of sex was foul. In the seventies, scores of American novels were published about the sex life of teenagers in the fifties, as grown-up writers recalled the high school divisions between bad girls and good. By the time those books were written, within ten years of the licensing of the Pill and the publication of *Sex and the Single Girl,* the pattern of women's sexual lives had been transformed. Women, like men, fucked around, got married or maybe not, fucked around some more.

Helen Gurley Brown had broken this taboo. She was given a syndicated column by the *Los Angeles Times,* setting herself up as a sophisticated older sister dispensing raunchy advice to the kind of mouseburgers she had once been herself. It was her husband who suggested she should have her own magazine; in the wake of the financial disaster of his production of *Cleopatra,* he had been fired from Fox in 1963 and the couple had moved to New York. She took a format to Hearst, but the company wasn't interested in launching a new publication. It was, however, prepared to allow her to take over as editor of *Cosmopolitan,* an ailing "family" magazine from the previous century that had once published the short stories of P. G. Wodehouse.

The first issue of *Cosmo* that Helen Gurley Brown edited was introduced by a perky little letter from the editor herself. "Come into My Parlor," it beckoned, as she has done in every subsequent issue. Helen Gurley Brown really does work in a parlor: a wallpapered sanctum with rows of Edwardian china dolls on the window ledges and tiny cushions embroidered with mottos about the good things in life like sex and champagne. And the editor herself sits in the middle of it all, with her strangely unlined face and withered arms, like the pleasantest spider in the world. "The stories and articles in this issue were picked for one reason only," she wrote. "I thought they'd interest you . . . knowing that you're a grown-up girl, interested in whatever can give you a richer, more exciting, fun-filled, friend-filled, man-loved kind of life!"[8]

The first issue of *Cosmo* bore Helen Gurley Brown's imprint, but it was still unsure of itself. It clearly aimed at the working girl and advised that it was just as easy to love a rich man, that psychoanalysis was not only for neurotics, that divorce could be painless, and that it was possible to break into advertising. There were no earnest articles about social legislation, no fashionable bogeymen to be assaulted. Women were capable of transforming their own lives by the administration of pharmaceuticals by male medics (*Cosmo* would have a long tradition of dispensing the advice of men with degrees). Its lead article in that first issue, in July 1965, was called "Oh What a Lovely Pill!" It was about estrogen, "a honey of a hormone," a miracle drug, a panacea that, if used from puberty to the grave, would promise eternal youth and sexual vigor. "My skin is fresher, my hair has more shine; the pill makes me feel and look more attractive," said one devotee. "I'm going to take these pills all my life," said another. "I wouldn't dream of giving them up. Even when I no longer need birth control pills."[9] Helen Gurley Brown was in her mid-forties. What she was describing was HRT.

The editor's age was showing. The magazine focused on the ghetto of New York singles, clustered in the apartment buildings of the Upper East Side. An early article went on an anthropological expedition:

> No other parcel of Manhattan real estate is so well geared to the frantic pace of the single girl than that bounded by Sixty-fifth Street on the south, Eighty-sixth Street on the north, Park Avenue on the west and across to the East River. Here amid a welter of banjo-and-beer saloons, discotheques, kooky boutiques, thrift shops, walk-up brownstones, and expensive apartment buildings is the domain of the single girl. Thousands on thousands of single girls flock to the Upper East Side, cramming themselves into small apartments, subsisting on an apple and a quart of diet soda a day, waiting for a telephone to ring and having a mad, wonderful time.

Inevitably they meet their men, and then just as suddenly as their ghetto existence began, it's over.[10]

But the New York singles ghetto had existed since the thirties. Indeed Jacqueline Susann, author of *Valley of the Dolls* and Helen Gurley Brown's friend, had lived such a life in the forties before she married. It had been the subject of innumerable films in the fifties, like *How to Marry a Millionaire* in which three schemers, including Marilyn Monroe, pretend to rent a swank apartment to catch their men.

Another early article, by a male writer, echoed the deep ambivalence toward the Pill of a media anxious about its effect on the family. "What the Pill Is Doing to Husbands" set up one of those phony trends so beloved of the magazine sector. It posited a syndrome by which men were made impotent by the newfound sexual freedom of their wives. A battery of doctors quoted statistics on how the Pill had improved women's sexual drive and "satisfaction." In response, their husbands, having lost responsibility for birth control, were succumbing to a disease that women had suffered from for centuries without it being medicalized into a syndrome: lack of self-esteem. One doctor, at the Institute of Psychoanalysis in Chicago, had recommended to a patient that he should remind his wife to take her Pill every night: "Thus by 'dispensing' the contraceptive, he felt he maintained control." Another wife was said to have driven her husband to "sterility anxiety": "He felt that because he couldn't possibly make her pregnant, he had lost control over his masculinity." Some right-wing doctors saw the Pill as a powerful agent in the emasculation of America by creeping socialism and government paternalism. A Dallas gynecologist never prescribed the Pill because he regarded it as castrating the husbands of his patients. But science could help, as always: "Right now," the author Theodore Berland wrote, "there is no test, no easy way to determine which husbands will flip when their wives go on the pill. Even wives can't tell in advance. But research being conducted now may result in some way to predict which men will have trouble. Until then, advise experts, physicians should interview and carefully examine couples before prescribing oral contraceptives."[11]

These early *Cosmos* seemed to reflect a failure of nerve on the editor's part. The articles were often coy and still jittery about the outright expression of women's sexuality. *Cosmo* seemed to be lagging behind the real changes that were taking place among readers, as if someone had switched on a short time-delay switch at the magazine's headquarters on Fifty-seventh Street. The problem, however, was the failure to find the right writers. Helen Gurley Brown looked abroad, to *Nova*, which had launched five months before: "About Alma Birk," she says: "In the early days there were very few people who got my message. There was a man named W. H. Manville who had more insight about my kind of woman than anybody. And then there was Alma, Lady Birk, rather prim, not spinsterish but rather correct, who knew exactly what I was talking about. I picked up the *Nova* stuff and still would if it were out there and I haven't seen many magazines to pull material from for *Cosmo*. She was invaluable and those articles she contributed were absolutely original. She was my personal pet." At this stage she was buying articles by Alma Birk from *Nova* and rerunning them. Then, when Birk was in New York with her husband, who was on business there, Helen Gurley Brown called her in for a meeting, to ask her to contribute directly. Birk was bemused. Helen Gurley Brown's philosophy seemed to be completely different from her own. Alma read, with disapproval, articles about looking to see if there was an attractive man driving in the next lane and she thought the practice was highly dangerous. She told Helen that, as a magistrate, she was shocked. *Cosmopolitan* represented, she thought, a relentless chase for men.

If you look at the contents pages of the early *Cosmo*s you will find that every so often one article seemed to lay out what was to become the *Cosmo* philosophy. These articles were wordy, literate, precise, lacking the zing and witty phrasemaking of American journalism; they were political and philosophical; they argued, cajoled, and convinced the readers that women's wrongs were structured into society and its institutions. They were all, of course, written by Alma Birk.

In February 1968 she wrote one called "The Sexual Drive in Women (Greater, Equal or Inferior to Men's?)." That women need sex less than men is a male-contrived myth, she began. Sex is an appetite that needs feeding and the sexual drive is a normal part of our biological nature. No one, she argued, would suggest that if a man and a woman were hungry for food, he should eat while she should starve. Only men who refuse to accept women as equals would take refuge in the stereotype of the sexually dominating woman. Then, from a simple enough point about biological need, she moves into the kind of analysis that would have been familiar to Carpenter and Russell. Society's way of preserving monogamy was to keep women insecure while conning them into believing they were free. It herded the single, the widowed, and the divorced into sexless ghettos while condemning the married woman to perpetual lack of confidence about her ability to perform or to be desirable. She spoke of a vast range of sexual possibilities, including masturbation, which she wanted out of the closet, and erotica for women, which she wanted made available. She looked the population trends in the eye coldly and suggested that if women outnumbered men, brothels for them should be seriously considered: "Disgusting? The quick answer is 'Yes.' But is it really worse than the numbers of lonely women starving for sex affection, who join cruises, holiday in hunting pairs, and try surreptitiously to pick up young men or other women's husbands? And with guilt oozing all over any transient pleasure they might find."

Finally, she tried to imagine a free woman, thinking classic utopian thoughts, a blueprint for the sexual millennium:

The free woman will be aware of her sexuality and unafraid of it. She will not have inherited inhibitions about sexual activity and stimulation and sex will be a natural part of her life. In fact, she will be integrated above and below her waistline. Men will then find their fears and anxieties are reduced for the sex war will be over and men and women will be able to live in true intimacy. Togetherness will mean something at last. Except for a minority, sexual monogamy is a myth. But monogamy as the basis of the family unit will be safer once the false theory of compulsive monogamy has gone. With its departure, I believe man and woman will show more wisdom in choosing their life partners, since they will no longer pretend that compulsive fidelity is the basis for successful marriage—or love. This freedom may come a bit late for the majority of the present adult generations to enjoy, but unless we have the courage to labor for it, the young ones will not stand a chance either.[12]

There were men and women in America who also thought these things, and we shall meet them in later chapters. But none were so close to the mainstream, to the sources of power, as Alma Birk was in England. *Cosmo,* like the rest of the American media, quickly became infatuated with Britain. America was suddenly self-conscious that its own suburban complacency as a postwar world power was beginning to look dated. The American wife with her crew-cut husband, dream kitchen, and god-fearing young'uns depicted in the sunny pastels of advertising color photography, was a stilted joke, a Formica prison for the spirit. "London is alive. London swings. London is youth, talent, vitality, creativity," wrote Elizabeth Downing in *Cosmo* in 1965. "As an American who has visited England every year for the last ten, I have seen London, in the manner of a nubile girl, suddenly make New York seem matronly." The author gathered evidence. She went to "Lady Q," who declared that the smart London dinner party now included some couples who were not married to each other. She walked down King's Road and found "Alice-in-Wonderland hair, little girl dresses and round-toed shoes. The craze was short, short hair last winter; it is just hitting New York. Other firsts were shift dresses and white, white stockings." The girls, British journalist John Crosby told her, "take to sex as if it's candy and delicious."[13]

Whatever was going on on the campuses or in the communes or the free-love movement in Berkeley, California, *Cosmo* was to draw its inspiration from Britain in the construction of the early model of the *Cosmo* Girl. The Swinging London dolly-bird, as an icon of the sexually free single woman, became gradually incorporated into emerging *Cosmo* philosophy, reinforced by those articles by Alma Birk that showed there was an intellectual rationale for such behavior. Yet sex continued to be treated gingerly, at arm's length. As late as 1969, W. H. Manville compiled a tame dictionary of "kinks"—"dirty language," fetishes for bras, a dollop of Hershey's milk-chocolate syrup on each nipple, dirty movies, porn, mirrors on the ceiling, one-night stands, and fantasies—reassuring the reader, heavily, *"It's not disloyal to your husband to have these fantasies."*[14] "Is Nude Psychotherapy for You?" another article asked.[15] A singles bar was tried, but the writer didn't like it. But such subjects were still assumed by *Cosmo* to be of minor anthropological interest. Unlike her English sisters, the typical *Cosmo* Girl was a big-game hunter and *Cosmo* was her guide. A map was drawn up of the United States advising women where to go find husbands: the number-one spot was Norfolk, Virginia, where men in the navy, shipbuilders, deep-sea fishermen, and automotive engineers outnumbered women three to one. Chicago wasn't a bad bet either, with its college professors, railroad men, conventioneers, meat packers, printers, butter-and-egg men, and ex-Big-Ten football stars entering business.[16]

It was very late, the sixties were almost over, before the final metamorphosis of the Swinging London dolly-bird/Upper East Side singles ghetto girl/*Nova* non-monogamous wife into the *Cosmo* Girl was complete. Despite her magazine's inherited title, with its In-Town-Tonight atmosphere of Stork Club and Polo Lounge, Helen Gurley Brown had always felt an affinity with small-town girls. Her readers would feel cosmopolitan even if they did not live in New York or Los Angeles. Nor, like the editor, would they necessarily have a college degree. But they were smart, earning their own livings, and having fun until they caught their guy. The British influence had created a shift in morality. It was smart to be sexy, not sluttish. But Britain was a small country and London only one city on a course to change its legislative framework of morality. It was remote from the real lives of working girls in Tacoma, Washington. The model for the *Cosmo* Girl had to be apolitical. Surveying the world, *Cosmopolitan* had ranged over dolly-birds, swingers, peaceniks, and surfers. It was telling its readers there was something else beyond their own small lives. What it now needed to do was to repackage the spirit of the age and market it into a total make-over course.

In 1969, *Cosmopolitan* found a new writer. To aid women in the hunt for a man she gave them new technological weaponry. One of the heavy guns was the Whipped Cream Wiggle:

> If you have a sweet tooth, this is the one for you. Take some freshly whipped cream, to which you have added a dash of vanilla and a couple of teaspoons of powdered sugar and spread the concoction evenly on the penis so that the whole area is covered with a quarter-inch layer of cream. As a finishing touch, sprinkle on a little shredded coconut and/or chocolate.

Then lap it all up with your tongue. He'll wriggle with delight and you'll have all the fun of an extra dessert. If you have a weight problem, use one of the many artificial whipped creams now on the market (available in boxes, plastic containers and aerosol cans) and forgo the coconut and chocolate.[17]

The Sensuous Woman by "J." was the book that taught American women how to do blow jobs. It was the publishing sensation of the end of the decade, the culmination of years spent in "liberating" single women from their virginity and teaching them to be good lays. In a section called "Penis/Mouth Technique," several methods for oral sex were suggested; not only the Whipped Cream Wiggle but the Butterfly Flick, the Silken Swirl, and the Hoover. It was cautious about Gnawing: "Rough handling here may give him a slightly negative attitude towards you as a future bed partner. Of course if you're tired of him, this is an excellent way to discourage further advances."[18] It is easy to be cynical about *The Sensuous Woman,* but it was brave in its insistence on the eroticization of women's lives, on their right to orgasms and the exploration of their sexual geography. I suspect that many American women, in the secrecy of their bedrooms, learned to masturbate with it propped up against the recommended jar of Vaseline or KY Jelly. If it seems hilarious now it is because of its fantastic combination of *Good Housekeeping* and *Playboy:* an attempt to render sex in a woman's language.

The book was a bestseller immediately, and it took only a year for the author to be unmasked. She had given hints of herself in her introduction:

> I'm sexy, all woman, that perfect combination of a lady in the living room and a marvellous bitch in bed, sensual, beautiful, a modern Aphrodite, maddeningly exciting, the epitome of the Sensuous Woman.
>
> Some of the most interesting men in America have fallen in love with me. I have received marriage proposals from such diverse personalities as a concert pianist, a best-selling author, the producer of three of America's most popular television shows, a bomb expert for the CIA, a trial attorney, an apple grower, a TV and radio star and a tax expert.
>
> Yet you'd never believe it if we came face to face on the street, for I am not particularly pretty. I have heavy thighs, lumpy hips, protruding teeth, a ski jump nose, poor posture, flat feet and uneven ears.[19]

Judging by the photograph on the back cover of J.'s 1984 autobiography, her success with men was due less to her physical imperfections than to the childishness of her features, a kind of sub-sex kitten look that many men find very appealing when accompanied by sexual sophistication, bringing out an allowable form of pedophilia.

J.'s name was Terry Garrity, and at the time of the book's publication in 1969 she was about thirty. Brought up in Missouri and Florida, she had arrived in Greenwich Village in the fifties to try to make it as an actress. On her twenty-first birthday she lost her virginity, arguing to herself that artists were not expected to lead traditional lives. Her lover had asked her if she had come. "I'm here aren't I?" she had replied, puzzled. She had never heard of an orgasm. Her sexual education had consisted of a confiscated copy of the 1940s bodice ripper *Forever Amber,* set in the reign of Charles II. Orgasms, she was told, were supposed to just happen. She waited. They didn't. She faked. She did a round of psychiatrists who told her she had a low sex drive and advised her to take up a diverting hobby. She asked one how he would feel if he had never had an orgasm. He told her that was different. Men did. She then attempted to track down an orgasm in the New York Public Library:

> I told librarians I was looking for books about "gynecological problems," because you didn't say "sex." . . . The few medical books that contained sex material were locked in glass cases in the library, and only "professionals" had access to them. . . . From my standpoint, the female orgasm was a secret more closely guarded than that of the hydrogen bomb. William H. Masters and Virginia E. Johnson had not yet published *Human Sexual Response.* They had begun to publish articles in professional publications like the *New England Journal of Medicine,* but I didn't know that, and I wouldn't have understood the terminology if I had come upon them.[20]

The orgasm was finally tracked down in the basement of Gimbels department store during a shoe sale. Terry Garrity was congratulating herself on having learned the technique of bargain hunting when it occured to her that perhaps sex also had to be learned. She went into two months' training back in her bedroom until one evening she suddenly shouted out, "Orgasm!" She had arrived. Inevitably, as most young women in their twenties do when they start talking about sex, she found out that none of her friends had had orgasms either. She had abandoned acting and now had aspirations to be a writer, but her unsolicited stories for the *New Yorker* were returned immediately. She went into book public relations organizing stunts and got a job with Lyle Stuart, a mainstream publisher who had a line of erotica. She later left him to set up her own PR company, but in October 1968 Stuart suggested that the time was right for a sex book for women by a woman.

She chose the "How-to" format, which she studied in *Play the Guitar in Five Minutes* and *How to Get Rich While You Sleep*. Lyle Stuart presented her with a jacket design that depicted a woman's face, against a black and chartreuse background, her mouth a welcoming O. Terry Garrity was horrified, and pointed out that women would not buy a book packaged in that way. She took him to the cosmetics department of Bloomingdales to show him "the kind of packaging women bought: tasteful, feminine, understated containers with pastel colors, elegant type styles and soft photography."[21] *The Sensuous Woman*, she suggested, should be presented like a fine French perfume. Stuart had been correct, however, when he predicted that the time was right for such a book. It became a bestseller and parodies of the title became a staple of copywriting the way "sex, lies and videotape" did in the early nineties. Datsun advertised its 240Z as "The Sensuous Car" by "D"; Hilton promoted "The Sensuous Inn" by "H." The *New Yorker* ran a Charles Addams cartoon of a monster browsing through "The Sensuous Thing."

Terry Garrity's subsequent story, which she told in her 1984 autobiography, *Story of "J": The Author of* The Sensuous Woman *Tells the Bitter Price of Her Crazy Success,* was of lawsuits, early hysterectomy, compulsive eating and shopping, clinical depression and a pathetic dependence on doctors and their medications, with an afterword by her current medical practitioner. When *The Sensuous Woman* had been proposed to her as a project, she had objected that she was not a "medical expert." During her feud with Lyle Stuart, whom she was suing for holding back royalties, she discovered what her former boss had been writing about her in *Screw* magazine at the height of her success: "But the sudden riches seem to have frightened away all the fellows she used to blow, and now she's hysterical because with nothing but bananas and overcooked frankfurters to suck on, her buck teeth are threatening to fall out."[22] Alone in her apartment in Florida, surrounded by towers of shopping bags and empty Sarah Lee frozen-pie wrappings, she was a classic victim of the sexual revolution, confident for a moment, trusting of male authority, probably used by her many lovers whose consciousness lagged behind her own. The men in her life indeed seemed to have dwindled and, unable to have children, she was frozen in time as the eternal swinger. Her autobiography ends with an empty horizon. She considered herself a liberated woman and an early supporter of women's rights. She "touted the book as a blueprint for the attainment of full sexual potential for all women."[23] Feminists, of course, denounced her, accusing her of teaching women to turn themselves into sex objects. But she had successfully helped Helen Gurley Brown complete the sexualization of the American woman.

Ironically, *Cosmo*'s success in normalizing sex as a subject for mainstream magazine fiction has not been duplicated in men's publications. Why do men love reading women's magazines? Because they are all about sex. And while a woman can sit on a bus or a train glued to a feature piece on the ten best turn-ons, a man must be content with *Car and Driver*. No wonder he's looking over her shoulder. Catch him reading *Penthouse* and he's branded a sexist. Triumphantly, *Cosmo* made sex respectable for women. Men still have to make do with pornography.

By July 1971, Alma Birk was clearly bewildered by the unleashing of a mindless sexual ethic, unharnessed to any vision of overall advancement. "Sometimes, I feel that if I see another sex book, I shall scream. . . ." she wrote. "The truth is that the sexual revolution is a myth: there has only been half a revolution. If there had been a complete, wholesome sexual revolution, there would be no need for books like *Everything You Always Wanted to Know* [*About Sex but Were Afraid to Ask*] or even *The Sensuous Woman*. In a really sexually emancipated society these best-sellers—and others like them—would be recognized for what they are: square as square."[24] But as the Swinging Sixties faded and London reverted to the dreariness of the fifties, American products started to make determined inroads into British life.

Hearst Magazines, the controlling company of National Magazine,

IPC's great rival, decided to launch *Cosmopolitan* in Britain in March 1972. It was also to be the testing ground for Helen Gurley Brown's latest revolutionary ideas—male centerfolds. Its early success was inadvertent. Brian Braithwaite, the managing editor, had looked around at other women's magazines and noted that none was selling more than 110,000 issues a month, *Nova* even less. He guessed that British *Cosmopolitan* would sell 150,000 and wrote an advertising rate card based on that figure. Given the magazine's international reputation, its status, and the stardom of its founding editor, the big cosmetics companies fought to advertise at what seemed low prices. The first issue was printed at 350,000 copies, depending on brisk sales from advance publicity. First, everyone thought that there would be a male nude in it; in fact that was not to be until the next issue. Second, the BBC current-affairs program "Man Alive" made a documentary about the magazine, "Who's Afraid of Helen Gurley Brown?" timed for the launch, followed by an edition of the prestigious arts program "Late Night Line-up" with Joyce Hopkirk, launch editor of the British *Cosmo,* and *Penthouse* owner Bob Guccione in the studio. The frail dissenting voices of the early *Spare Rib* collective were plaintively heard denouncing a juggernaut. The first issue was sold out from the newsstands by lunchtime. The second issue, with a print run of 450,000, disappeared the second day.

Paul de Feu, the unknown, quickly-to-be ex-husband of Germaine Greer (he later married Maya Angelou) was the first centerfold, a bland, anodyne, sheepish nude, knee bent up over his genitals and his navel air-brushed out. The first American was Burt Reynolds, naked on a bearskin rug with a big cigar. Helen Gurley Brown was astonished to discover that centerfolds did not seem to capture the imagination of her readers. Editorially, she believed that only very famous men would be interesting, but a mere handful were prepared to risk their careers. However, another magazine publisher adopted the idea, and so *Playgirl* and the crop of other mid-seventies soft-porn magazines for women were launched.

In 1980, *Cosmopolitan* undertook a major survey of the sex lives of its readers. It discovered that 28 percent had had between two and five lovers, 25 percent between eleven and twenty-five.[25] A twenty-year-old college student said, "At this point in time, I have had 134 lovers. I am proud to say that I remember the names of all but three of them."[26] A forty-year-old declared: "I've had upwards of a hundred lovers, have never married or lived with one, and don't expect I ever will. Why should I? Why should I put up with the inconvenience of men, their sloppy habits, their snoring, their stinginess, when I can have the best thing of all: sex whenever I want it, and no strings attached."[27] Nineteen percent had had group sex, the majority with two men.[28] When Helen Gurley Brown had coyly written *Sex and the Single Girl* in 1962, it would have been impossible to imagine that any woman other than a professional prostitute could have had this kind of sexual experience.

As an afterthought, the *Cosmopolitan* sex survey had asked its readers what they thought of the sexual revolution. This was one reader's response: "There are the nights when I say goodbye to a lover to whom I've just given the greatest ecstasies in bed, and I think to myself, here I am in my dangerous Greenwich Village apartment, with its fire escapes and dingy staircases. Maybe someone will break in and rape me during the night. Or kill me. Will this guy I'm saying goodbye to ever wonder about me in the morning? Will he wonder enough to call and discover I don't answer the phone? Will he notify the police? Probably not. That's the sexual revolution for you."[29] In 1975, the *Cosmo* Girl was recast as Woman as Victim of Her Sexual Desires in Judith Rossner's faction novel, later filmed. *Looking for Mr. Goodbar* was the story of a woman whose lonely and compulsive search through singles bars for temporary filling of the emptiness results in her murder by a casual pickup.

Seven years later, *Cosmopolitan* asked "How Has AIDS Changed Your Sex Life?" and a reader wrote: "I'm adamant about making a man use condoms. It's not an issue for discussion or compromise. The first time I went to a drugstore to buy them, I thought I'd feel funny, but there they were, in full view, boxes and boxes of different brands. The one I chose had a picture of a sunset with a silhouetted couple running through a field on the front. It was as easy as buying a roll of film!"[30] I can think of no more fitting symbol for the *Cosmo* Girl, frank, open, direct, unintimidated about her right to her condoms with their romantic promise not of sex but soft-centered intimacy and the gentle balm of nature, forever running into the carefree future.

Witness

Someone Keeps Poisoning the Well

Richard Ogar was born in Detroit, Michigan, in 1941. In 1966 he moved to Berkeley, California, which was to become, in the aftermath of the Free Speech Movement of 1964, the focal point of radical student politics in the United States. From 1967 to 1970 he wrote for the Berkeley Barb, *one of the first underground newspapers in America. In May 1970 he joined two other dissident* Barb *staffers in founding the* San Francisco BALL, *a soft-core sex tabloid with one foot in the hippie market and the other in the adult bookstore market. He continued editing sex tabloids until 1973. He is currently the Head of Photoduplication Services at the Bancroft Library, University of California, Berkeley.*

I became a teenager the same year rock and roll came into being; I take great pride in this fact. I spent my entire childhood in Detroit, Michigan, and the world that I grew up in was one in which sex simply didn't exist as anything more than vague ideas associated with masturbation. I'm absolutely amazed that young women I know now were giving blow jobs when they were fourteen years old. I cannot imagine an event of that kind. When I was fourteen that would have been the grandest dream of my life, and one that could never be realized. Feeling a breast under three layers of clothing was enough to keep one's imagination fired for months. Sex hardly seemed to exist for women at all, except as something to defend against. Among guys it was a subject that we all talked about but not seriously. We pretended—through exaggeration or outright lie—that we had engaged in it, but no one really had (although there was always the envious fear that someone you knew might actually have done something). There was no real awareness of homosexuality beyond the generalized notion that somewhere in the world there were men who fucked men and they were effeminate. Lesbianism simply didn't exist as a concept. As for women in general, it seemed likely that the only ones that would go to bed with you were riddled with diseases.

I remember as a teenager going down to Hastings Street in the black section of Detroit with three of my buddies to find a prostitute. I was scared shitless and hoped to God that we couldn't find one. In fact we couldn't find one who would take on four of us for the amount of money that we had collected. I was incredibly relieved by that, because I felt sure that if I were to have sex with a black prostitute I would inevitably catch an incurable disease. Even if it were curable, I'd die from it eventually because I wouldn't have been able to tell anyone that I had it. The level of ignorance was staggering. There were simply no sources of sexual information, at least not for males. I got into trouble once in high school for stealing a copy of a booklet that Kotex had put out for young women, ostensibly to educate them on the changes going on in their bodies, but actually to peddle Kotex pads. I had some vague idea of what menstruation was—women bled every month—but this booklet seemed a gold mine of contraband information. A friend and I each put a copy under our shirts, but as we were lining up to leave class, he told the home economics teacher I had something hidden. I was searched, the sweat-stained booklet pulled from under my armpit and held aloft. I said my friend had one too but he didn't; I'd obviously been set up. I was suspended from school for having delved into the secrets of a woman's biology.

So of course when the sixties and the so-called sexual revolution came along, I wanted to be at the forefront. Even in high school I had been arguing in favor of legalized abortion and prostitution and getting into a good deal of trouble for it. My father was a labor journalist, so I was brought up hard-line liberal, the strict union line. I remember meeting Harry Truman when I was very young, being caught up in Democratic Party politics and the American labor movement. But of course I had to take it further, into socialism and other fringe philosophies. It caused a number of violent arguments with my father from my high school years on. He had battled the Communists who tried to infiltrate the American labor movement in the 1930s and 1940s, and now he had a son who was espousing Marxist-Leninist principles. For my father, the enemy had invaded his own home; to me my father was simply bourgeois, a sellout to convention and capitalism. These protracted battles continued almost until the time he died in 1976.

High school was a sexual wasteland, but college wasn't much better. I entered the University of Michigan in 1959, and discovered that, for all intents and purposes, the main role of a university was to keep males and females strictly segregated. Privacy simply did not exist. I was eighteen before I had any sort of orgasmic contact with a woman (a hand job through my pants), twenty before I had my first blow job, and twenty-two before I fucked anyone and that woman I married. Why? Because she wanted me to and I felt that having taken her virginity I was obligated to make good on it. Besides, given my past, it seemed that if I let her go I'd likely never have sex again. I really thought that was a possibility. But it seemed a cruel outcome. I had this bloated agenda, a mental list of all the women I wanted to make love to—short, tall, thin, fat, white, black, Asian, whatever—and I suddenly realized I wasn't going to make it past number one. But I was presented with an ultimatum: marriage or no relationship at all. I was horribly depressed by the whole business, but there didn't seem to be any way out. I had one of the more questioning and liberated minds around, yet I found myself still running along those very narrow tracks. Of course after we got married she lost interest in fucking, and I met a lot of women who probably would have fucked me anyway if I hadn't been married. So it was a comedy of errors all round. I had my first extramarital affair nine months after the wedding with a woman who had also been married less than a year. I guess those were early-warning signs of the sexual revolution—1964 to 1965. Both of us had gotten into these marriages and realized, "Oh my God, I have to fuck this same person and no one else for the rest of my life." Neither of us could stand the idea, so we decided to fuck each other. But that made no sense to me and the relationship ended when I came to California.

The first sexual reporting I did was for the Berkeley Barb. *It was a long series on the emerging porn industry in San Francisco. It was supposed to be a single article but I threw myself into the research, one might say, and the thing went on and on until I finally had to kill myself off in print. I was still working for the* Barb *when I began editing the* San Francisco BALL *(as in balling chicks) but I left shortly thereafter. The BALL's motto was: "To ball is to live, everything else is just waiting." The sixties were full of mindless slogans like that—"It's easy being easy when you're easy" or "If it feels good, do it"—but ours was as good a watchword as any. My suspicion is that, at the time, to fuck was in and of itself a form of liberation. And to do it outside the conventional bounds of dating or marriage. It was hip to be promiscuous and square not to be, it was a defying of convention. And it was all tied in with these sort of treacly and nauseating concepts of love and peace and brotherhood. Sex was being seen as physical liberation, as psychic liberation, as a union between people, even to the point of being a tool for world peace. It almost lost all personal connotations. Certainly if you were involved with somebody you were with them in a personal way but there was also this pan-sexual element. The implications went far beyond whether or not you were getting laid or if you were enjoying the sex you were having.*

It was a principle of liberation in and of itself. There was some sense that it was a legal psychedelic, that the more you did it the more your consciousness expanded, the more you were able to encompass, the more love you were able to express. It was a cheap and easy, legal form of LSD. And of course it was to be enhanced by drugs whenever possible. That was doubling your chances for enlightenment.

But it was really seen as far more than something merely recreational. In the sixties you almost had to fuck for the good of the human race. It was your moral duty to keep this thing going like a transcendental chain letter in order to improve our lot and save the planet. There was a general idea that people who controlled the world and created all the evil did so because they couldn't fuck. Guys had to go out and build super penises to compensate for other shortcomings. All the ugliness and uptightness came from people who couldn't gain sexual release. So we thought, if everybody starts fucking we won't be uptight, we won't have the aggressiveness and the violence. We won't need symbolic penises and vaginas because we'll be able to use the real ones. It was loosely, sloppily, but definitely messianic and programmatic. It was a panacea along with drugs and rock and roll. It would lead us to a better land. Sex, drugs, and rock and roll were a very real triad. Those were the three paths to liberation and if you embraced them all you could not become one of those tight-assed bastards in the Pentagon.

What happened? It was bullshit. That simple. The problems were a little more complex than we saw them. We didn't realize at the time that sex, drugs, and rock and roll could be as easily incorporated by the power structure as anything else. The power structure co-opted all of that shit, it made all the money. The mob comes into the drug trade and introduces harder and harder drugs; the pornographers come out with definitely non-liberating products that are aimed at the older generation; and rock and roll gets completely taken over by the big record companies. We lost the whole thing to the enemy, whether they fucked or not. The truth is, they probably fucked more than we did—I'm sure John Kennedy got more than I did. It was all naive, a false premise.

Looking back on the sexual revolution, I don't think there was a hell of a lot in it for women. I'm not so sure that I would go so far as to say that women were conned by men, but I think they definitely got the short end of the stick. If the sexual revolution worked to anyone's benefit, it was men's. The great liberating ideas were that, yes women can fuck, yes women can choose who they want to fuck, women can be orgasmic, they can have a sex drive, they can enjoy erotica, those are the sorts of ideas. But it never went much further than that. And all the things that women could do, it was assumed they would do with the guys who had wanted to do those things all along. When the women's movement came on the scene, it didn't do men any good. We paid the price of the sexual revolution by having our balls busted for several years. When my son was born in 1973, I got out of the sex business and turned to free-lance writing and editing. Since my wife had a secure job at the University of California and I was a man of uncertain income, it seemed logical that she would continue working and I would take care of Jeffrey and the house. So for five years I was a housewife and I was stupid enough to think that this would earn me some points with women. I remember my wife once got a call from a total stranger who remarked on her unusual last name, and asked if she were related to the guy who had written about pornography for the Barb. *My wife said yes, and the woman said, "How can you live with such a sexist pig?" My wife said, "He's not a pig. He takes care of our son, he looks after the house, does the cooking and all that." And the woman says, "So you have to go out and work while he sponges off you?" I thought, wait a minute. I can't win here.*

I left my wife in 1978 and the following year I took a job at the University of California. I've been there ever since. My political ardor has cooled considerably. I don't think the human race can be rehabilitated. I certainly don't think that I can rehabilitate it. Over time, I opted out and looked more and more into ways to put my own life together. If I couldn't save the world at least I could save my own ass. And I didn't try to do this by joining the system and trying to make a lot of money. I don't think working in the Bancroft Library photocopy office can in any way be called joining the system. It was just trying to retain in my own head the sorts of values that I cherished personally and I'm closer to doing that at this point in my life than I have ever been at any other time. Sexually though, I'm very far from realizing my ideals. At the moment I'm very happily involved with a twenty-two-year-old woman who happens to be far more sexually advanced and more experienced than I am. Or, I suspect, than I will ever be.

I have this almost cosmic sense that there is a conspiracy against sex at work in the world. The window of sexual freedom—between the Pill and AIDS—was quite short, about twenty years. That beautiful window! Along comes herpes, then AIDS and it's all fucked up again. Every time it seems you can actually do this thing, something comes along that says no, you can't. I don't know whether it's a divine plot or a CIA plot or a right-wing Christian plot but something keeps poisoning the well.

My son is eighteen now and off at college. I know nothing at all about his sexuality. He clammed up and went very straight after he hit puberty. I think my relationships with much younger women are difficult for him to deal with. For the past several years, he's been an absolutely phlegmatic Reagan-Bush Republican. Just the other night he was flipping TV channels and turned on something about the People's Park riots and said, "Hey dad, it's your people." Even though my own views have tempered a good deal, we still have political arguments. He's a real hard-liner and very intent on going into politics. His mother says she won't vote for him if he runs for office, but he figures his biggest obstacle is explaining away his parents. And he doesn't even know the worst about his old man. People ask me how he got this way and how I manage to deal with it. One thing I can say is that it made him the easiest teenager in the world to deal with—no sex, no drugs, no rock and roll. The kid's an absolute straight arrow and to him his major values are what kind of car he drives and how much his suit cost.

7

A Clarion Call to the Strenuous Life

Bell-bottoms have to be worn to be understood. They express the body, as jeans do, but they say much more. They give the ankles a special freedom as if to invite dancing right on the street. They bring dance back into our sober lives. . . . No one can take himself entirely seriously in bell-bottoms. Imagine a Consciousness II university professor, or even a college athlete, in bell-bottoms, and all of his pretensions become funny, he has to laugh at himself.
Charles Reich, *The Greening of America* (1971)

"The Love Force" & "Group Marriage," Talk. 21 Oct. 7–9 p.m. 13 Prince of Wales Road, London W8. Admission 5s.

The notice appeared in the classified section of the *New Statesman* in 1964. It was spotted by Derek Ive, a reporter for the muckraking Sunday newspaper, *The People*. Ive took himself off to Kensington where he found a large dusty room with thirty-seven men and three women sitting on steel chairs facing the lecturer, Emanuel Petrakis. The family, Petrakis declared to the audience, was completely out of date. Women under present marriage laws were just a form of property and male jealousy was nothing more than fear of a man stealing what rightfully belonged to another. A skeptic arose from the floor. The trouble was there was too much sex today. Sex, sex, sex, that was all he got. Speak for yourself, someone else called out. Petrakis pressed on. Group marriage was the answer. Communities would form where everyone would share wives and husbands and the children would be brought up communally. At the mention of shared wives, the audience sat up. When Petrakis called for questions, half a dozen hands shot into the air. An elegantly dressed man of about forty-five caught his eye. This communal marriage, he was all for it, but how was Petrakis going to get the ladies to take part? After all, they were poorly represented at this meeting. Petrakis had a solution. If everyone in the room tried to convert all the ladies of his or her acquaintance to these views, that would soon give the movement more converts. Leaflets were offered to hand out as ammunition.

A few days later, Derek Ive called on Petrakis at his bedsit in Finsbury Park. He answered the door in a dressing gown and showed the reporter into a room where his wife and two children were sitting on a double bed watching television. Mrs. Petrakis was one woman of her husband's acquaintance who had not been won to the cause. Ive asked her what she thought about the utopian plans. She looked uncomfortable. She didn't want anything to do with it, she said. Ive left, well-pleased with himself. Here was a spokeswoman for what any self-respecting female would believe. So much for Petrakis and his bright ideas.[1]

Undeterred by social disapprobation, Petrakis's organization, the Sexual Emancipation Movement, continued to meet throughout the second half of the sixties. The meetings were small, lugubrious events. A social held in January 1968 attracted a turnout of only thirteen, attributed to the flu epidemic. Newsletter No. 22 was delayed after Mrs. Petrakis broke her leg and had to spend a month in the hospital. "I had to look after our three young children as well as keep my teaching job and run the home, leaving me with practically no time for anything else,"[2] he complained, then reported enthusiastically on an Anti-University forum on Love Communes, which must have seemed a glitteringly utopian alternative to the double day of the British working mother that he had just experienced at first hand.

Petrakis was obliged to inform new members that the movement "does not organize sexual activities of any kind, nor does it introduce people to each other for sexual purposes. We are a social reform association concerned with spreading enlightened attitudes on sexual matters. What people do in private is their own affair, but we should be clear not to confuse our private lives with our role as members of S.E.M. The movement has far more important goals than just the satisfaction of personal sexual appetites (as important as these are)."

The sexual utopianism of Russell had burned out by the time its advocates of the 1930s had reached the 1960s and middle age, when many found themselves intellectually and socially stranded in a society they no longer understood. A visitor from California found Britain far from swinging in the late sixties, as he reported when he wrote home: "London seems to be about 5–7 years behind S.F. [San Francisco]. Everything is behind closed doors. British women are reserved and seem to maintain a 1950s cool. . . . You have spoken of a British sexual freedom group. Can't find it! . . . Much to my surprise there is not much religion here. Same 1950s cool. Maharishi has not caught on anywhere in Europe."[3] The Sexual Emancipation Movement, for which the writer was looking, would have been as difficult to find as a corset on King's Road. *The Observer, Guardian, British Medical Journal,* and *Teachers' World* had all refused its classified advertising.[4] Petrakis pined for America, for his sister organization, the Sexual Freedom League, at its headquarters in San Francisco. For by the late sixties, the passionate millenarian spirit of the early sexual-freedom movements had taken root in California, where it was to flourish for many years.

While Petrakis was canceling meetings because of viruses or inclement weather, the Sexual Freedom League, under sunnier skies, was organizing nude wade-ins and orgies. On September 2, 1968, a piece of wedding reporting was submitted to an underground newspaper:

> Throughout the seaside cottage, naked bodies thumped and quivered through the several acts of love. The roar of surf and wind at Pacifica was diluted with sitar music and broken by cries of passion.
>
> Having had their reception already, the guests assembled for the wedding itself. They cooled themselves down by meditation and chanting "Hare Krishna." Jeannie sang a sentimental song in [a] high, clear voice.
>
> The bridal pair, Joseph ———, 33, and Joyce ———, 20, stood up and shared champagne from a new goblet, never used before, then shattered it. Instead of a ring, Joseph hung a sexfreedom yin-yang amulet, hand-wrought of brass, around Joyce's slender neck. The couple kissed each other on their mouths and then their genitals, and were declared wed by a Neo-American Boo Hoo.
>
> After more mantra chanting, the partying resumed.[5]

The author was Jefferson Poland, then twenty-six, who the year before had placed an advertisement in *Maverick,* a traditional girlie magazine:

NEED IDEALISTIC FREE LAWYER to help me change my name from "John Jefferson Poland, Jr." to "Jefferson Fuck Poland."[6]

In the sixties, Poland was one of the marginal figures on the Berkeley scene, part of San Francisco's local color, a long-haired, black-bearded hippie who progressed about the city followed by a retinue of high priestesses from the Psychedelic Venus Church whose impecunious divine was Poland himself. From the mid-sixties to the early seventies, Poland was the archivist for the Sexual Freedom League, and when, dispirited in the mid-seventies, he abandoned activism, he donated his papers to the Bancroft Library at the Berkeley campus of the University of California. Their thousands of pages—letters, memos, notes of meetings, correspondence from abroad, newspaper cuttings, copies of underground magazines, flyers, and posters—form an extensive insight into hippie sexual idealism.

Sex took off in California as it did nowhere else. Californians were far removed from the legislative center. Three thousand miles west of Washington, they had little chance of influencing politicians. Nor could they take over the existing major media unless, like Helen Gurley Brown, they moved to New York. Californians were always, to some extent or another, pioneers. The immigrant experience had been to light out for the territories, to continue to head west to find Utopia—land greener, more hospitable, unclaimed. The instinct of those pioneers who came to California was always to keep going—they had passed through so much country already. At the West Coast they hit the sea and had to stay put. It made those struck with the greatest wanderlust a little crazy. In place of the physical frontier, Californians substituted the only remaining freedom left to them, the sole way that they could be transgressive—crossing the borders of sexual convention and internalizing what had once been a quest for political and religious freedom. California must have seemed purpose-built by God for sex-freedom dreamers. Nature poured forth blessings like the Garden of Eden, and the prospect of a return to a prelapsarian state of nature, a sinless world that the Ranters might have constructed in their millenarian tracts, appeared highly viable, even inevitable. California acted as a laboratory for ideas of sexual freedom to be tested out in practice. Nudism was obvious, as was the vaguely defined "free love." In the mid-sixties, the Alpine Liberation Front, an early gay organization with which the apparently bisexual Poland was involved, attempted to buy up Alpine County in the Sacramento area to found a gay town and commune.

A René Guyon society was established to put into practice the ideas of the 1930s French philosopher who argued that sexual taboos derived from religious fear of supernatural beings. As a modernist, Guyon could find no adequate scientific motive for any sexual prohibition. He held that Freud's notion of the child's polymorphous perversity was not only normal but should be instituted into a sexual practice of childhood, with family friends initiating the young. The Californian followers of Guyon lived out these beliefs, albeit in great secrecy, and their children grew up, one supposes, having sex with a variety of "uncles" and "aunts." At the same time, an American advocate of Summerhill, the progressive school in Suffolk, was campaigning in the United States, having enthusiastically endorsed the mild observation of Summerhill's founder, A. S. Neill, that there was not much wrong with his pupils having sex with one another. "Summerhill" became another Californian movement for the sexual "freeing" of schoolchildren.

We understand the sixties through visual images. Our eye has been trained by Andy Warhol, who detected the pleasurable emptiness of surfaces. The hippie chick of Haight-Ashbury* stood for the sexual libera-

---

*Originally an obscure neighborhood, Haight-Ashbury was first identified by the media in a *San Francisco Examiner* story of 1965, which described it as "A New Haven for Beatniks." For two years "the Haight" became synonymous with the acid culture Tom Wolfe was to document in *The Electric Kool-Aid Acid Test*—the "acid tests" (LSD parties) held by Ken Kesey and the Merry Pranksters, who strove to turn on America. The progenitors of the Haight were only a few years younger than the Beat poets of the early fifties (Ginsberg, Orlovsky, Kerouac, etc.), whose own scene had been at North Beach near the center of the city. At the apotheosis of Haight-Ashbury, during the 1967 Summer of Love—an antidote to the Vietnam War—the Grateful Dead were performing at Bill Graham's Fillmore Auditorium, Augustus Owsley Stanley III was manufacturing acid in his secret laboratory, and dozens of self-styled light artists were producing the psychedelic light shows that completed the trips. Rain Jacopetti, of the Berkeley-based Open

tion of the West Coast. The hippie chick had the same curtains of bottle-blond hair, the same blankness as her British sister. But the body is naked; onto her are projected the patterns of the psychedelic light show, particularly onto her breasts, which more than legs evoked the beneficence of Mother Nature that unalienated Californians invoked. The mandalas and concentric patterns were formed by liquid pigments in motion, changing from moment to moment, abstract expressions of the disintegration of order, the yearning for the East and mysticism, imposing holiness on the body. The hippie chick's gaze was turned inward into her own unconscious, which she explored through drugs. Although the image functioned as mild pornography, in a way the hippie chick violated the rules of the centerfold—she didn't look outward to a male gaze.

Sex in California had a major intellectual guru, a figure as important then as Michel Foucault would be in the eighties. Herbert Marcuse, who had come to America in 1933 as a refugee from Nazi Germany, arrived to teach at San Diego in 1965. From the thirties onward, as a member of the Marxist Frankfurt School of critical theory and philosophy, Marcuse had considered sexual repression one of the most important attributes of the exploitative social order. Under capitalism sex was commodified, stripped of the element of play and spontaneity. Love was reduced to duty and habit. Sex for the workers was even further restricted by their brief periods of leisure. In a society in which all value is based on the exchange value of labor, pleasure is devalued.

These ideas were already well known through Germany's other great philosopher of sexual freedom, Wilhelm Reich, who had also fled to America. Reich was in many ways a conservative who regarded the genital orgasm produced by sex between opposite genders to be the only "normal" form of intercourse. His view was that people were sick because they did not come. But Marcuse saw the whole body as a generalized instrument of pleasure in revolt against its appropriation by capitalism as an instrument of labor. Perversions were the body's expression of resistance against

---

Theater, is said to be the first woman to have a light show projected onto her body by standing up during a Scott Paper educational film about menstruation. Delighted with the effect of an animated diagram of physical processes all over her, she stripped.

the institutions that maintained the established order, particularly those that insisted on sex solely for procreation.

Initially, like the rest of his generation, Marcuse welcomed science and technology, in which he had faith as agents of the liberation of man from alienating work, freeing him from the sexual repression the industrial revolution had required. But in 1964 he published *One Dimensional Man*, in which he argued that capitalism had co-opted the sexual, had made work sexy. Secretaries, sales girls, and junior executives were all sexualized images of the attractiveness of the company. Sex was integrated into work and appropriated by public relations. Libido had been mobilized in the service of the economy. Faced with capitalism taking possession of the sexual in this way, the worker could only answer in the extreme, with an absolute refusal: against war, racism, imperialism. The old left of the Communist Party and orthodox Marxism had hardened into a purely economic force. The New Left, neo-Marxists influenced by Maoism and the revolutionary movements of the Third World, did not worship the proletariat with the same phallocentrism of Stalinist socialist realism. Hippies, civil-rights activists, writers, intellectuals, and students were the true descendants of the proletariat, Marcuse believed. At a lecture at the Free University of West Berlin in July 1967, he spoke of an antiwar demonstration at Berkeley when the police barricaded access to the military railroad station:

> . . . as usual there were several people at the head of the march who yelled that the demonstration should not stop but try instead to break through the police cordon, which naturally would have led to a bloody defeat without achieving any aim. . . . After two or three scary minutes the thousands of marchers sat down in the streets, guitars and harmonicas appeared, people began "necking" and "petting" and so the demonstration ended. You may find this ridiculous, but I believe that a unity spontaneously and anarchically emerged here that perhaps in the end cannot have failed to make an impression on the enemy.[7]

Young America loved the politics of play. Marcuse's ideas echo through passages of the Yippie Jerry Rubin's book *Do It!*, published in 1969:

"Puritanism leads us to Vietnam. Sexual insecurity results in a supermasculinity trip called imperialism. American foreign policy, especially in Vietnam, makes no sense except sexually. America has a frustrated penis trying to drive itself in Vietnam's tiny slit to prove it is the man."[8] Marcuse himself was not a flamboyant figure. As a European intellectual, he could have hardly realized the extent to which philosophy could be put into practice. "I sometimes suspect that there's a barely repressed strain of puritanism in Marcuse's make-up, a fastidiousness which allows him to treat sexuality with great abandon at the level of theory, but results in a squeamish 'That's not what I meant at all!' when confronted with the untidy reality of sex,"[9] wrote Paul Robinson, a Marcuse scholar, in a post-AIDS study of sexual radicals. Marcuse's appeal, however, was enormous. *One Dimensional Man* was a key text of sixties political consciousness. Together with Frantz Fanon's *The Wretched of the Earth* and Paolo Freire's *Pedagogy of the Oppressed*, it was to be found on every politically correct campus radical's bookshelf. One suspects that it was, like *A Brief History of Time* in the nineties, one of the great unread bestsellers of the sixties; it was not easy going, formed as it was by the language of Marxist philosophy, but a crude approximation of its ideas permeated many levels of society. Bertrand Russell had sanctioned sex as an object of political attention. Marcuse elevated desire into a revolutionary act. California was ready.

Jefferson Poland was born in Indiana in 1942; beyond these meager facts, little is known about his origins. He seems to emerge fully sexed in 1962, when he moved into the San Francisco household of two anarchist women "who practised nudity and promiscuity."[10] Poland was a student of Gandhi and his philosophy of satyagraha, nonviolent direct action, and he proposed a program of civil disobedience on sexual issues. He distributed leaflets at Lenny Bruce's obscenity trial. At San Francisco State College, where he seems to have been briefly a student, he ran for the student legislature on a platform that included selling contraceptives in the college bookstore. In the summer of 1963 he temporarily despaired of the cause of sexual freedom and went to Plaquemine County, Louisiana, as a CORE volunteer helping register black voters, one of the important campaigns of the civil-rights movement and from which he must have learned a great deal about political activism. The summer over, he moved to New York. Two days after the assassination of President Kennedy, he went to see Dr. Leo F. Koch. Koch was briefly famous for a celebrated skirmish in the battle to de-virginize American girls. A biology professor at the University of Illinois, he had read an article in the student newspaper, *The Daily Illini*, on March 16, 1960, in which two male students argued that campus dating was nothing more than impersonal encounters between male and female "sex units." Koch believed that society encouraged such superficiality by condemning premarital sex and wrote a letter to the paper saying so. Three weeks later he was suspended and later fired. The case made national headlines.

Poland suggested to Koch that they form a political-action group that would bring the tactics of the civil-rights movement to the cause of sexual freedom. They chose the name "League for Sexual Freedom" because they thought that Wilhelm Reich had led an organization of the same name. An early statement laid out their philosophy:

> . . . a lasting and thorough emancipation—the much discussed "sexual revolution"—requires a movement and an ideology, and cannot happen in secret. It is not enough for people to violate the puritan ideology furtively and to see themselves negatively as "no better than they should be." We need a positive alternative, a model of generosity and liberty, to explain and justify our desires and actions to ourselves and to our children. . . . Puritanism is promoted and enforced by social institutions—school, church, government. The individual, especially the developing child, needs help in resisting these massive pressures.
>
> The Negro freedom movement shows that action is the best means of starting discussion, not vice versa.[11]

The League's first members came from Greenwich Village bohemia and Columbia University: Beat poets Allen Ginsberg, Peter Orlovsky, and Diane de Prima; John Wilcock, the Yorkshireman who started the *Village Voice;* Judith Malina and Julian Beck of the Living Theatre; Tuli Kupferberg and Ed Sanders of the Fugs (a band that was the primitive ancestor

of Frank Zappa and Alice Cooper); Paul Krassner, editor of *The Realist**;
Dr. Franklin Kameny, a gay astronomer fired by the government because
of his sexuality; and Rey Anthony, author of *The Housewife's Handbook
on Selective Promiscuity*. Most of the members took a straight civil-liberties
line, calling on the state to keep its hands off their genitals and sanctioning
anything done voluntarily in private by adults. "Very few members then
had the orgiastic orientation which was to emerge two years later in
Berkeley," Poland wrote.[12]

The League embarked on a number of campaigns. The city, they
claimed, was cleaning up the arts in New York in preparation for World's
Fair tourists. Filmmaker Jonas Mekas and three assistants were arrested
for showing allegedly obscene films, including Genet's *Un Chant d'Amour*.
On a deserted windswept canyon in the Wall Street district the League
picketed the District Attorney's office and learned an important lesson:
case the location in advance. Next, joined by "beautiful anarchist actresses
from the Living Theatre," they marched to the women's prison in Greenwich Village singing a song derived from the current round of Beatlemania: "We love you prostitutes, Oh yes we do, when you're locked in
jail, We're blue . . ."[13] Their most successful demonstration was at the
New York Public Library, which restricted access to 150 books, like the
Kama Sutra and the novels of Henry Miller, to academics. After a picketing and letter-writing campaign, the books became generally available,
though not listed in the library's classification system.

Poland moved back to San Francisco in February 1965. The campus of
the University of California at Berkeley, across the Bay Bridge from the
city, had become the hippest, most revolutionary college in the country
the year before. Students returning from a summer of civil-rights work in
the Deep South in the fall of 1964 had been told that they could not

*A magazine that focused on conspiracy theories, counter-cultural politics, and lots of sex,
including publicizing the work of Margo St. James, the founder of the prostitutes' organization
Coyote, who described herself as a Realist nun and accompanied Krassner on speaking engage-
ments in full habit. In one issue of the magazine Krassner published an interview with her—
conducted, he claimed, while she was sucking his cock.

distribute leaflets that advocated direct action or collect money for organizations that did so. Mario Savio, a student and civil-rights activist, became the leader of mass demonstrations in what came to be known as the Berkeley Free Speech Movement. At a demonstration on December 2, 1964, Savio gave the speech that was the clarion call to the strenuous life for a generation of student revolutionaries: "There's a time when the operation of the machine becomes so odious, makes you so sick at heart, that you can't take part . . . and you've got to put your bodies on the gears and upon the wheels and you've got to make it stop."[14] Joan Baez sang "Blowin' in the Wind," the police came in and arrested 800 people. Three days later the university administration held a mass meeting. As Mario Savio walked to the podium, a cop grabbed him round the neck and dragged him from the stage. The next day, the students' demands were met in full.

A month after Jefferson Poland arrived back on the West Coast, John Thomson, "barefoot poet,"[15] walked round the campus carrying a small card bearing the phrase "Fuck (verb)," intended, as he said, as a protest against the Vietnam War. An hour later he was arrested. Six months before, the mere sight of a cop on campus had been enough to inflame accusations of police brutality. The students, however, didn't feel that the right to swear was a cause of much importance, not compared with the institution of the draft. The Sexual Freedom League's next action, and the only one for which Poland was ever to receive national attention (in the form of a small item in *Time*) was a nude wade-in to dramatize a campaign for nude beaches that continues to occupy Poland a quarter of a century later. Clad initially in bathing suits and a flower behind the ear, circled by the press, Poland and two twenty-one-year-old women, Ina Saslow and Shirley Einseidel, waded into the water at Aquatic Park in August 1965. A large crowd formed. "Take 'em off or I'll rip 'em off,"[16] someone cried, though probably not to Poland. Surrounded by rowboats full of camera crews and two bronzed lifeguards, identical twins on surfboards, the trio removed their undergarments in fifteen feet of water. Back on the beach they were arrested for swimming without proper attire and received ninety-day suspended sentences and six months' probation. The lunch counter sit-ins in the Southern states, to oppose segregation, had taught Poland a good lesson. It was a public-relations victory.

For some, however, picketing was not quite enough. In September 1968, Poland received a letter from upper New York State:

> As a new member of the SFL, last May while I was revisiting my old seminary (Church Divinity School of the Pacific in Berkeley), I met Tom and Irene at an Open House, then, thanks to Irene's finding me a female friend, attended a very pleasant party in the Walnut Creek area, went home to San Francisco with the dame and had a delightful twelve days combining seminary with semen! Took in a Visual Delights, beholding my first pornographic movies (believe it or not!) with my girl friend; participated in reading Lulu at the Drama Circle (they complimented me on my performance); attended a wild SFL party in San Francisco (at 1019 Ashbury) where I not only made it with this wonderful girl I was spending most of my vacation with, but satisfied my curiosity as to what cocksucking would be like and got a good suck by a cute girl who didn't want to fuck. It was very thrilling to have these experiences in the presence of others, some watching, but most doing their own thing. . . .
>
> My wife and I have been nudists since 1952 (I am a youthful 46), but are aware of how stodgy the nudist camps are—forbidding any physical expression of intimacy. . . . My wife knows that I have SFL membership, and she knows about the parties I attended in May, but she won't approve or participate. . . .
>
> I'd love to help people, as you apparently do. I can do it in the ministry (I'm an Episcopal Priest), and can even work indirectly for the cause of Sexual Freedom. But I can't work openly, as you are doing. And the chances are that I may never repeat the ecstatic experiences of May. But I have only the SFL to thank for them, and know that you are the one person who deserves the greatest credit.[17]

The writer made a donation to Poland personally of five dollars.

The political activism envisaged by Poland, Ginsberg, and other leftists was not destined to have a wide appeal. Poland himself was the most liberal of men, enthusiastically endorsing campaigns for the legalization of abortion, prostitution, pornography, and homosexuality, a member of the National Organization of Women and a speaker at their state meetings, an opponent of censorship and champion of a wide range of reforms, including of prisons and farm labor. His was a global, eclectic vision. But the majority who were won to the cause were more interested in the parties. When Poland had started the San Francisco Chapter of the SFL, he led a tiny group of a dozen or so, mainly hippies aged between seventeen and twenty-five. Early in 1966, another member, Richard Thorne, suggested holding nude events. Poland excitedly regarded these as a form of civil disobedience and anticipated arrest: "We'd all be busted for indecent exposure, ride to the city jail singing 'We Shall Overcome' and then there would be a big test case in the courts," he hoped.[18] But although the parties were reported in underground newspapers like the *Berkeley Barb*, as well as the *San Francisco Chronicle* and *Time*, they were tolerated by the police throughout the Bay Area. The organization's questionnaire suggests why:

> Indicate below which activities you are interested in:
>   Nude parties with fifteen or fewer present?
>   Nude parties with more than fifteen present?
>   Husband-and-Wife-swapping affairs? If you are interested in the last named affair, how many couples would you want such affairs to include when you are invited?
>   Do you have a home at which you might like to invite other members?
>   Do you have such facilities as a private swimming pool, tennis court, billiard room, barroom etc at which you might like to invite members? Name facilities.[19]

A movement of middle-class suburbanites was not what Poland had imagined:

> Once the trail was blazed by hardy pioneers, we began to recruit more timid members. They were afraid of their employers, afraid of their neighbors, afraid of their relatives. So they wanted assurances that their membership would be kept a dark secret—"discreet," as the wife-swappers say. They often joined under phony names. Many members followed the first-names-only custom of conservative nudists. They had no interest, beyond lip-service, in taking public action to spread sexual freedom and to repeal archaic restrictions. They mainly wanted to attend these parties.[20]

Sexual Freedom League meetings soon came to resemble those of the Sexual Emancipation Movement: single men who turned up in hope of meeting permissive women. The parties had to be restricted to couples. Single men were advised to advertise in the *Berkeley Barb* for a girlfriend, convert her gradually by bringing her to clothed events, then nude beaches, finally to a party. The middle-aged new recruits didn't enjoy body painting or art movies. What they wanted was group sex. "At every League party, one room is cleared of furniture and carpeted with mattresses from wall to wall. It is available (as is the whole house) for sexual activity," Poland wrote.[21] Sadly, he recalled a Berkeley party in which the hippie spirit had still been untrammeled: ". . . we kept the lights on in the mattress room and played a rough and tumble game of horsie, which is more innocent than perhaps it sounds. That is, the men crawled around the room on their hands and knees with girls riding them. We had races and jousting tournaments. Bareback, as it were. But normally a mattress room is dark and more directly erotic. There are often one or two persons sitting quietly and unobtrusively watching, which is OK unless one of the watched persons objects, in which case the voyeur goes elsewhere."[22]

As he dreamed up wilder schemes to challenge the state, Poland was increasingly marginalized from his own organization. He had succeeded in adopting "Fuck" as his middle name (nothing is known of any action taken by the Polish ambassador to the United States) then dropped "Poland" and had a protracted battle with the Wells Fargo Bank, which refused to print his name on their checks. He attempted to have the League designate 1969 "Clitoris Appreciation Year." On January 22, 1969, he put forward a resolution to the League:

> Whereas, Each person should be allowed to live his private life as he sees fit; and
>
> Whereas, Aphrodisiacs are useful to many persons in relaxing inhibitions or directly stimulating the genital organs; and
>
> Whereas, Marijuana facilitates sex and love sharpening the senses and reducing inhibitions; therefore,
>
> Resolved, That the Sexual Freedom League urge society to tolerate and legalize all aphrodisiacs including marijuana.[23]

He decided to branch out and start his own organization, announcing it with a press release to the *Berkeley Tribe,* another underground paper:

A new sex-pot church will attempt to bridge the gap between suburban swingers and hippie heads. This Psychedelic Venus Church, chartered Nov. 24 by the Shiva Fellowship, worships Aphrodite "as our symbol of hedonic pleasure, in her psychedelic aspect symbolizing direct spiritual revelation. We see her presiding over nude orgies of fucking and sucking and cannabis: truly Venereal religion."

"Half my friends are into sex, and the other half into dope," muses Fuck. "There's not enough overlap, at least not up front. So Psychedelic Venus means we'll try to combine the trips, get hedonism back together in the Old Time Religion."[24]

Within a month he was publishing a new organ, *Intercourse,* claimed to have seventy-five members, and hoped to outrival the Catholic Church by the turn of the century. Sackcloth was to be the official uniform of the church until the end of the Vietnam War; members were advised to make a burlap dress out of a hundred-pound brown rice bag. Poland, thus attired, had attended a Gay Liberation symposium where he had attracted appreciative attention. Some members were recruited from the puritanical rigors of the early ecology movement when they found that sex was regarded as non-macrobiotic. The last known sighting of the Psychedelic Venus Church was by *Berkeley Barb* journalist Richard Ogar, when church members appeared on a float during a Berkeley parade: "The float with the naked priestesses did not get far—the police diverted it onto the first available side street (I was lucky enough to be in the first block!). At least one of the priestesses was fond of dancing naked in Lower Sproul Plaza on campus, attracting a good deal of attention at first, but eventually becoming simply one more part of the scene."

Around that time, Ogar interviewed Jim and Artie Mitchell, two hippies who were in the process of building a career for themselves making porn movies. Other San Francisco experimental filmmakers such as Alex de Renzy and Jerry Abrams had made sex films, but they were documentaries, like de Renzy's *Pornography in Denmark* or Abrams's film about the Sexual Freedom League. In between they made porn—what they called "beavers"—to finance their fantasies of themselves as cinéastes and auteurs. The Mitchell Brothers, however, were intent on producing erotica. Artie ("husky, with a full bandido moustache, long hair and receding forehead") had got out of the army in 1968 and found that Jim ("tall and thin, with a shock of dark blond hair which he kept under a stocking cap"), while studying politics at San Francisco State University, had learned the rudiments of filmmaking. The Mitchells' early shorts were influenced by both the politics and the culture of Haight-Ashbury. They described one film called *Paul Is Dead, the Walrus Is Paul* (a title based on the widespread belief that Paul McCartney had died before the release of *Sergeant Pepper* and that messages confirming this could be heard if portions of empty disc were played backward); it was this hippie sense of fun, they claimed, rather incoherently, that informed such a film: "Why, when you're shooting a balling movie, do you introduce a guy coming down off a ladder with all those yellow lights behind him, you know? Here's a chick intercut with all these shots of McCartney and the Beatles on the wall—Art shot her with a yellow filter, and she's squeezing her tit and her milk's shooting up in this real nice spray . . . it was pretty trippy." Art pointed out that there was a distinct difference between L.A. and San Francisco porn: "You know, in L.A. beaver there's blood and there's violence. In San Francisco beavers, there's fucking and peace and tranquillity usually. You hardly ever see any bondage. People don't like it."[25]

Twenty years later, guests were invited to a bereavement party at the Mitchells' O'Farrell Theater, where they dined on finger sandwiches and raw oysters while exotic dancers simulated sex on fur rugs. The wake was for Artie Mitchell, who had been gunned down in his house by his brother. The Mitchells had not only survived the sixties but prospered in the seventies and eighties, establishing a cinematic language and syntax for pornography. A year after the Ogar interview they made *Behind the Green Door* (1971), the porn industry's first-ever feature-length movie with plot and character development (based on a story that had circulated for many years by means of typed carbon copies, an original underground classic). The Haight-Ashbury porn industry parlayed the icon of the hippie chick into the topless go-go dancer. The dreams that had been imprinted on the hippie chick's body, like the psychedelic light show projected onto her, were stripped down to drugs and sex. It is possible that some of the "high priestesses" of the Psychedelic Venus Church drifted into the Mitchell Brothers' sex empire.

The Mitchells were probably the first pornographers to use the First

Amendment to fight their frequent arrests under obscenity and anti-prostitution laws, and they won nearly every case. As hippie porn kings they made no attempt to operate furtively, as the mainstream sex industry had always done. They saw the attempts to ban pornography as another manifestation of straight culture with its authoritarian distrust of pleasure: "I'm more interested in the fact that people have the freedom to see any film they want to see," Artie and Jim told Ogar, "especially since it seems so easy to prove that they're not going out and hurting anyone else after they've seen them. It's just the straight fascist trip again—wanting everyone to be like them, you know? . . . Like, if all the students would go home, [they think] everything would be great all over. Nixon would be happy. Agnew would be happy. Yeah, if everyone would cut his hair, [they think] everything would be great."[26] By paying market rates to lawyers committed to progressive causes, their fees bankrolled the legal defense of well-known radicals like Angela Davis and the Black Panther Huey Newton. The Mitchell Brothers were the future of the San Francisco sexual-freedom movement.

Many of the most encouraging offshoots of the movement, dedicated to escaping the weight and authority of mainstream society and giving a voice to the counter-culture, drifted into the sex industry. It was as if once sex was identified as a subject for personal freedom, sleaze overwhelmed the politics. It was not just the atavism of sexuality but the philosophical underpinnings of pluralism that guaranteed everyone could do his or her own trip, whether that be the campaign for the legalization of abortion, the opening of gay clubs, or the transformation of Vice into a major U.S. industry. Counter-culture politics urged everyone to do their own thing. Politicizing sex legitimated it for the apolitical. The solitary wanker with his girlie magazine was now a member of the oppressed.

The *Berkeley Barb*, started in 1965 as a response to the Free Speech Movement, charted a classic decline. It had been launched by Max Scherr, a fifty-year-old ex-lawyer, union organizer, and bar owner, and reflected his credo: "I'm into all the little movements that are divergent from the mainstream of culture," he wrote in the first issue.[27] Like the Mitchell Brothers, Scherr was against all forms of censorship, which he believed had no place in what used to be called the Movement. But once the heyday of the hippies had passed, the *Barb* could no longer sustain itself on advertising revenue. It had to compete with a new kind of underground newspaper produced by a different kind of rebel—Al Goldstein, who started the New York sex magazine *Screw,* denounced by *New Yorker* cartoonist Jules Feiffer as "dildo journalism . . . about as pro-sex as the clap."[28] The *Barb,* like other underground papers, began to accept personal ads from "deviants" and display advertising from the Mitchell Brothers. It became the only newspaper in the Bay Area to accept sexual advertising, which quickly became the paper's main source of revenue.

In New York, *Rat,* another underground magazine, was proposing a sex-and-porn special issue. Radical feminist militia made up of women from groups like Redstocking, the Weatherwomen, and WITCH, invaded an editorial meeting and demanded to produce their own issue. San Francisco feminists pressured Scherr to remove his sex advertising. At home, Scherr was a domestic tyrant who struck his wife in front of staff at dinners she was obliged to cook for them at the Scherrs' house. "He knew full well that if he cut off that advertising he was out of business," Richard Ogar remembers. On principle Scherr detested censorship, though he had refused to accept advertising with a sadomasochistic content. But the pressure became so strong that he segregated the sexual advertising into a four- or six- or eight-page center section, depending on the amount in any issue, which could be discarded from the newspaper if the reader found it offensive. The tactic went awry: readers were discarding the newspaper and keeping the supplement. Scherr was close to retirement; he was reputed to have money squirreled away in foreign bank accounts, his marriage was falling apart. He sold the paper and fled to Europe, where his wife could not get hold of his assets. The sexual section of the *Barb* was purchased as a separate company called the *Spectator.* And as Scherr had known in his bones, within months the *Berkeley Barb* had died while the *Spectator* flourished and still exists to this day.

What, if anything, did the sexual-freedom movement of San Francisco achieve in the end? Very little. By the early seventies Poland had seen his organization stolen from him by straight suburbanites. The last Sexual Freedom League chapter died in 1983, but by then Poland had dissociated himself from what had become a swingers' movement. He proceeded to dedicate the rest of his life to the pursuit of claiming strips of sand for nude beaches. In 1974 he appeared in San Diego, campaigning to turn Black's Beach into a haven for skinny-dippers. At some point during this period he changed his name again, to Jefferson Clitlick. He vanished to Australia in the eighties and reemerged in La Jolla editing a guide to the nude beaches of the Third World and acting as proofreader for the *Sex Maniac's Diary*, which lists each year's calendar of sexual events. He is researching the nineteenth-century sex-freedom movement and signs his letters "For planet and liberty," with the name Jefferson Poland. He sent me a cutting from the *San Francisco Examiner* dated September 30, 1992. It showed a photograph of ten young people, in various shapes, sizes, and colors, backs to the camera, wearing, at most, Nikes or thongs. They were participants in a campus "nude-in" at Berkeley. One man had decorated his chest and shoes with the phrase "Free our bodies" in blue paint. I was reminded of the various clubs at Oxford in the sixties and seventies whose members affected to be characters from Evelyn Waugh novels, going to hell with a cigarette holder and a cocktail while the Noël Coward songs on the gramophone were drowned out by next door's Grateful Dead.

Hippies themselves have left few enduring marks, though the nostalgia for many of their ideas, which permeates retro-grunge, suddenly surfaced in the nineties as a reaction against the money culture of the previous decade. Flares are back and a whiff of patchouli oil, the pungent perfume that drifted across the air in communes, mixed with the scent of joss-sticks and the odor of joints, can suddenly assault the nostrils in the most unlikely of contemporary locations. But the vision of an alternative lifestyle that would overwhelm straight society withered because of the hippie disinterest in existing political movements and structures. To them we owe little more than the presence of a health-food shop in almost every town. The brief reign of the hippie ethos seems to have been a particular moment in postwar culture, unrepeatable because it depended upon a combination of prosperity, which indulged experimentation in lifestyles, reinforced by a national consensus about the breakdown of prudery.

But just as the pot-and-acid lifestyle fostered, inadvertently, a market for hard drugs, so the hippie notion of the freedom to do one's own thing sexually was co-opted by the emerging sex industry, which commercialized the new sexual freedom. Porn cinemas, brothels, gay bathhouses, which were previously known only by word of mouth or through cab drivers or from wandering the seedy areas of town, were able to advertise under the guise of sexual liberation and gained respectability. North Beach, the old Beat area of San Francisco where Ginsberg had lived in the fifties, was taken over by porn theaters and massage parlors. Poland's sexual-rights campaign and Max Scherr's repugnance of censorship (doubtless drilled into him during the days of the McCarthy witchhunts) legitimized sex businesses, gave them an outlet to reach their public, and turned them into the multimillion-dollar industries they are today. The politics were discarded like the clear plastic wrapper on a dirty magazine. Magazines like the *San Francisco BALL* did represent a new direction in porn, escaping the control of the Mob. Their descendants are the gay magazines *On Our Backs* (the lesbian parody of political correctness), *Anything That Moves* (for bisexuals), and *Diseased Pariah News* (for gays with AIDS). The humor and the sense of play echoes down from the counter-culture. But the boys and girls in the movement grew older, settled down, had kids. Feminism, with its rigorous analysis and increasing sense of history, challenged the wisdom of "trips."

A few hippies, the walking wounded, were sucked into the sex industry, victims of Post-Traumatic Sixties Disorder. Dropping out of school or college without qualifications, they believed the world would be remade into a place where careers would have no role. The women appeared on screen until their nubile bodies began to bear the marks of too many screws, too many drugs, and what hippies never thought they would have to face—age. Like Janis Joplin, the archetypal hippie chick, they went under. If they were male, they wrote scripts, recruited the "talent," acted as agents, as hustlers. You can see the men today in Los Angeles with their balding heads and graying ponytails, still believing sex is beautiful. But not that it is free.

8

Sister Kerista Saves the World

*It was never, in our minds, an experiment. We believed we were living under
a system which the whole world would sooner or later adopt.*
Pierrepont Noyes, *My Father's House: An Oneida Boyhood* (1937)

*Utopian communities are of necessity utopian but where else can we run from
the Wipeout Gang but into each other's arms?*
David Widgery, "Here Come the Wipeout Gang," *The Observer
Magazine* (1967)

Ska was the first black person to join the Kerista commune and stay.
She was the first black person who could stand being the first black
person. When she came along to the rap sessions she thought people
would be a lot more hippy-dippy than they were. What did freak her out,
though, was that some of the guys were "kind of chubbed out and stuff,
their figures weren't actually together." She had to deal with a voice in her
head that said she should be going out with a really svelte, built stud.
Except that if the truth be told, she was kind of chubby herself and had
a really big case of acne. So she was going to fall in love with some of these
dudes and live with them for the rest of her life. Ska was committed to
polyfidelity, the non-monogamous movement that had been tried out in
various forms since the sixties. Before she joined the commune, when she
was still living in Los Angeles, she had fallen in love with a gorgeous,
really artsy guy from Palo Alto who had wanted to be non-monogamous.
He wasn't the first man she'd slept with, but he was her first boyfriend.

He was a babe, he was really cute, and if he slept with someone else he would maybe find out that her vagina wasn't special. So she was insanely jealous and started to act like a macho, backwoods redneck. Turned off, he disappeared home to Palo Alto and she wrote lost-love poetry. Finally someone asked her, "Why are you whining about this guy? It sounds like you treated him like a piece of meat." This was when she was eighteen.

She moved to San Francisco. It was the first place she'd lived where it was okay to be mixed-race. San Francisco had its place in American pop mythology as a hippie town, but among the L.A. punk types it was also known as a city where you could get a job in a coffee shop and no one cared that you had purple hair. The Sex Pistols had played their last gig there. Ska went to work in a trendy clothes store for minimum wage and thought about jealousy. She decided that it wasn't cool. The principles of the women's liberation movement could also apply to the liberation of men. Men didn't deserve to be objectified either. She met Dimitri and they decided they would be an open couple. But when she started seeing other guys, he became jealous and insecure. Someone dropped off the Kerista newspaper at the place she worked and she figured out there was a community attached. She guessed she figured it out because she was looking for it. She decided that if she was going to be non-monogamous, she should get involved with some guys who could handle it. It took a while for her to find her B-FIC at Kerista—her "Best-Friend Identity Cluster," the family of friends/lovers whom she would fall in love with and live with for the rest of her life. After many combinations, she wound up with Buff and Bet. Bet took some getting used to. He was forty-seven. She was falling in love with this guy and her friends were seeing her walk down the street with him, a fat, bald-headed dude. Bet and Buff had joined the commune back in the seventies; there were pictures of them from those days, with long beards down to their chests, like the guys from ZZ Top. Ska worked on them. She was their B-FIC's style police. She cut their hair and took them shopping. She made them watch MTV.

What did Ska get in return? Security. Her parents had met in college in the sixties. Ska's mother was part Cherokee, part black, descended from slaves on an Irish-owned plantation. She was very dark-skinned and at eighteen no black man had found her attractive. The guy who sat behind her in class, admiring her figure, was seven years older, Jewish, the grandson of pogrom immigrants from Warsaw and Odessa. Ska was conceived in 1967, during the Summer of Love, and born in March 1968, two months before the student riots in Paris. Not long into the marriage her father began to have affairs. Her mother retaliated and got herself a boyfriend. Ska, at three, came down to the basement and found her father hanging from the ceiling. She yelled to her mom to come and cut him down. He lived. They divorced. He got into heroin. Then he met a new girlfriend with a twelve-year-old son from a previous relationship. He was called Alexander and he would do sadistic things but promised Ska he wouldn't do them to her if she let him feel her up. Ska's father's brother was gunned down by the Los Angeles Police Department during an altercation over drug prices. Her two-year-old cousin came to live with them. One day Alexander took the little girl into a room and locked the door. Ska told her mother about Alexander, so she denied her ex-husband access to their children. He stopped making child-support payments.

Ska's mother took her two kids and went back to live with her mother in Compton, a poor black neighborhood. She joined the Scientologists and Ska and her brother went to work in the Church's youth-labor program. Between the ages of eight and eleven she supported her mother; the two children managed to bring in $400 a month. After a few years there was a reconciliation between Mom and Dad. He took his ex-wife on holiday to Thailand and promised her lots of money. When they got there, he revealed that he was importing heroin to the United States. He later stiffed her over her share of the deal. She went back to Thailand to try smuggling herself, got caught, and was sentenced to life imprisonment. She only spent six years in jail, after a royal pardon, but while she was inside Ska and her brother moved to Hawaii to live with their father who was trying to kick heroin. She would skip school to help him over the cold turkey. By her teens she was a young basket case, playing in a rock band for the attention of the guys who thought she was hot because she played guitar, editing her own fanzine.

This little history of an American hell was commonplace in the eighties. The pioneers' dreams of a new life had degenerated into sex, drugs, shopping malls, and freeways. The hippie cause had failed. If the earliest immigrants had escaped from the decadent corruption of a sick European society, where could their descendants hide? There was no place further to go. Yet people still thought of an ethical life. The reaction against materialism in the sixties had created a commune movement of temporary idealists. Few communes had survived more than a handful of years, yet the idea of intentional communities had stubbornly persisted for centuries. Millenarianism had first been pronounced a heresy at the Council of Ephesus in A.D. 431 when communities of "perfected" men set themselves apart from degenerate society, owing no allegiance to the secular state.[1] Monasteries offered many of the possibilities of communal living: standing outside society, autonomous and often egalitarian, they were units of radical social engineering, structuring the day around physical labor and the quest for spiritual perfection. They regulated an unorthodox sexual arrangement, celibacy, and while they often experimented successfully with new economic forms, their goal was always a higher one. Thomas More lived for four years in a monastery and the monastic order is apparent in his *Utopia*.[2]

Through all communes runs a millenarian vision: the call to forsake a former life, abandon all established institutions, and light a beacon for the future in which the small band of the regenerated will survive while the unenlightened meet their doom. The Millerites sold all their belongings and gathered on hilltops to await the end of the world, proclaimed for January 1, 1844. On the day on which I write this, newspapers report the expected Second Coming in Korea. Koreans "are jettisoning their worldly goods to earn a ticket to heaven. Families are breaking up, businessmen are leaving their jobs and selling their assets. One woman reportedly had an abortion because she was afraid she would be too heavy to ascend to heaven bearing a child."[3] Religious millenarian cults tend toward authoritarianism and the single, all-powerful cult leader. The success of Hare Krishna and the Moonies was achieved by imposing thoroughgoing ideologies and rigid structures. In contrast, secular communities are wedded to antiformalism and a modern, post-Enlightenment outlook.[4] For these, the millennium is to be achieved not through the imminent coming of a supernatural being but by a radical restructuring of social and economic forms. In 1948, the year *1984* was published, the behaviorist B. F.

Skinner wrote *Walden II*, a polemic about a fictional utopian community based on a scientific theory of human behavior that solves the problems of personal relationships that bedeviled nineteenth-century experiments.

All utopias have addressed the most significant social institution, the family: Plato, in the *Republic*, forbade marriage and advocated a community of wives. Children were to be under the supervision of the state, by which they would be reared anonymously. Early millenarian communities in America, like the Mormons, adopted polygamy until forced to abandon it by the outrage of mainstream society. In *Walden II*, sex takes place freely between adolescents; when a young couple wish to marry, they maintain separate rooms since, as children are reared communally, the family has no function.[5] The vast majority of the thousands of communes that were established in America in the sixties were no more than attempts at dropping out by relatively affluent young people who readily dropped back in again when the fashion for antimaterialism passed on. Our common image of the commune is of the earth mother hippie chick, a brood of unwashed children and tow-haired men in overalls sullied with chicken shit. Communes turned out to be serious hard work, made insupportable by the weight of a messianic desire to abandon modern technology.

In the 1972 novel *Where the Wasteland Ends* a portion of the Pacific Northwest breaks off from the United States and declares the independent state of Ecotopia, based on E. F. Schumacher's "small is beautiful" philosophy, combining medieval street entertainment, ritual war games, the banning of cars, bright peasant clothing, naked massage, communal open-air hot tubs, and marijuana. The reality of ecotopias was either a harem for male dope smokers or the politically correct communes of the Vermont lesbian movement, a form of latter-day Stalinism. One lesbian commune, committed to smashing romanticism and reasoning that one falls in love because of various agist, sexist, racist, and able-bodiedist conditionings, chose lovers by drawing names from a hat. In 1977, after purity had reached such dedicated extremes that chainsaws had been banned, one woman ran away.

Kerista, however, survived against all the odds. In its earliest incarnation, it had appeared, a year before Ska was born, in a front-page story in the *San Francisco Chronicle*, under the headline RAID ON NUDE HIPPIES.

A deputy sheriff in Marin County had investigated an old summer house in search of a runaway from Daly City. Smelling the "unmistakable odor of 'pot,' " he discovered twenty-five hippies "cavorting in the nude" and sequestered the runaway. "It was a typically Haight-Ashbury crowd—sandals, beards and bare feet," the *Chronicle* reporter wrote. Before they were marched off to jail, a sign was stuck to the door: "We've been busted. Play it cool. Love you all." One girl complained that a woman officer had confiscated her birth-control pills, a sign of the Marin County Police Department's unfamiliarity with dangerous narcotics. "We call the house the Kerista House," one girl told the reporter while waiting to be booked. "Kerista means love. Don't say how dirty the place is—tell the people about the spirit of the place, how it's a place where people can come and go and how they all love it."[6]

Kerista did not quite mean love. A quarter of a century later, by the time Ska had been living a polyfidelitous life for three years, Kerista had become a shadowy organization that ran the thirty-third-fastest growing corporation in the United States, an ethical company dedicated to using the capitalist system to divert funds into philanthropic enterprises and sustain alternative relationships for its members. Kerista had metamorphosed into Sister Kerista, a comic-book heroine and goddess of rock and roll, worshipped by commune members, particularly when she took earthly form in the body of Joan Jett, leather-clad rock chick of the eighties. Sister Kerista's devotees described themselves as fun nuns and punk monks; they needed a religion and this one was as good as any.

Kerista seems to have put in her first earthly appearance in 1956, when she delivered a message to the effect that her cult would be the next great religion of the world, a stepping-stone to higher evolutionary consciousness. The recipient was John Gruen, a friend of Allen Ginsberg and Peter Orlovsky born around 1924. Gruen served and was decorated during the Second World War, married four times, and fathered six daughters. The first two marriages were traditionally monogamous; during the third and fourth he got into the early swinging scene in New York, holding weekend parties where couples fueled Gruen's fantasy projections of a sexually enlightened community.[7] Around 1965 he changed his name to Bro Jud and set up a household of five women and five men who lived in the nude, later moving to San Francisco, where he began a commune that consisted of himself and a harem of girls.

Jud was inspired by the kibbutz movement of modern Israel and by the traditional Jewish concept of *tzedakhah,* which combines the ideas of charity, justice, and righteous living. Jud looked to Joseph Perl, a leader of the Jewish Enlightenment in Galicia, who had transformed the notion of the messiah into a symbolic construct containing ideas of redemption, universal peace, and freedom from oppression. Rummaging around in rabbinical history, Jud discovered the Edict of Worms of 985: under the leadership of Gershom ben Judah, a thousand-year prohibition had been placed against multiple-adult, non-monogamous households. The purpose of the ban, Jud wrote, was to avoid persecution by conforming to Christian values. It was about to come to an end.[8] At first Jud dreamed of a homeland for his followers in what was then British Honduras. The expedition seems to have failed and any fantasies about rural living were abandoned for good. Kerista found a storefront office in Haight-Ashbury, members began to occupy a number of apartments in the neighborhood, and they turned their attention to constructing their polyfidelitous lifestyle and building the business empire that would enable them to enact the principles of *tzedakhah.*

None of these great aspirations would have been possible if it had not been for Eve Furchgott—"Even Eve," as she decided to be called—and her high school friend Blue Jay Way Konigsberg, or Way, as she is now less cringingly known. When Eve arrived at Kerista in 1971, Jud's harem was living off his war pension. Eve wrote to her parents and informed them that since she had no intention of going to college, they should hand over the money they would have spent on educating her so she could start her own business. It was a typically hippie venture—a bunch of people doing odd jobs to scrape together enough money to live. In the meantime, Eve, Jud, and Way developed an erotic philosophy. Jud had been in the habit of going to an occasional porn movie. Eve went along and saw an interview with the Mitchell Brothers. Back East she had been involved in the women's movement: Artie and Jim proved too much. Porn had to go. Masturbation involved fantasy and turning someone into a porn object in your head. No more diddling. Sucking nipples was regressive and promoted inequality. Pop music had romantic lyrics and should not be listened to. These attempts at imposing cultural and erotic purity went on until 1978 when, between Eve, Way, and Jud, the notion of polyfidelity emerged. Each commune member would join a "family" or B-FIC, an evolving unit of individuals, ideally composed of equal numbers of both sexes (though there is a bisexual Kerista B-FIC). B-FIC sex is structured by sleep schedules. In a B-FIC of three women and three men, a member would sleep with person A on Monday, person B on Tuesday, person C on Wednesday, person A again on Thursday, and so on. In Ska's B-FIC of two men and one woman, Buff or Bet would have to sleep alone every other night. Sex is not mandatory every night—it is a sleep schedule, not a fucking schedule—but fidelity to the members of one's B-FIC is.

B-FIC sex poses fascinating speculations. What if a particularly good-looking young new member isn't attracted to older people in his B-FIC? "If this babe wants to sleep with me but not a woman who's a lot older, I don't want to sleep with him," Ska says. "I don't want some guy who's going to dump me as soon as my breasts start to sag. I'm going to get older too. One of these days I'll be the forty-eight-year-old woman and there'll be some twenty-three-year-old chick coming along." And if a super-good-looking dude turned up whom the other members of her B-FIC vetoed? "The two guys in my family aren't going to have to sleep with him, all they have to do is get along with him. He'd have to have a major personality defect and then I'd have to figure out why I was attracted to some guy with a major personality defect." One of the obvious advantages of the Kerista sexual practice is that it overcomes the agism inherent in relations between men and women. Kerista women in their forties have firm-bodied young lovers at the peak of their sexual energy, redressing an imbalance that exists in the wider society. The onus is on these women, however, to keep themselves in shape—the commune as a whole is extremely appearance-conscious. With the exception of Jud, the hippie patriarch, members are encouraged to keep up to date with fashion.

Unlike most communes, there are almost no children running around underfoot. Eve had decided that the reason why there were so few great female historical figures was that women were assigned a lifetime role as child-carers. At first members were allowed to have a child each, until it became apparent that the commune would quickly be overrun with kids. The rule was then changed to one child between two people. Finally, Kerista decided to make a complete separation between sex and reproduction. There were to be no children at all. Vasectomies became mandatory for all male members, though there is an option of having one's sperm frozen. This left the commune free to pursue its second millenarian ambition: an autonomous economic community dedicated to the redistribution of wealth, using capitalist economics to finance philanthropic activity: a business-driven Peace Corps. In the long view, it aims to be the seedbed of an international mega-commune network "that will function as a civilian branch of service and generate huge amounts of philanthropic funding that will be used to solve global problems." The framework of ethical Jewish thinking is clearly discernible here—its internationalism, the importance of the community to it, its pursuit of justice, its post-Enlightenment modernism and aversion to a rural way of life.

By the beginning of the eighties, Kerista had acquired its first computer, an IBM, and a typesetting system. The two did not interface, so Eve and Way set up a development team to hardwire them. Finding out later from the industry that this was something of an achievement, they decided to become consultants. In 1984 they were introduced to Apple's Macintosh systems. For Eve, it was comparable to a visual artist never having seen paint before and then going to Italy in the middle of the Renaissance. By 1991, Eve and Way had recruited over a hundred employees, two-thirds from outside the commune. The company had become the fifth largest Bay Area computer retailers, with fourteen million dollars in sales in 1990. Corporate publications were beginning to take an interest. Way and Eve were giving interviews, dodging the issue of their unconventional lifestyle by selling themselves as yet another example of ethical business. Yet in 1987 Eve had written:

[This] is the most urgent and important thing because the welfare of humanity and our planet may be at stake if our plan—or some plan, and we don't know of any others—fails to work. But my guess is that the way we're going to get people to join us and help us make the plan succeed will be by appealing to them on the basis of the things that really hit home, no matter how stone-cold intellectual they may be: sex and eroticism. The world will be liberated from the yoke of economic oppression and ecological suicide through sex. How's that for a hippie concept? It's 1987, twenty years since the Summer of Love, and the spirit of Haight-Ashbury lives on.[9]

This mission to save the world has, at the time of writing, twenty-eight members, fourteen men and fourteen women. Forty percent are Jewish. The median age is thirty-four. The youngest person is twenty-one and the oldest woman forty-three. It seems likely that the world's problems will have overwhelmed everything before Kerista succeeds in its global vision. Everything Kerista stands for has failed in the wider society: the communal structure, the sexual experimentation, the utopianism, the attempts at social engineering and a mixed economy. One can easily laugh at these earnest hippies, with their naive belief in the transforming possibilities of individual action. Yet in this tiny experiment one finds the millenarian spirit still vital, still concerned with its twin goals of world transformation and sexual freedom. With its Gestalt group dynamics, its commitment to the future, its ability to make fun of itself, its capacity to adapt and survive and to provide a safe haven from the horrors of the worst of Californian living, Kerista is a small light in the darkness that marks the end of our millennium. And as we construct our own frail relationships in which we invest so many of our hopes for the future—our own happiness and that of our children—we might remember how utopian our more conventional family structures are.

Polyfidelity was not restricted to the communes. From the mid-sixties to the beginning of the eighties, non-monogamy was an underground movement, largely among youngish, middle-class Americans with homes and careers. The 1963 French film *Jules et Jim* presented an eternal triangle of three lovers—two men and a woman who cannot choose between them. The film was a landmark of cinema in the sixties, influencing a generation. Its penultimate scene depicts Cathérine resolutely driving Jim across a bridge, the center of which has collapsed, sending both to their deaths. It was an image that seemed to stand for a final leap of daring, a defiance of the impossible. Audiences gasped. Jim tells Cathérine, "To be a pioneer you must be unselfish." The politics of relationships in the French *nouvelle vague* defied the conventions of bourgeois marriage. By contrast, the British films of the period—*Alfie, The Knack, Georgy Girl*—exposed the sexual ethics of Swinging London as a charter for philanderers. For the political radical, non-monogamy represented a chance to move beyond possession and jealousy, which seemed to dehumanize partners and turn them into impersonal objects. Non-monogamy, on the other hand, claimed to respect the integrity of the individual and the variety of his or her desires and choices, which should not be limited to one lover. Through influential novels of the period like Lawrence Durrell's *Alexandria Quartet* (1957–1960), readers learned that identity and events were not fixed and limited; we all play out differing roles and differing versions of reality. And if so, why not have different partners for these multiple selves?

Most viewers of *Jules et Jim* had no intention of abandoning their way of life for an inflated agenda of macroeconomic change. But the nuclear family, particularly as it had evolved in Britain and the United States, felt to some like a prison for the spirit, an inappropriate system for childrearing and a failing economic unit. The nuclear family had been hijacked by capitalism until it was no more than a tightly structured market for commodities, its identity manufactured by Madison Avenue. Faced with rising life expectancy, the two partners in a nuclear family could expect to be shackled together for fifty years with all the sexual ennui that entailed. Suburban housing imposed a terrible isolation on women stuck at home with their children, divided from their neighbors by consumer envy. Anthropologists became enchanted with the extended families they found in southern Europe and the Third World. They hailed, for example, the Nyars of the Malabar Coast of India, for whom the family was a *taravad*, a permanent, multigenerational clan of relationships, a matrilineal structure within which marriage was a nightly visit from one of several changing husbands of another *taravad*.[10]

Three years after the release of *Jules et Jim*, the notion of group marriage gripped America through the publication of *The Harrad Experi-*

ment, a thinly imagined novel that proselytized a supposed sexual experiment among the students of a fictional New England college (the name was of course a compound of Harvard and Radcliffe, the then male and female Ivy League colleges in Boston). The novel proposed that Harrad encouraged communal living between the sexes, culminating in a group marriage when the various couples finally graduate.

The author, Robert Rimmer, was a middle-aged Boston businessman whose wife Erma had, in the mid-fifties, discovered he was having an affair with a neighbor. After a few permutations, the Rimmers ended up in an open marriage with another couple that lasted until the wife's death, when the husband quickly found a younger woman. Rimmer, born in 1917, was trapped by his father's authoritarian insistence that he should enter the family business (a printing firm) and early marriage at a time when premarital sex was virtually impossible for young men of his class. Rimmer envisaged himself as Pygmalion to his wife's Galatea, insisting that she acquire "cultural literacy." He led her through an interminable course, of which she seems to have been an unwilling student, in Indian yoga, tantra, and tantric sex, socialism, chamber music, art.

The Harrad Experiment suggests Rimmer's yearning for the freedom of the student life, particularly as it was lived in the affluent and expansive sixties, that he had never enjoyed in his own youth. After trying unsuccessfully to publish the novel himself, Rimmer discovered Sherbourne Press in Los Angeles, a mail-order porn distributor. The front of the building was a former nightclub and the back was a warehouse for sex aids. Sherbourne had a huge mailing list, of which six thousand names were doctors. *Harrad* was advertised with a four-page publicity flyer. The man who wrote it told Rimmer he could make Charles Dickens sound sexy. Seventeen thousand copies were sold in hardcover by mail until Sherbourne sold the paperback rights to Bantam, which put up billboard advertising in university areas. Within a month, Bantam had sold 300,000; within a year it was on the bestseller lists. When it finally went out of print in 1976, it had sold three million copies. It was filmed with Tippi Hedren and Don Johnson and still shows up on late-night television.

Rimmer was too old to join in the party that his book had unleashed. Harrad groups began to form. When Massachusetts sociologists Larry and

Joan Constantine began their academic study of group marriage, which was eventually published in 1973, they found that only one group marriage was known to have predated the publication of *Harrad* (and that of Robert B. Heinlein's *Stranger in a Strange Land,* a science fiction work that addressed the topic from a Martian point of view, in 1961). Two young couples, with husbands both studying under the GI Bill, shared a house or apartment for about six months in 1952, and this had led to a stormy sexual involvement. But "so significant were the Rimmer and Heinlein novels in serving as releasing mechanisms (or such was the masterful timing) that we have been unable to trace the start of the experimentation with actual group marriages prior to 1966,"[11] the Constantines wrote. For the Constantines, the explanation for the interest in alternative forms of relationship was to be found in a reaction to the Eisenhower years and their emphasis on conformity. The groups they studied, mainly men and women in their thirties, sought authenticity of experience—a concept that was finding its way into everyday language through the popular writings of humanistic psychologists.* When the

---

*Authenticity in sexual relationships found its guru in the sinister figure of John Williamson, who, for a few years in the early seventies ran Sandstone, a sexual retreat for couples in Topanga Canyon, California. Williamson was an engineer in middle age who set himself up as the head of a kind of sect run on encounter-group principles. In the "ballroom" couples were encouraged to have group sex, taking them beyond individual anxiety about possession or performance. The activities at Sandstone were documented in Gay Talese's book *Thy Neighbor's Wife,* which on publication in 1981 caused indignation among reviewers: the furore was one of the signs that the sexual revolution was over. Talese had labored over the book for ten years, and in that decade the psychological exploration that had been commonplace in the seventies came to seem dated, self-obsessed, and boring. Alex Comfort had written enthusiastically about Sandstone, at which he had done thorough and painstaking personal research, in the second edition of *The Joy of Sex* (1977): "Most important for couples was the exorcism of all the custodial anxieties about conventional marriage. In shared openness . . . both couples found that the sight of a lover relating sexually to someone else—often while holding their regular partner's hand—was moving, exciting and finally immensely releasing. There was nothing to be afraid of. Afterwards they were often more tender to each other because of a feeling that the parts of their personhood which they felt had been taken had been returned as a loving gift." The section on Sandstone did not appear in subsequent editions. Williamson was sighted by Erma Rimmer in the late eighties looking "sleazy, all screwed out."

Constantines asked their sample for their reasons for participation in multilateral marriage, the strongest that emerged was the desire for greater companionship. And while the quest for a variety of sexual partners was cited everywhere, vague notions like the need for opportunities for personal growth, intellectual variety, a richer environment for the children, and even more people to talk to recurred. If the nuclear family closed in on these couples, the group marriage seemed expansive, a window to a more variegated landscape of reality.

Harrad West, in Berkeley, was an immediate and public offshoot of the Rimmer book. It published its public statement in the Winter 1969 issue of *The Modern Utopian:* "Our basic idea at Harrad West is that perhaps six, eight or even a dozen or more adults can form 'marriage' relationships with each other as a means of attaining far more than monogamous marriages can offer. (There are presently six adults, three male and three female, plus three children living here.)"[12] Of the six adults, Dub, a commercial artist, and Claudel had been married for fourteen years before trying group marriage as an alternative to the swinging scene they had tired of. They had sold their home in the suburbs and were ready to try anything. Wayne and Ruth "appeared super straight . . . Wayne in his suit and tie, very stiff and formal, his words well guarded; Ruth in her best party dress, more conversational, but very proper." Hyam was "pushing sixty, separated from his Black wife and overly sensitive to the feelings of others ever since his mind-blowing encounter weekend at the Esalen Institute." Dorothy, "recently separated from her husband, seeing her analyst and wearing the gaudiest colored dresses you can imagine, joining the Sexual Freedom League and being the life of the orgy—and doing quite well at it in a comic sort of way."[13]

This ill-assorted group began by formulating a credo, always one of the easier aspects of the experiments in radical lifestyles of the sixties. They wanted to learn and grow together and their children to have a larger number of adults to rely on. All adult members were to be considered married to all others. Sex was vital in a successful marriage, helping them to become more affectionate people; it would deepen their friendships, enrich their lives, and allow them to become—that all-important attribute of the authentic life—more honest with themselves. A certain number of possessions would be shared, but private property would be retained. Couples who wished to join were advised to try swinging first. Claudel did most of the housework. Dub and Wayne were the intellectuals inasmuch as they spent a great deal of time theorizing about the experiment. It lasted for only a few months. Later, under the influence of encounter groups, Dub determined that he should give up work in order to devote himself more fully to personal growth. After locking himself in a closet for two weeks, he was committed to a mental hospital. Claudel was sent out to "rip off some welfare."[14] Wayne liked systems and had set up an elaborate rotating sleeping-partners schedule in which members had to spend the night with whom they were assigned to on the list. He proposed a position based on the "concrete positive reinforcement of the other real person," which could be deconstructed as "any girl whom I want to fuck should fuck me, and any girl who wants me to fuck her need only ask me."[15] He joined the swingers. The subsequent activities of Hyam and Dorothy are not recorded, nor is the effect on the children.

This ghastly ménage was probably typical of many hastily abandoned attempts at group marriage. Others lasted a little longer, when more serious effort was put into solving the group dynamics of an untested system. The Constantines were optimistic in 1973. The family's future, they believed, was sure to be pluralistic, and "the ramifications of multilateral marriage and other emerging family forms will reach to the very foundations of modern family life. Few families will not be affected," they wrote.[16] Before the book was published they were contacted by Udi Eichler, a producer from Thames Television in London, who was making a documentary, exuberantly titled *California 1970. Sex, Love and Marriage: Do What Turns You On.* The Constantines passed on to Eichler the names of two couples living in a group marriage in Orange County, California, near Los Angeles. Linda and Bob Corson and Didi and Jim Cluffs were members of a radical Unitarian church that was supporting group-marriage experiments. The two men had gone into business together and the wives jointly ran a handicraft store. The couples had effectively swapped partners but occasionally swapped back again. Sitting in their suburban garden, the wives in their already dated Pucci prints, the four chatted amicably but with a certain submerged anxiety about their lifestyle. Even to Eichler at the time, the tensions underlying the relationship were obvious. The program's narrator, Peter Williams, was clearly appalled by the setup: "At the moment the group marriage of Linda and Jim and Didi and Bob is too much for even this society to accept," he opined. "At the moment California boasts that what it does today everywhere else copies five years later, which, having seen the swingers on the other side of paradise, is for me a depressing thought."

Eleven years later, Eichler received a phone call from Didi, who was on a visit to London. Was he interested in hearing how it all turned out? He was. Alcoholism and attempted suicide were mentioned.

Very little research was done on the long-term effects of group marriage. As far as the Constantines know, none of the marriages they studied is still together. Commonly, some kind of dramatic flare-up served as the immediate cause of dissolution. Group marriages of more than two couples were the least stable since the more individuals, the greater the problems of an equal fit. Many of the women the Constantines met found group marriage a convenient way of sharing child-care responsibilities and came to use the family arrangement as a way to make an advantageous transition from one marriage to another without a period as a single parent. The effects on the children were mixed. At the time, the Constantines felt that children growing up in communes and group marriages showed higher levels of emotional maturity, self-esteem, and social skills, a premise borne out by the many multidisciplinary studies that were carried out. But in later years, the Constantines were to meet young adults who had grown up inside these relationships, and they were to tell a different story. They felt ignored and lost in the intensity of the adult experiment. When the marriages failed, they were abandoned by the partners who left. Often they never heard from them again. Most group marriages collapsed because of the exactions of the emotional business required: the endless Gestalt meetings, the working on feelings, the devotion to group dynamics; in the end the commitment to grow turned into another prison. The experimenters no longer had lives, they had a marriage that devoured their time and energy. The experiment was never widespread, perhaps a few thousand people at most. Those clustered along the West Coast were most committed to the ideology of alternative

lifestyles—the drugs, the mysticism, the radical therapy. As those preoc-
cupations fell out of fashion, so did group marriage. The Constantines
found that the East Coast "families" were less bound by ideology, more
by happening to meet other couples with whom they became intimate.

One California network of devotees of open marriage survived into the
nineties. Family Synergy was started sometime in the early seventies and
had as its statement of purpose that "people can live fuller, more reward-
ing lives, achieving more of their potential, if they developed an awareness
of their freedom of choice concerning interpersonal relationship styles; and
that given an increased awareness, many will select open, multiply committed relationships." One member, who attended the 1991 conference
with his ill wife, used the group newsletter to remember how it had once
been:

> I felt very nostalgic, since the first Family Synergy Conference we attended
> was at de Benneville in 1979. Much has changed since then. I remember
> Gloria-Sue was the first nude person we saw, of many who spent most of
> the Conference nude. She was very enthusiastic about being nude; an
> intense feeling of freedom emanated from her. I remember the nude
> dancing Saturday night and the colored slides played on the bodies.
> . . . I remember my intense feeling of being part of something awesome
> and revolutionary, a really different life-style, in which grouphood and
> individual growth seemed to be more important than couplehood, espe-
> cially possessive couplehood. We were full of common purpose.
>
> This year the atmosphere was quite different. The warmth was based
> primarily on the fact that many members present had become friends in
> varying degrees over the years and a kind of old-home week flavor
> prevailed. . . . Many of the people who in 1979 were enjoying an open
> life-style have now chosen a monogamous orientation. . . . The interesting
> and informative keynote speech . . . dealing as it did with AIDS, was at
> best a left-handed tribute to the open life-style. Some members considered
> it a "downer," not a good prelude for Saturday night dancing. I would
> have preferred a talk celebrating multiple intimate relationships, with "safe
> sex" as a footnote.
>
> I assume that this is not our last Conference, though I think our
> organization is running out of steam.[17]

In the "Sunshine and Showers" column it was reported that one member was recuperating at home from a recent heart attack while another had had orthoscopic surgery on her other knee.

Today, in post-AIDS America, few people would admit to an interest in non-monogamy. Yet the grandest old alternative of all still flourishes; monogamy with affairs on the side, which we call adultery, the way that even the most conservative American politician faintly echoes in his submerged life the freethinkers of twenty-five years ago.

The sexual revolution of multiple partners is not dead. It lives on in an underground culture, on housing developments, in suburban enclaves, behind mock-Georgian doors lit by carriage lamps, ranch-style houses with shag rugs, immovable mobile homes cemented into trailer parks. Sexual freedom triumphed in swinging, which carefully filleted out the politics and made unconventional sex palatable for the middle-aged and middle-class. The sexual revolution envisaged by Jefferson Poland and Bro Jud stood apart from capitalism; it was a defiance of what it called straight society. It could not see itself existing outside a framework of a radical political agenda. It proposed a total transformation along gender, race, and class lines in which desire would be liberated from its chains along the way. It celebrated a phrase reputedly seen daubed on a wall in Paris in 1968: "Revolution is the orgasm of history." Swinging was capitalism's way of co-opting the dreamers. Swinging was a free-enterprise activity by which the emerging sex industry could open clubs at which like-minded people could meet and mate. Swinging made no demands on its adherents other than the sexual. There was no call to a new life, no urge to abandon the structures of one's security—home, job, or marriage.

Swinging was much studied and many how-to guides were published. One of the earliest was *The Swinger's Handbook*, an insiders' account by the pseudonymous "Carol" and "Tim." They both claimed to work in the "communications field in very straight institutions"; they had both been married but not to each other. They described themselves as "friends and lovers,"[18] but they did not live together. In this they were atypical. Most swingers were married couples in their thirties or older whose sex lives were drained of energy. Carol and Tim tried to explain the historical and cultural factors that led to swinging. They suggested that the Victorian era had ended with the First World War, that Prohibition had led to a disrespect for the law, and World War Two had encouraged the urge to live for the moment. But a variety of technological factors were also important: the retooling of domestic automobile production during the peace led to a car culture that gave sex an alternative venue to the marriage bed; the motel boom; penicillin; the Pill; the new mobility of the jet age, which created the notion of travel as a liberating experience; and finally, America's adulation of technology, with its emphasis on efficiency and quality, had led to endless analysis of and efforts to improve sexual technique.[19]

The earliest swingers, before the commercialization of their scene, were scientific utopians, as the population controllers had been. Science, they believed, would liberate sexuality for them. A sociological study of swap clubs written in 1964 (and published by the same porn distributors that awoke a sleeping nation to the possibilities of Harrad) looked at private groups in the Midwestern states, including one in Denver, most of whose members were employed by a large missile manufacturer. The authors, William and Jerry Breedlove (yes) breathlessly anticipated the scientific transformation of the body:

> . . . pharmaceutical scientists predict the physical evidence of menstrua-tion—the natural hemorrhage and the absorbent pads or injectives—will be eliminated within the next twenty years. We are on the threshold of a revolution in body chemistry as fantastic and beneficial to the comfort of humanity as the Industrial Revolution little more than a century ago. Government-conducted studies on the human digestive system for example may completely eliminate fecal waste and urine from the body: the question in the near future will not be how far a man *can* go with these changes, but how far *dare* he go, when rapid evolution incurred by any one of many great changes could change man's entire physiological make-up. . . . These are the questions that may very well occupy our minds later this century.[20]

If the body could be transcended, why not laws, religious scruples, conventional morality?

When the Breedloves were writing, in forty-five out of fifty states the police could break into a private home and arrest two people under fornication-and-adultery laws if they were having sex outside marriage. In fifteen states, a couple could be arrested for living together. In forty-seven states oral sex was illegal. There was a maximum penalty of twenty years in jail for anal sex. In five states you could be sent to jail for practicing mutual masturbation. Arkansas, California, Louisiana, New Mexico, and Tennessee had no laws against swap clubs, providing that the members adhered to the missionary position.[21] The Breedloves aspired to greatness, to an appeal to the Gettysburg Address and Lincoln's phrase, "government by the people for the people." They cited the Nazi Party as an example of what happened when people were not encouraged to think for themselves. They gestured grandly toward "scientific progress" that was in the process of creating a reasoning society, now directed inward to the psyche in which, reason told them, we would discover our true selves. They set in motion an appeal to the First Amendment to guarantee rights to sexual expression, which was to become the rallying cry of pornographers, in the eighties and nineties, against the censorship of the Moral Majority.

How swinging worked in practice was another matter. Perhaps there were dedicated visionaries fucking for the technological revolution and the Enlightenment. But most swinging came down to husbands putting pressure on wives; the wives agreeing reluctantly; going along to a club or party or putting an ad in a contact magazine; hating it and telling their husbands they would never go again; or loving it, terrifying their husbands into threatened anger. Carol and Tim show the distorted psychological pressures men placed on women: "For Carol, it was chiefly a desire to please Tim in the beginning, followed by her own growing curiosity. She has finally realized what Tim has told her from the beginning: she is simply too much woman for one man, unless she is willing to sublimate her sexuality (as she did for years)."[22]

What all this boils down to is that Tim is frightened of the power of Carol's sexuality, which he believes he cannot satisfy. He tells Carol she is abnormal, a nymphomaniac. The only way she can be satisfied is by a number of men. The only solution to the problem of her sexual appetite is for Carol and Tim to swing. Carol suffers from occasional bouts of what Tim calls ambivalence, which Carol describes:

There are times—even many times—when I feel I can't do this at all. Those are the times when I'm on my way to a swing, particularly when I'm going to meet new people. I moan and groan and think of excuses and tell Tim I'm *completely* out of the mood, so why don't you just run along, dear, and I'll see you later. And he laughs, and says, there I go with my famous ambivalence again, and he'll remind me of my words later on the way home—if he can get me to *go* home. I groan some more and say that I really *am* ambivalent, or at *least* that, although maybe I'm just completely out of place in the whole swinging thing, and he should go and find himself another partner or do a single act—there are enough ads by women alone, heaven knows . . . "Look," Tim complains, "you don't have to buy a man's entire life-style and voting record to enjoy his lovemaking."[23]

But Tim needed Carol. Single men were never welcome at swing parties. There were too many of them. Women were at a premium. All studies of swinging agree that while bisexuality among male practitioners was so rare as to be almost unheard-of, women were enthusiastic about sex with other women. Two British swingers, interviewed in 1976, indicate the gender differences:

Bob: "I always feel a bit uneasy with the men, and I'm scared stiff that one day one of them's going to try something with me. If we're sharing a bed in a foursome I try to keep as far away from the man as possible, but obviously you do come in contact, and sometimes it puts me right off . . . It could be an outlet for people who have homosexual feelings but don't want to risk anything. You often hear about happily married men suddenly turning queer, and so perhaps some people like to have a safety valve." . . .

Kitty: "As a woman it's easier for me to accept my homosexual feelings and not have any shame about them, but it's harder for a man—it all involves his virility and everything."[24]

So prevalent is the use of swinging by wives as a way of finding lesbian sex that it seems that under cover of suburbia there is a shadowy empire of gay housewives as yet untapped by the lesbian community.

Most swingers, though, are conventional people who nonetheless do not wish the sexual revolution to pass them by completely. "Modern" is a word often found in contact ads. From the sixties, *Playboy* sold suburbia a fantasy life. One investigator of the swing scene in America talks of a recurrent rumor that film and pop stars would turn up at parties. Swingers had a dream of being among the Beautiful People, jet-setters at a bacchanalian feast. The word "penthouse" entered the language as a place where such parties would take place. Derek Bowskill, a British writer who tried swinging in the mid-seventies, found a consistent self-image: swingers thought of themselves as attractive, well-educated, happily married, liberated, guilt-free, and in the vanguard.[25] The reality, he thought, was that they were orthodox in dress and conventional in behavior: acquisitive, bourgeois white Anglo-Saxon Protestants who rejected Bowskill from one group because he was an atheist. They lived by the words "discreet" and "confidential."[26] They desired to be "with-it," "liberated," "experimental," and "modern," "namely anything other than what most swingers are—bourgeois in mind, body, soul, sex and class,"[27] Bowskill wrote.

Like all other sexual revolutionaries, swingers believed themselves to be harbingers of the new life. Carol and Tim shared the belief in a visionary utopia: swinging would split through the fabric of society and become so commonplace for the majority that it would no longer have the name "swinging," the way few people now speak of "premarital sex." "And finally . . . organized swingers and the free souls in the larger society who see sex as a marvelous recreation will eventually melt together in the same stream of sexual liberation. 'Swinging' will be no more. But in the land will be a new openness to physical joy."[28]

Over the Labor Day weekend of 1991, I went to a three-day swingers' convention in San Diego attended by around 6,000 people. The event was dedicated to the spirit of the 200th anniversary of the Bill of Rights and its ten amendments of which the first laid down the freedom of speech, of the press, of the people to peaceably assemble and to petition the government for a redress of grievances. Some months earlier a disgruntled nightclub owner had attempted to use the First Amendment's guarantee of freedom of speech to defend his topless go-go dancers. The convention's keynote address was titled "Sexual Repression as a Means of Political Control." It was delivered by Albert Z. Freedman, Ph.D., the cofounder of *Forum* magazine, vice president of Penthouse Films, publisher of *Penthouse, Omni, Longevity,* and *Compute* magazines. Freedman was perhaps the last living sexual revolutionary. *Longevity* magazine still believes in the potential of the human body for transformation and its capacity to cheat death.

Before the convention culminated on the Saturday night in an Erotic Masquerade Ball (rumored to be attended by a number of "stars from L.A." in disguise), conventioneers participated in a variety of workshops: The ABCs of Swinging; The Sexuality of Aging: Tri Weekly, Try Weekly, Try Weakly; Latex and Lace: Fun Ways Through Safer Sex; S&M 101: How to Start; Tantra: Ecstasy Through Sexual Union; Erotic Spirituality; Swinging in Review: the Sexual Recreation of Today's Playcouples. The Friday session opened with a workshop, Science Fiction & Group Living/Group Marriage, run by an organization called Live the Dream. About a dozen heavyset people in their early fifties took the stage, the women voluminously robed, the men's bellies held in by coveralls or braces. They were descended from a proud lineage—the last remnants of the Harrad movement. For an hour these unappetizing middle-aged hippies talked about their grandchildren and their surgery, pleading for young blood to join their doomed enterprise. One man who had joined an early Harrad group marriage now ran a travel company specializing in Southeast Asia. He was proposing to organize group marriages consisting of American males and a bevy of Thai beauties. Otherwise, living the dream turned out to involve nude picnics and a study of the state laws governing triads. The embarrassed, giggling audience drifted out to sit around the pool where the silicone implants, at rest, resembled a landscape of small lumpy hillocks. In the marketplace every kind of fantasy was being sold. I bought an icetray that in inverted bas-relief depicted a line of penises. You could buy bondage gadgets, leather underwear, porn movies, contact magazines like stamp collectors' publications in which men showed pictures of their wives: "I've got this, what can you swap it for?"

The convention had been organized by Robert McGinley, who had built a million-dollar business from his string of swing clubs and his holiday resort, Hedonism II, which offered "modern," "mature," "adult" vacations for the liberated in spirit. Before I left, a suave black man in a gangster suit and jaunty hat asked me if I'd got laid. I had, in truth, spent much of the convention retreating to my room to catch up with the attempted coup in the then-Soviet Union and the independence demands of the Baltic states. I said I had not. Had he? Why else did one come to a swingers' convention? he wondered. How many times? He counted up. Thirteen between Thursday and Saturday night. I took a step backward. Wasn't he worried about AIDS? Didn't I go to the workshops? The message had been clear enough. *You can't get AIDS from heterosexual sex.* These people planned to live forever.

Everything that was idealistic about radical movements for sexual freedom disintegrated. Even swinging, which survived the years of reaction, remains underground, circled by discretion and first names only. Did society become more open about sex? In many ways not. Politicians continue, as they ever did, to have extramarital affairs. Few survive exposure with their careers intact. In the early seventies a Birmingham housewife opened the first Ann Summers sex supermarket in Britain, which provided sexual aids to couples on the high street. After a brief period of fashion, the shops retreated back to Soho, where their wares had always been sold in less salubrious surroundings. Teenagers went on holiday to fuck as much as possible in the ravaged resorts of Spain and Greece. But the working class had been doing that for centuries, only in cooler climates and with less exotic food and drink. The British tabloids introduced nude pinups. But film magazines of the thirties and forties had similarly aroused men's lust with their glamour photographs of the stars in partial states of undress.

Where couples did become more sexually adventurous was in the privacy of their bedrooms. *The Joy of Sex* has been a continual bestseller since its first publication in 1973. *The Joy of Sex* taught a generation erotic techniques that were once the closely guarded secrets of the most expensive courtesans. The most recent Kinsey report estimates that the average age of loss of virginity in America is sixteen or seventeen[29]; that between 50 and 80 percent of American women perform oral sex (though less than half like doing it)[30]; around 35 percent of men have had an extramarital affair; the same numbers of women have had anal intercourse. These figures come from a 1990 Kinsey publication subtitled "What You Must Know to Be Sexually Literate." It is no longer enough to do it; you need a course in talking about it.

The breaching of the silence imposed on women's sexual desires from the nineteenth century to the 1960s must have enriched relationships between men and women as the latter became more knowledgeable and confident about their own erotic needs. But there is little evidence that couples regard their sexual lives as anything other than private. And as those private lives are outwardly manifested, sex has slipped down the agenda of needs. The ritual of the white wedding has been reinstated, as if to substitute for the downgrading of the importance of the loss of virginity. In the eighties, families found that the sensuousness of sex could be replaced by the hedonism of possessions—of designer clothes and decorator interiors, exotic foodie morsels and foreign holidays. Finally even sex grows boring. Great sex in marriage, once curiosity and tension has been eroded, is an event that depends on an intangible number of variables: a mood, a moment, the making up after a row, a quality of intimacy that is touched for a brief while before more humdrum concerns rush in. Its magic is impossible to schedule and organize. In the place of great sex there is the dinner party, the evening out at the theater, the guests in for drinks, the weekend in the country, the shopping trip. Through good food and wine we share sensuousness with our neighbors in a public expression of pleasure. This has the added benefit of establishing our wealth, showing off our possessions. The poor, of course, just fuck. It is fun and it is, above all, free. Them we call irresponsible. The group expression of desire, as a metaphor for the discarding of privacy and possessiveness, has never seemed more utopian to our acquisitive age.

9

The Future Has Been Postponed
Until Further Notice

I have never had a climax.
No! I swear!
It's the clitoral truth.

Margaret S. Chalmers, *Spare Rib*, September 1975

It was not AIDS that ended the sexual revolution—it was what had started it, the Pill. In 1971, Carol Downer stole a speculum from her doctor's office in Los Angeles and, aided by a mirror and a flashlight, became possibly the first woman in history to see her own cervix. Within twelve months she was running a women's self-help health group, turning to alternative medicine to treat vaginal discharges with such household remedies as yogurt. The clinic was subsequently raided by the Los Angeles Police Department and she was charged with entering a vagina without a medical licence. The LAPD attempted to seize as evidence a pot of yogurt, but was restrained by a woman who insisted it was her lunch. The incident quickly became known as the Great Yogurt Bust and went on to make its appearance in court as the Great Yogurt Trial. Downer was acquitted, thus establishing a precedent in California: women's genitals were no longer territory reserved for men. This concept, known as women's control of their bodies, had come about in direct reaction to the Pill and the sexual revolution. It was one of the most profound principles of the women's movement and one of the few feminist demands to attract widespread support beyond the confines of activists. It would, in time, revolutionize medical practice. It transformed how women thought of themselves sexually and how they related to men. The campaign against the Pill went to the very heart of women's autonomy. At the end of it, the sexual revolution would be reviled as a male conspiracy. Sex is only just beginning to recover.

Alice Wolfson was living in a commune in Washington, D.C. in 1970. Nobody in the house worked, apart from her husband, whose paycheck supported everyone else. They believed in example. If everyone shared a washing machine and a refrigerator, somehow that would change capitalism. Sometimes they tried to break down monogamy—they would rent a cabin in Vermont for Christmas and have a rotating bed schedule. One of the women was starting to come out as a lesbian and one night a radical feminist group called the Furies burst into their living room in an abortive attempt to "liberate" her.

Alice had started out in the antinuclear movement, moved to civil rights, then got involved with an early feminist group. It was a common political trajectory. But she was living in a black city where the people were not pro-choice. And the reason why they were not pro-choice was because they didn't want the white medical establishment controlling their bodies. Black women in Washington were dying from illegal abortions and being sterilized without knowing it, and Alice wondered who ran the health system and for whose benefit. Population control, she thought, was evil. It was not an innocuous movement. If all the world's resources were redistributed, population control would not be necessary. Population control kept power in the hands of the few. It allowed the West to overconsume. D.C. Women's Liberation was divided into different interest groups focusing on campaigns such as daycare or women and imperialism, but Alice joined the one on health.

Then she was in a meeting—everyone spent their lives in meetings. It was ten o'clock in the morning and someone said, there's some hearings going on about the Pill. So they started to talk about that. They had all had side effects, not terrible ones, but Alice was losing her hair and two of the doctors she had been to see had said it had nothing to do with the Pill. So she had gone to a dermatologist and asked him, "Could this have anything to do with the Pill?" And he had said of course it could. Alice had gone on Enovid in 1962, when it first came out, ten milligrams of it.

It had been prescribed for her by a boyfriend of a friend who happened to be a doctor. She later thought that the more comfortable you are with your sexuality, the less you need a contraceptive like the Pill. But back then, she had been embarrassed and the Pill smoothed away the difficulties of having to talk about contraception and hence sex. Sometimes it was easier to fuck than to say no. She would think, "Oh God, do we have to go through this again? Okay, let's just fuck and get it over with." Then they all got up and went down to the hearings. They did not go there to change the law. It was just that they had some suspicion in the backs of their minds that the Pill might not be good for them.

The hearings had been convened by Senator Gaylord Nelson, who was earning a reputation as a whistle-blower to the pharmaceutical industry. At first the women's group just sat and listened. They watched man after man come out and testify; they talked about women as if they were guinea pigs. They discussed risk versus benefit. It seemed that all the risk was to the woman and all the benefit was to population control. Alice can no longer remember who was the first to put up her hand: "Senator Nelson, I have a question. Senator Nelson, I have a question." You don't ask questions at Senate hearings. The women persisted: "But Senator Nelson, why aren't there any women testifying? Why aren't there any women who took the Pill up there talking about what it feels like?" And at that moment, all the news media, the cameras, and the columnists rotated on their axes and turned from the podium to the audience.

It was so simple to begin with. They just wanted to tell the government that they didn't know what was going on. In that first question was to develop the mass consciousness of the battleground between women and the state over control of their bodies. Roe versus Wade, which legalized abortion, was about to be won. At the Nelson hearings the feminists, veterans of the political movements of the sixties, began to organize. They handed out leaflets, held placards with slogans like: WHY DO WE HAVE TO DIE FOR LOVE? and FEED THE PILL TO YOUR GUINEA PIGS AT THE FDA NOT LIVE WOMEN. They set up alternative hearings. They wouldn't let a single hearing pass without a demonstration, their twenty-five-dollar bail money hidden in their boots. They would have a person placed in every third row, the first at the end, the second at the other end, the third in the middle. Every time a guard came to remove someone the person on the other side of the room would ask her question. They couldn't be contained. It was chaos. Other women turned up. One group came from Boston, handing out a mimeographed booklet called *Our Bodies, Ourselves*, based on a course of workshops that a number of women had run.

The most prestigious woman at the Nelson hearings was Barbara Seaman, and it was because of her that Washington was talking about the Pill at all. She had started out in journalism, as a columnist at *Brides* magazine, then at *Ladies' Home Journal*. She had never been on the Pill herself; married in the late fifties, she was a young diaphragm matron for whom the method then dispensed by the Margaret Sanger clinic and countless family doctors would not lose its appeal or convenience. By the mid-sixties she had started to receive letters from her readers worried about the side effects of the oral contraceptive. The stories were heartrending. Even in Dr. Pincus's files there were seriously worrying accounts of the Pill's effects on a woman's health, as in this letter of April 10, 1967:

My problem is this: I dislike the diaphragm for aesthetic reasons and the "condom" is unfair on my husband; for the last five years I have been on the "pill." I started with Enovid and when a steady increase in my weight began to be noticed I was given Narinyl which gave me violent menstrual cramping. I was then prescribed Oracon which seemed fine except my weight steadily increased despite a diuretic I was also given . . . two months ago I was given an IUD, which I believe was a "Lippes Loop." The actual insertion was so painful that I went into shock. I kept it in me for the full monthly cycle but experienced violent pain or at best great discomfort at all times . . . and finally when codeine and a tranquilizer became ineffectual in preventing the cramping I had my gynecologist remove it. I continued to bleed heavily for an additional 12 days. I have left myself without birth control medication for the last month in order to let my body normalize after this above ordeal. . . . Also, and most important, I now realize that although I "climaxed" during intercourse before, my desire for my husband is almost as great as when we first met and I lubricate so readily I am loath to give this up when I once again must shortly start the "pill."

Thank you so much for your time in helping me. If you would advise me on my dilemma I, and my husband, would be eternally grateful.

P.S. In 1955 I went to Dr. ——— ——— of Billings Hospital but frankly at that time the interns with him rather upset me.[1]

The letter appears to be signed by the writer's husband. Pincus replied a week later. He referred her to a gynecologist who would help her experiment with low-dosage Pills. This was the kind of subservience women had then to male experts.

Despite the letters that occasionally came in from doctors with patients suffering from thrombosis (a complaint later acknowledged by the medical profession as a leading side effect of oral contraception), Pincus always denied that his Pills were anything but wholesome. Yet within a year of Enovid's licensing in 1960, its manufacturer, Searle, had a file of 132 reports of thrombosis and embolism among users, including eleven deaths. There was some talk that the U.S. government might withdraw Enovid for general contraceptive use. Searle then called the first major conference to discuss its safety. The conferencees met in a jocular mood. One death was attributed to a tight girdle. The chairman was anxious to wind up and proposed a resolution stating that there was no causal connection between the Pill and clotting disorders. Only one doctor spoke against the motion. It was not until 1968 that the British Dunlop Committee on the Safety of Drugs finally established a firm connection between the Pill and thromboembolic clotting disorders.[2]

Barbara Seaman lacked the medical training to make a professional evaluation of the Pill, but she was tenacious and well-connected. Her husband was a psychiatrist with extensive contacts in the medical world, and she doggedly tramped around New York cajoling, questioning, and investigating. She came to believe that women were taking the Pill with consent, but that this consent was uninformed. She set out to write a book for her *Ladies' Home Journal* readers that would arm them with the information they needed to properly assess the risks they were taking when they agreed to an oral contraceptive prescription. She called it *The Doctor's Case Against the Pill,* and it was probably the last feminist book on women's health that was to invoke the male medical establishment in its title as a gesture toward professional credibility. She simply didn't have the confidence to call it "The Women's Case Against the Pill."

In the course of her research, she found that the principal source of information for women about the Pill came from booklets written for the drug companies and distributed free to doctors who gave them out to their patients. They were usually illustrated with flowers. Hugh Davis, director of the Contraceptive Clinic and Assistant Professor of Obstetrics and Gynecology at Johns Hopkins University, had observed in 1969: "I have looked at these lovely little things which range anywhere from 15 to 38 pages. I saw pictures of roses, tulips and peach blossoms. I saw not a word about thorns or worms."[3] Eight million American women were estimated to be taking the Pill. All, Barbara Seaman concluded, as she discovered more about the Puerto Rico clinical trials, were guinea pigs for a form of medication that had not been adequately tested. Only a tiny proportion of adverse side effects that women reported to their doctors were passed on to the FDA.[4] *The Doctor's Case* produced several histories of women who had died as a result of clotting associated with Pill usage. There seemed to be an additional link between oral contraception and strokes, cancer, heart disease, jaundice, thyroid disfunction, weight gain, urinary infections, arthritis, skin and gum problems, depression, and irritability. Is there a better way? the author asked. There was. It was the scorned and discarded diaphragm.

As soon as the book was published at the end of 1970, Barbara Seaman sent a copy to Gaylord Nelson, whom she knew was interested in the drug industry. He convened his Senate hearings. So when the women from D.C. Women's Liberation began their campaign of disruption, Barbara came over and asked them to lunch. As an officially invited guest, she knew the schedule. She told them that a secret meeting convened by the FDA was to take place behind closed doors. The feminists tried to gate-crash it and were threatened with arrest. They would say, "That's fine, arrest us. You're having a meeting to talk about the effects this Pill is having on our bodies and you won't let us hear. What's so secret? If we can take the Pill, why can't we have the information? We'll tell that to the press." As the Nelson hearings continued, the women focused on the demand that warnings should be inserted inside the packets—the formalizing of informed consent. The suggestion sent tremors through the ranks of doctors. If you told a woman she was going to get a headache, you could be sure she was going to get a headache. "Meanwhile," Alice Wolfson protested, "they were sitting there with data implicating the Pill in strokes and heart attacks in young women and they're debating whether to tell you what to look for." The insert became the focal point of the rest of the hearings. The debate was no longer whether there should be a warning, but how long a warning. "And the only reason there was a warning at all was because of the demonstrations, the pressure that we were able to bring to bear because the media were so interested. Without the media the demonstrations wouldn't have done anything. We learned how to use the media and we used it well, very well."

The protests at the Nelson hearings were one of the most important feminist actions since the riots for the vote fifty years earlier. That they have been forgotten is a disgrace. Winning legislative changes to provide information about medication was a concrete victory and it led to a generally accepted practice that all drugs should advise users on possible side effects. But the protests went beyond the Pill itself to a fundamental alteration in consciousness about the body. The Pill had released women from the stress of worrying about conception and gave them the potential to liberate their sexuality. The reaction against the Pill spawned the widespread distrust of the orthodox medical establishment that persists to this day, popularizing what became the massive growth industry of alternative forms of healing. The feminist health movement, which began at the Nelson hearings, argued that the male-dominated pharmaceutical corporations were using artificial hormones to colonize women's bodies. There was a close analogy with the larger political situation: women were being bombarded with lethal chemicals just as the Vietnamese were being bombed by Agent Orange, the dioxin-laden defoliant that was to produce such deadly long-term consequences in the fetuses of Vietnamese women. The Vietnamese, at least, were fighting back. By contrast, not only did American women expose themselves to dangerous substances every time they took a Pill, they were complicit in the surrendering of their own autonomy. They internalized the system of patriarchy. Capitalism enslaved women through their bodies by feeding them artificial hormones that in turn made them willing victims of the lust of men. They surrendered to men not just as lovers but as doctors who harnessed them to technology.

In her second book, *Free and Female*, published in 1972, Barbara Seaman asked:

> Why are American women shaved, humiliated, drugged, painted and stuck up in stirrups to deliver their babies? Why are they pinned into a position which is so totally unnatural and inconvenient for the mother?
>
> Why are delivery rooms managed and run for the convenience of the doctors, not the patients? . . .
>
> Why would a man consecrate his life to the female organs?
>
> What leads a physician to specialize in reproduction and female disorders?
>
> Isn't it hard to believe that voyeurism or some special love-hate relationship with women doesn't play a part?[5]

This analysis was taking place at the same time as the development of the early environmental movement, but it was a feminist discourse that first began to investigate alternative medicine and health foods. In the same year as the Nelson hearings, *The Greening of America* by Charles Reich and Alvin Toffler's *Future Shock* were published, both sensational bestsellers with a global vision of a society that must reject or restrain technology if it was to survive. Toffler used an ecological model to argue that there had been unforeseen consequences of oral contraception in loosening traditional ties of relationships in the Third World. Like an oil spill that threatens the life-forms of a coastline, upsetting the overall ecological balance, the Pill was a potential threat to world peace.

The diet of the average Western family then consisted of meat with a few wilted, overcooked vegetables, or salad smothered in bottled dressing, and various sugar products. It was before the aerobics and running boom, before the scares about cholesterol and carcinogens, when women routinely had children by cesarean section or immobilized from the waist down by drugs. Before America in particular discovered Health. The campaign against the Pill required a shift in political analysis. It meant that women should seize power over their bodies from doctors. They should trust their instincts, always be deeply skeptical about any form of treatment or medication produced by the male-dominated military-industrial-pharmaceutical complex. They should turn away from the manufactured and processed to the alternative, the "natural," the old-fashioned.

From the very beginning there was a text that spelled all this out: *Our Bodies, Ourselves* taught the second-wave feminist generation about their physical beings. The book had developed out of a Boston women's group workshop whose members were concerned that they did not know enough about how their own bodies worked to evaluate the medical care they were getting. The workshop was held in 1969, and the majority of presenters, like the members of D.C. Women's Liberation, had come through what shortly came to be known as the "male-dominated left," the same civil-rights, antinuclear, and anti–Vietnam War organizations that had politicized the women who went on to become feminists. When the course was over, it was suggested that the experiences be written down. The New England Free Press, a radical left-wing publisher, printed it, and it was sold initially for seventy cents. The women who came to the workshops knew almost nothing about their own bodies. Many had never had orgasms, but even the most sexually experienced, the liberated chicks who partnered the hippest activists, had not seen their genitals, never talked with anyone about their sexuality.

One of the workshop leaders was Eleanor Stephens, who had come to the United States from Britain with her boyfriend, who was on a scholarship to MIT. She chose to talk about sexuality. At the end of the session a woman with two children came up to her and said, "You talked about orgasms, but what is an orgasm?" At the next workshop she decided to ask the women who attended how many had ever climaxed. It was no more than 60 percent. When she asked how many women had had an orgasm during intercourse, the numbers were much smaller. The women's health movement uncovered an alternative reality to the version of the sexual revolution that cast women as liberated chicks or swinging dolly-birds. There was a deep-seated ignorance among women about their own anatomy and their sexual response that called into doubt the long-held belief in women's frigidity peddled by sexologists. Women failed to derive the pleasure they needed from sex not because they were incapable of sexual response or psychologically repressed, but because their orgasm was more complex and had, for too long, been subject to male interpretations of what it should resemble. The male climax is much of a muchness; the erogenous zones are pretty well limited to the genitals. All men coming sound and behave about the same. But a man who had had sex with a woman who shouted and thrashed about would then go on and tell the next woman he slept with that she hadn't come "properly" if her response was different. And women were so polite then. They fucked men they didn't fancy, as Alice Wolfson had, worn down by their persistence, just wanting to get it over with. They rarely came: they must be frigid, male reasoning concluded.

While *The Sensuous Woman* had emphasized "lovemaking"—how to become a great fuck—Stephens was interested in how the women gave pleasure to themselves. Back in England, she wrote an article for *Spare Rib*. "The Moon Within Your Reach" described how she had lived with a man and their small child, enjoying a happy sexual relationship, with one small problem, the fact that she was never sure whether or not she had had an orgasm.[6] The article produced, not surprisingly, a huge response from readers, for she wrote about the "pre-orgasmic workshops" she had helped run in California and how their participants had learned how to come through masturbation and the use of a vibrator. Women wrote asking where the workshops were to be found. The Family Planning Association did some sex therapy, but there was a nine-month waiting list. Eleanor decided to run her own workshops in London, and she was soon approached by Udi Eichler, the television producer who had earlier filmed group marriage in California. He was making a series to be called *Sex in Our Time*, which would examine the extent of the permanent changes to sexual relationships that the sexual revolution had brought about in Britain.

The program was taped during the brilliantly hot summer of 1976, and the women sat around in their cheesecloth smocks and tan marks, watching as their workshop leader showed a slide projection of the female genitals and cervix. Just before transmission the managing director of Thames Television viewed the program and was shocked by what he saw. The depiction of sexual organs on television was, he believed, obscene.

The entire series was canceled and not shown until 1991, when one episode appeared in Channel Four's "Banned" season: even then the genitals were blacked out. You could go into an art gallery and see the male form plainly depicted (although never in a state of sexual excitement—taboos have always existed in depicting men as well as women). Yet the representation of women's bodies had been restricted to the interpretation of the male gaze, through painting or pornography. It would not be an overstatement to argue that women's bodies were free for men to see, but denied to women attempting to understand their own anatomy.

Our Bodies, Ourselves changed that. It was a map. It drew diagrams of the clitoris and explained its function. It urged women to get hold of a speculum and with the aid of a mirror and a flashlight examine their own cervixes. It gave instructions on how to masturbate. It also destroyed the image of the orgasm that had been built up through literature—the cataclysmic experience in which the earth would move. There was no right or wrong orgasm; it can be "a very mild experience, almost as mild as a peaceful sigh, or it can be an extreme state of ecstasy with much thrashing about and momentary loss of awareness. It can last a few seconds, or for half a minute or longer."[7] *Our Bodies, Ourselves* was not only concerned with sex but with all the issues connected with reproduction. It explained how conception worked and examined the politics of contraception. It argued that the Pill was big business, that in 1968 women had taken a hundred million dollars' worth of oral contraceptives, and that with such huge profits it was easy to see why the pharmaceutical companies would want to cover up any findings that linked the Pill to serious illnesses. The purpose of the book was not, however, to proselytize, however much its tone when read now seems clearly linked with the political activism of its origins. Its mission was not only to demystify the body but to help women to make informed choices, a major redistribution of power that had long-term consequences for the health of the west.

Within two years of its underground publication, local demand was so great that a quarter of a million copies had been sold and the resources of its publisher were outgrown. The collective had to take a decision to sell out to what it defined as the capitalist system—in the guise of Simon & Schuster—and allow the book to become a mainstream text. It retained the proviso, however, that the royalties would be used to promote women's health and that the collective would have editorial and advertising control.

By 1975, Barbara Seaman, Alice Wolfson, and another woman, Belita Cowan, had formed the Women's Health Network, a national alliance dedicated to monitoring the existing system on women's behalf. The principles of this movement, which spread in spirit throughout the world, argued that modern medicine regarded the normal reproductive processes as "sickness." Obstetrics and gynecology had become a male preserve in which patriarchal power was exercised in the examination room. The poor in particular received little care. The Network edged toward a holistic analysis of health that criticized the emphasis on the symptom in isolation from the mind and the body. Childbirth was excessively technologized, women were not allowed to trust their own instincts or make their own decisions. At the furthest extreme, such theory became radical feminism in which reproductive technology was demonized as a torture chamber for men to act out their misogynistic fantasies on women. The manufacturers of the Pill still cast women in traditional roles. An advertisement for Ovulen-21 in 1968, aimed at family doctors, showed a woman with her head divided into segments, each with a picture—a joint of meat, a shopping cart, an iron or a hair dryer—and labeled with the day of the week: "Whether it be 'shopping day,' 'bridge day' or 'housecleaning day,' a woman is accustomed to thinking in terms of days of the week rather than in 'cycle days,' " doctors were advised. "Ovulen-21 lets her remember the natural way. Once established, her starting day is always the same day of the week . . . because it is fixed at three weeks on–one week off and is independent of withdrawal flow."[8] The whole system by which health was underpinned by the assumptions of patriarchy needed to be questioned.

The medical system, in other words, reduced women to the status of children and elevated doctors to that of paternalistic dictators. Mary Daly's 1978 book *Gyn/Ecology* was the theoretical text for this understanding:

The title of this book, *Gyn/Ecology,* says exactly what I mean it to say. "Ecology" is about the complex web of interrelationships between organisms and their environments. In her book *La Féminisme ou la mort*, Françoise d'Eaubonne coins the expression "eco-féminisme." She maintains that the fate of the human species and of the planet is at stake, and that no male-led "revolution" will counteract the horrors of overpopulation and destruction of natural resources. . . . The title *Gyn/Ecology* is a way of wrenching back some wordpower. The fact that most gynecologists are males is in itself a colossal comment on "our" society. It is a symptom and an example of male control over women and over language and a clue to the extent of this control. . . . Gynecologists fixate upon what they do not have, upon what they themselves cannot do. For this reason they epitomize and symbolize the practitioners of other patriarchal -ologies, and they provide important clues to the demonic patterns common to the labor of all of these.[9]

For radical feminists, the only hope that this power structure could be overturned was by developing an alternative system of health care that relied heavily on self-help. Carol Downer, who had seen her vagina through a stolen speculum, set up the first clinics that taught women to diagnose and treat their own ailments: simple infections like thrush, self-examination of the cervix and the breasts, pregnancy testing, and the use of a period-extraction device that also functioned as a method of early abortion. Soon evening classes in abortion were being offered that included in the curriculum anatomy of the female reproductive organs, methods of abortion, dangers involved, and how to deal with police questioning.

But self-help would never be more than a middle-class movement of highly motivated, educated, and mainly white women with access to feminist information networks. The poor still took the Pill and there were other political divisions. Black women in a feminist group wrote an open letter to the Black Panthers: "So when Whitey put out the Pill, and poor black sisters spread the word, we saw how simple it was not to be a fool for men anymore. . . . That was the first step in our waking up! . . . Now a lot of black brothers are into the new bag. Black women are being asked by militant black brothers not to practise birth control because it's a form of Whitey's committing genocide on black people. . . . For us, birth control is the freedom to fight genocide of black women and children."[10] Women in America began to divide along class lines as the best informed began to subscribe to the cult of the natural. At its most extreme, in the radical feminist interpretation that Mary Daly popularized, women turned to nature worship. Nature was the goddess, beneficent, caring, abundant. Women were somehow part of Mother Nature, they partook of her qualities. Men were the hands of the devil, technology, the artificial. This was not just a nightmare scenario of biological determinism but left out an important observation: that nature was also responsible for earthquakes, floods, typhoons, droughts, and famine, a force that men and women had tamed because of its cruelty.

Natural childbirth, natural health foods, natural fibers, natural remedies, naturopathy, and natural birth control became the hallmarks of a civilized life. Fast food, acrylic carpets, general anesthetics, artificial hormones, gas-guzzling cars, polyester pantsuits were the giveaway signs of the unevolved, the politically unengaged, the powerless. Reproductive technology was replaced with reproductive choice. For a while women were urged by feminists to abandon tampons (especially in the aftermath of the outbreak of Toxic Shock Syndrome) in favor of blood-rags, an old pioneer remedy. Sponges were another solution, which, attached to strings, you were to insert in your vagina and wash out every few hours, which made for unpleasant excursions to the bathroom. In birth control too the search was on for natural methods. The demonization of the Pill led to the elevation of the diaphragm as cult object around which a whole movement for its reinstatement was born. Germaine Greer, never one to do things by halves, felt she should go along with this celebration of the technological counterrevolution "to the extent of wearing the springs from worn-out ones as ceremonial jewelry and marks of caste."[11] By the mid-seventies, *Cosmopolitan* was announcing in a cover story: "The Diaphragm Is Back in Town!" *Newsweek* wrote about it, talk shows discussed it, and in 1976 the diaphragm was The Method of the Year.[12] To Barbara Seaman, the diaphragm was "for disciplined women . . . a better than 99 percent reliable method."[13]

It was the diaphragm that Isadora Wing, feminist heroine and seeker after zipless fucks, carried with her at all times in Erica Jong's *Fear of*

Flying. Many women, however, had mixed feelings. Here is Germaine Greer again, describing hers:

> No one who has ever been forced to carry her dilly-bag with spermicide and diaphragm at all times and gamely tried to squirt and insert in the woods and on the beach, who has not cudgeled her brains to know when one occasion of sexual intercourse ended and another began so that she could decide whether or not to squeeze more cold glop into herself (a procedure which necessitated the carrying of a plastic applicator—never totally clean—as well as all the other impediments of the dilly-bag) has not longed to do away with the whole kit and caboodle.[14]

Diaphragm women reverted to a state of nature, clomped about in platform shoes, somehow more "sensible" than stilettos, their breasts bobbing out of the sides of overalls worn with no T-shirt. They ate brown rice and had meaningful relationships with New Men. This parody of feminism dragged on long after its brief period of fashion. On the whole, women did not take to the diaphragm. In the 1989 General Household Survey, only 1 percent of British women said that they used it, making it even less popular than the rhythm method, which claimed 2 percent of users. Despite the Pill's decline in popularity, it remained the most frequent contraceptive method at 25 percent.

Yet the feminist response to technology took hold and was swiftly incorporated into general consciousness. There was more than one form of medication to which women had learned to become addicted. Valium and other antidepressants, prescribed chiefly by male doctors for the use of women, were subjected to an analysis arguing that it was women's oppression, particularly in the home, that led to disorders of the spirit and the psyche. The answer was not more pills (and Valium was found to be particularly addictive) but a holistic psychotherapy that became a boom industry for the middle classes and a favorite midlife career choice for feminists involved in women's health campaigns. The cult of the natural was quickly co-opted by the beauty industry through the conduit of another former left-wing activist, Jane Fonda. Her workout program had been developed out of the actress's revulsion with a youth spent consuming barbiturates disguised as diet pills. Health foods and aerobics, she argued, were the way to vitality and a slender body. To be sexy a woman need no longer be dieted and drugged into an approved shape. She had to be fit. It was natural and it involved the resurrection of the Puritan work ethic. The enormous irony of this wholesale rejection of science and technology in favor of natural healthiness, jogging, and aerobics was the way Americans came to believe that they could cheat the aging process and even death itself altogether. Death is something that should only happen to poor, unlucky, malnourished people.

In the long term, the women's health movement played a crucial role in the final demolition of a visionary technological utopia. Its impact was primarily upon the U.S. Food and Drug Administration. In December 1990 the first new contraceptive since the IUD was launched in America. It was called Norplant, a few fingers of soft rubber that are inserted under the skin, where they remain, secreting hormones, for five years. It had taken twenty-four years for the Population Council to research and develop it, stymied by a climate of negativity toward artificial methods of contraception that, according to Philip J. Hilts, a *New York Times* journalist, had left America in the Dark Ages when it came to birth control. For Carl Djerassi, one of the Pill's progenitors, "The United States is the only country other than Iran in which the birth control clock has been set backwards during the past decade."[15] Hilts cited RU-486, the abortion pill, as an example of a viable contraceptive method that had "been kept by its manufacturer, Roussel, from all countries except France for fear of the political and economic consequences."[16] In the eighties, all four American manufacturers of the IUD pulled their products off the market when the Dalkon Shield was found to cause serious and sometimes fatal infections. More than 300,000 claims were filed against A. H. Robins, the Dalkon Shield's manufacturer, and its compensation cases led it to bankruptcy and an order to pay out over two billion dollars to women who had used the method. Depo Provera, the injectable contraceptive widely used in the Third World, has never been available in the United States. Behind this litany of shame, Hilts argued, lay an unholy alliance between the anti-sex Right and the women's health movement. The Women's Health Network had effectively lobbied against RU-486 and it was about to register formally its disapproval of Norplant.

But within six months of its introduction, some state officials were suggesting that the insertion of Norplant should be mandatory for women claiming welfare payments. When the *Los Angeles Times* asked readers whether they thought female drug users of childbearing age should be forced to have Norplant implanted to prevent them breeding, over 60 percent approved, leading *The Economist* to predict a revival of popular interest in eugenics.[17] The early socialist analysis of the health activists seemed to have been correct: birth control was a plot to oppress minorities, poisoning the blood with chemicals, and denying black, working-class, and addicted women control over their own reproductive freedom. Norplant had all the Brave New World qualities of the compulsory sterilization programs of the Deep South in the 1930s. The power of feminism had put the pharmaceutical industry to flight, Hilts insisted. In 1974, the FDA had decided to approve Depo Provera as manufactured by Upjohn. But the agency deferred action after a campaign led by the Women's Health Network. "Among the companies, the feeling was that if they could throw out this one, they could throw out anything," Richard E. Edgren, director of scientific affairs at Syntex, the company that had first synthesized progesterone, told Hilts. "It was tainted forever. This said to the companies that after 100 million dollars of work, women can throw it out, even after the FDA approved it. . . . Upjohn said, 'We'll never do it again.' . . . I can't believe how fast and completely they shut down. They fired people and retrained the rest for other areas."[18]

Products aimed at women are the most sensitive to litigation. Roderick L. Mackenzie, chairman of Gynopharma Inc., a small contraceptive manufacturer in New Jersey that markets one of the only two IUDs now available in the United States, revealed that drugs that treated other illnesses did not have to be 100 percent effective or 100 percent safe: "You don't have a sea of bad publicity endangering your other drugs and your researchers can get Nobel Prizes."[19]

When the generation of sixties activists reached menopause, it discovered that another hormonal treatment was awaiting it—HRT, the honey of a hormone that the first issue of *Cosmopolitan* had promised them for their middle years. In April 1990, Schering, the· European market leader in Pill and HRT brands, took a party of British journalists to its headquarters in Berlin for a four-day press junket to acquaint health writers with the newly freed city and to brief us on HRT. Put up at a five-star hotel, taken to nightclubs every evening, driven about the city with an official guide and gathered in seminar rooms every morning for "scientific lectures," we saw Schering demonstrating the importance pharmaceutical companies place on public relations when it comes to products aimed at women. The purpose of the expedition soon became apparent. Changes in the management of GPs' budgets meant that some doctors were refusing to prescribe HRT on the grounds that it was too expensive.

Schering had commissioned Insight Research, an independent market-research company, to evaluate menopausal women's perceptions of their doctors. Those doctors who were uninterested in menopause, believed that the "change" was inevitable and belittled their patients' symptoms (particularly those involving painful intercourse) were less likely to prescribe HRT, and were regarded as less oriented toward women's concerns. Doctors who did prescribe HRT were regarded as more caring, more able to make a female patient feel valued. Schering was using the lessons of the women's health movement to persuade journalists that HRT was a feminist cause; that GPs who regarded the treatment as in some way "cosmetic" belonged to the old school of medical practices that denied women the right to health and autonomy. Needless to say, HRT unavailable on the National Health Service would dramatically reduce Schering's sales in the U.K.

But gynecological medicine was not the only sector affected by the climate of consumer skepticism the women's health movement had helped to create. Saul Kent, director of the California-based Life Extension Foundation, is one of the last of the technological futurists who believes that people could live forever with the right medication. What about overpopulation? journalist Jay Rayner asked him in *The Observer*. "By the time we've conquered ageing we'll be living in outer space. There's room for 1000 times the population on this planet just in this solar system."[20] What is foiling Kent's efforts to develop drugs that would prevent aging is, of course, the FDA. In order to have a new drug approved by the agency, over 200 million dollars needed to be spent in research, Kent argued, which meant only the very largest companies could play the market. Saul Kent's longevity dreams are the farcical curtain opener to the main event: the fight to approve drugs that claim to treat AIDS. Guerrilla clinics are being set up to administer experimental drugs to people with HIV or the full-blown disease, part of an AIDS underground grapevine. Since the existing FDA drugs will not keep people alive, the desperate feel that they might as well try something else. America is dividing into two constituencies: those fearful of medication, demanding ever tighter controls, and the ones who cry out for science to produce a magic bullet, something to make AIDS go away.

Alice Wolfson moved to San Francisco and became a lawyer. She is now working on the issue of women who want to have breast implants removed after links between implants and breast cancer were revealed but whose medical insurance will not cover the procedure. Her boss has freed her to organize public meetings. His hope is that everyone who has an insurance case will bring it to his company. In her resides the irony of those who fought the drug companies to ensure that never again could untested medication come on to the market without thorough research into its side effects.

Some years ago, her son died of leukemia: "Because I had a child that died, I know I would probably have tried any experimental treatment for him that I thought could have helped without harming too much," she says. "In fact I did go to a psychic healer, I went to a Chinese herbalist. We did traditional treatment, he had a bone-marrow transplant—I schlepped him everywhere. The AIDS movement is asking for drugs that haven't been tried or tested. It is willing to sacrifice the protective functions of the FDA out of a desperation brought on by terminal illness. The Pill brought into a focus a lot of stuff about the morality of the drug industry. The AIDS movement, for better or worse, may be undoing some of those important aspects. On a human level, it may be that the kind of protection you need from a government agency like the FDA differs according to whether you're sick or healthy. In other words, if you're giving a medication to healthy women who can use other, less intrusive means to obtain the same results, you may want more protection. You may apply a very different standard than when you consider releasing a drug to a terminally ill patient whose death may be days or months away."

There is a final, macabre note to the tale of population control. According to epidemiologists, AIDS may have a greater impact on population than the Black Death and could reduce Third-World growth rates to zero.[21] The xenophobic fears of the fifties that Southeast Asia might one day swamp the West could prove groundless: the workers in the Thai and Filipino sex industries, created to provide rest and recreation for American GIs during the Vietnam War, are infected with HIV or AIDS. Unable to work, they take their diseases back to the villages from which they came. An estimated two to four hundred thousand people in Thailand are HIV-positive. Cause and effect is seldom simple, but there may be a grisly logic in the way the dream of solving the population explosion through pharmaceuticals failed. The sexual revolution that the pharmaceuticals created may, horribly, do the job instead.

Witness

There's Something in the Genes

I was born in 1948 and grew up in East Anglia. My father was a farmer and a Methodist lay preacher. Then my parents moved to Suffolk to a tied cottage, but to get enough money to bring up a wife and two kids my father went to work in a factory. I used to listen out for signs of their sex life. My bedroom was next to theirs and I would listen at the wall hoping to hear bumps and thumps but I suppose they were listening for me, waiting out to hear if I'd gone to sleep. So there we were, them listening on one side of the wall and me listening on the other. I went to the local village school. The head teacher was a bit ahead of his time because it was totally free. From seven onward there were no set lessons, so for most of the day I wrote and illustrated stories with pictures. By eleven I had written my third novel. Sometime last year my mother found it. She thought it might be published because a child had written it and maybe children would be interested in reading it. I said, "Mother, a children's book no; Mills and Boon maybe." It was ninety pages long and it had everything there. Suicide, death, implied sex, a tart with a heart. All written at eleven and three-quarters. Real TV miniseries stuff. But then I failed the eleven plus and twelve plus because I'd done so little mathematics, went on to secondary mod, took O-levels at a polytechnic, and went to art school.

When I was about twelve I had this thing about not marrying. I would say to my mother, "If I marry, I'm not going to marry an Englishman." I think even then I saw them as a bit too staid and boring. Most of my friends at school married and stayed in the area. One of them had her first child at fifteen and has three grown-up children and probably grandchildren by now.

I lost my virginity at college when I was seventeen. It was classic; he was a lecturer, sixteen years older than me, married of course. I remember going to this big hall where you could choose which subjects to do for general studies and I saw this guy who was lecturing in international relations, very appropriately. He was Pakistani, very good-looking, and had amazing charisma. I was an incredibly unconfident, shy person, but I think I've always been my own person, been aware of my own actions and that I could take the consequences. One morning we got to chatting and he said he'd got some tickets for the theater and would I go? So I did. Except we didn't make the theater and I don't even know if he ever had the tickets. He used to give talks for the BBC and we had to go there first and we ended up seeing a film. So it was a bit of snogging in the back row. It was sort of consummated in the most peculiar situation, in the backseat of a car in his garage. The car belonged to people who were having dinner in his house with his wife. You could actually see the light on in the dining room from the garage. I found it amazingly uncomfortable. I did say to him, what happens if her guests don't like the pudding and want to leave early?

Okay, he was into the power thing and God knows how many other women he was doing the same with—it might not have been with anyone else but it might have been with a load. I did the very conventional thing of getting real excitement out of it and that's what I still need. Which is why I still haven't settled down to a cozy marriage situation. Marriage itself has never been something I've needed or wanted. This first relationship lasted for two years from 1965 until 1967 and I've no regrets about it. It did cause me an awful lot of pain but in some ways it set a path in that after that I didn't want anything too dull or boring. If that's your first relationship where do you go from there? I probably was used but I feel I got something back. Sexually it probably was appalling, though it seemed wonderful at the time. He did encourage me to go to the Margaret Pike Centre for contraception but I didn't, so it was all the coitus interruptus stuff. Basically it probably was awful. He liked my body but I wonder what satisfaction he got out of it because it was very limited in that way.

There was a really good feeling of optimism then. You really did feel you could do anything you wanted somehow. You could go out there and do it. I'm very grateful to the sixties, I'm very pleased to have been born at that time because ten years either way could make a vast difference to you. I can

*remember from being a fifteen-year-old, wearing a Moygashel costume, want-
ing to be grown-up—you have to be pretty old to remember Moygashel, it was
pre-Crimplene, I think—so I had this green Moygashel suit and was trying
to look like a grown-up lady. Three years later from wearing a little suit and
trying to look thirty-five, I was in a miniskirted smock trying to look fifteen
again. It was a very extreme change.*

*My sexual life in the sixties was limited to a married man and then a
boyfriend. I had had a couple of other lovers when I was with my main
boyfriend. He was a doctor. There was a cultural problem in terms of settling
down. He was Sudanese and his family had paid for him to be educated and
he was torn between the two cultures. There were times when I thought that
I wanted to live with him and I had these fantasies about how it might work
out. I was initially on the cap and then I went on the Pill over a period of about
twelve years with apparently no physical side effects. But I even had a vision
of a child, of myself rushing around juggling my career in one hand, baby in
the other. Once when I thought I might be pregnant, he made some comment
about how it "wouldn't take long," meaning abortion, and I was quite upset
that he was so dismissive. It was a false alarm but I was surprised at how
upset I really was. I caught a glimpse of that biological thing that can take
a woman over that I didn't think I had.*

*I did all my sleeping around in the eighties, which was a slightly dangerous
time to do it, in retrospect. Several years ago a friend insisted I add up all
the men I'd slept with and it came to over forty so I guess it would be nearer
fifty or so by now. At the beginning of the eighties I was in my thirties and
putting myself about a bit after ending my long eleven-year relationship. I
remember one time: the date's clearly fixed because it was the best experience
of my life sexually. I went out with some friends to Dingwalls, a club in North
London. There was this guy who was extremely good-looking, quite beautiful
in fact, and I think I did a bit of a chat-up on him really. I even said things
about his beautiful blue eyes, I did a male chat-up. I asked what he did and
he said he was a taxi driver and he'd drive me home and I said no but he took
my phone number. He rang me up the next day and I was amazed because he
hadn't written the phone number down. So he came over straight away. We
talked but not for very long. He said, "Do you want to go for a drink?" and
I said, "Oh do you really want to go for a drink?" Several hours later when*

we paused for air he confessed he'd remembered my telephone number but forgotten my name. He traveled a lot. I think he was on speed when I met him. As a human being he might have been shit, I don't know, but he had an amazing body. After having made love for almost twelve hours, he went off at seven o'clock the next morning and I made some comment like, "Well thank you, that was wonderful," not asking anything, not "What's your phone number, can I see you again?" Almost not expecting anything. I was sitting at home the following evening willing the phone to ring and it did and it was him. And we did it all over again. He left the next morning—it was February 14, Valentine's Day, 1979—saying, well it seems as if I'm going to have to see you again. I actually thought he meant it. And that was the last I ever saw of him.

I was in physical agony. Because it was so good sexually. Long afterward I would let out an occasional scream walking along the street. It was like there was this coil of physical tension and desire caught inside me. For the first week or so after he left I could smell him in the lobby of this little studio flat I had and it was such an intense smell I could practically get an orgasm by smelling the air. Sexually it was perfection. I've never had such good sex before or since. Mind you, if I'd got to know him it probably wouldn't have been as good. I knew very little about him. He did have a very good sense of humor, though. He came from Tasmania and I knew his name and that his mother drank pink gin, but that was about all. But I had more orgasms with him than with anyone else ever. They were coming out of my ears. It was amazing. I didn't have to say anything. I did tramp around Pimlico on a couple of occasions because I knew he had been working on a building site there, but he'd probably gone off traveling, to Bangkok I think. I was aware that if I'd seen him a few more times we wouldn't have fallen in love because I would have found out things about his character that I probably wouldn't have liked.

I've never done anything thinking this is going to be a one-night stand. I don't think anything was ever negotiated. I don't recall a single one-nighter, though I've had half a dozen two-night stands. They've been situations where I've started off by thinking this might lead to something and discovered that it didn't. About five years ago I'd thought I had (and did have) herpes and went to a clinic and the woman doctor there had a young male medical student with her. She asked me when my last sexual experience was and whether it was a permanent relationship and I said, no, but I thought it might be. And she asked for the one before that and I said no, but I hoped that would be as well. And she said, "Men are bastards aren't they?" That medical student's face fell.

My past doesn't embarrass me, but it has worried me occasionally. In 1981 I went and lived for a couple of months with a known IV-drug user in Texas. And there were two other guys, one a two-night stand, the other someone who was in and out of my life for a year or so whom I'm sure was very promiscuous, and a drug user. And this was all on the Pill and then the cap. I haven't had a test. I did think about it last year when there was a program on TV about AIDS. If you do find out you're HIV-positive there are certain drugs that will help delay the process of full-blown AIDS. But in the end I came down to thinking, no, I won't. I think if I was about to get into something that was going to be serious and I hoped might last then obviously I would talk about it. I would like to have another long-term relationship with someone, which can seem like a contradiction in terms when it seems so difficult to get to know a man. I would like a very equal relationship with someone of equal intellectual capacity. I'm not sure if I could cope with living with someone. I haven't for any great length of time. Six months with one person, two months with another guy, a couple of months in Texas. My sum total of living with men on a day-to-day basis, seven days a week, has amounted to just over a year, so doing it now would be very difficult, I imagine. I very much need my own space but if there was somebody who had their own space and could interact with mine from time to time, that could be good.

I think our sexual behavior is genetically determined. When a woman makes love, she really opens up, physically, psychologically, and you're there, open, whereas a man just deposits himself and somehow it's a relief, there it's done, it's over with for a while and a woman is left open and somehow that's the beginning for a woman. It's a fundamental mistake in the design of human beings. Men do in general seem to be less concerned with sensuality. For me, it's about the way you travel. Arriving is great but the way you get there can be just as good. If men spent less time worrying whether you were going to come or not and spent more being concerned about two bodies having a good time you'd both end up having a good time.

Another fundamental design mistake is that women supposedly reach their sexual peak in their late thirties while men have been going downhill since eighteen, so you're there, all peaked, looking for a suitable sexual partner and unless you want to pick up a teenager, most of the decent grown-up men are married or in a relationship. I know loads of nice, interesting single women in their thirties and forties who would like a relationship, not necessarily marriage. But where are the equivalent men? They're usually married and living with Mrs. Wrong or gay and with Mr. Right.

Vietnam Tango

[Sex is] inconvenient, time-consuming, energy draining and irrelevant. . . . Erotic energy is just life energy and is quickly worked off if you are doing interesting, absorbing things. . . . [If] genital tensions persist, you can still masturbate. Isn't that a lot easier anyway? This is not a call for celibacy but for an acceptance of celibacy as an alternative preferable to the degradation of most male-female sexual relationships.

Dana Densmore

The sexual culture of the sixties ended in 1972 with the release of the film *Last Tango in Paris*. An American man and a French woman meet in a room to fuck, in an attempt to separate sex from everything else. In the room there are no names; what stands in for them are animal noises. He requires her to strip away her identity to the simple essentials of lust. They tell each other stories in the room. He says he has been a boxer, an actor, a journalist, a bongo player, a South American revolutionary. He demands from her sex without phoniness. He demands that she prove her authenticity by subordinating herself to his wishes so totally that she is prepared to eat vomit for him. He believes that this is the *real thing*. But life, inevitably, floods in. Outside the room, the woman's boyfriend is making a modish, fragmented film about her, a work of cinema verité that is to culminate in their own wedding; he offers her "pop marriage"—a relationship for a new age constructed out of advertising images. So outside the room are the first intimations of postmodernism: that there is no real life, only art and contemporary culture.

The man is mourning the unexplained suicide of his wife in the flop-house they both managed, where middle-aged prostitutes bring their pickups. The "truth" he thinks he enacts in the room is, as the critic Pauline Kael observed when the film came out, "an intensified speeded-up history of the sexual relationships of the dominating men and the adoring women who have provided the key sex model of the past few decades— the model that is collapsing."[1]

When I first saw the film, I could not understand the relationship. What was the beautiful young actress Maria Schneider doing with the fat, middle-aged Marlon Brando, a figure from an earlier generation? A "straight," as we used to call them. When they finally meet outside the room, on a bridge (that most useful prop of sixties cinema), and exchange names—he is Paul, she is Jeanne—she looks at him in his blue blazer and gray slacks and clearly wonders the same thing herself. They have one drunken lurching dance in the middle of a tango contest; he is at his most wretchedly virile in the middle of that fake, ritualized passion. Outside the room she reverts to being the colonel's daughter; when he follows her to her mother's apartment to declare his love, she takes her father's service revolver and shoots him. The film's release was a watershed in the cinema, the first truly erotic movie, Pauline Kael thought, and one that launched a debate about whether it was pornography. The attempt by the press to cast Maria Schneider as a new sex kitten was thwarted; the actress had fallen in love with an American woman who had been detained in a mental hospital after throwing a hundred dollars' worth of lire at an airport-reservation clerk in Rome. Refusing to be separated from her lover, Maria Schneider had herself certified, as well.[2]

Inside the room, the woman is mesmerized by male power, by his version of reality, his definition of what constitutes desire. Outside the room, Paul is menacing, a violent, coercive threat. Intimacy, on the streets, now looks like rape. The character of Paul was a portrayal of the last of the sex modernists who strove for authenticity of experience and for whom sex was one of the most personal, asocial acts one could commit (together with pointless violence). Sex for the modernists had been impaled on the sensibility of disgust, a nausea provoked by dykes, pimps, flappers, booze, automats, other emblems of the Roaring Twenties; many of the modernists, D. H. Lawrence in particular, were appalled by modernity itself, by the imposition of civilization over nature (hence the popular exoticizing, in 1920s Paris, of that savage place of cultural mythology, "Africa").

In his earliest novel, the eponymous *Crazy Cock*, Henry Miller expressed the sense of emasculation and disorientation that gnawed at the modernist: "Society had complicated the relations between men, had so enmeshed the individual with laws and creeds, with totems and taboos, that man had become something unnatural, something apart from nature, a phenomenon which nature herself had created, but which she no longer controlled."[3] Nowhere was this condition more deadly than in America, where "somehow a cocaine atmosphere wouldn't produce literature. America was producing gunmen and beer barons. Literature was being left to women. Except everything was left to women, except womanhood."[4] Even fucking his wife is left to another woman: she has her own lover, on the threshold of whose room the narrator stands, broom in hand, symbolically in every way one can think of:

> Everything about this place smelled of decay, depravity. It was here in this foul, moist den that she wrestled with the demons of her dreams, or rolled off the cot when the walls heaved and bulged. Here, when she got drunk, that she curled up like a fetus and lapped up the ashes of her cigarettes. Here that her friends came and, standing on the cot in their dirty shoes, expounded their moth-eaten theories of art, or pinned bloomers on her fleshy nudes, or added a missing nose or foot. A dirty womb of a place, spewing darkness and poison, slippery and lurid as the opalescent mucus of Michelet.[5]

Miller's physical aversion to this symbol of autonomous female sexuality, Jeanne's murder of Paul, Maria Schneider's own surprising lesbianism, all these were symptomatic of the draining away of male power. All sexual politics, I believe, began to be transformed by what *Last Tango* had so eloquently understood; "authenticity" had passed from a male to a female discourse and then was finally lost.

The logical conclusion to the feminist critique of the sexual revolution, its refusal to continue to accept the male agenda with its delight in sex divorced from emotion, was separatism. The Black Panthers had already taken the lead in arguing that oppressed and oppressor could not work side-by-side in the same movement. The black activists who had once taken white wives discarded them for the darkest-skinned women they could find to affirm their "Africanness." Out of radical feminist separatism developed the political lesbian, who slept with women not because of the sex but because of the politics. The feminism of the seventies began to recast male sexuality as little more than the legitimation of violence and power. Eventually, the bold if crude logic of radical feminism made intellectual sense to many women. It made common sense to those who had been deeply wounded by men—hurt by their insensitivity or inability to communicate, hurt by abortions and rape. And for most feminists misogyny was a palpable presence in the world. Women walked the streets in fear. At home they might not be much better off if they were tied by bonds of financial dependence to a battering man. In the warmth and shared experience of women's relationships with each other was not only safety but a sense of power and of personal growth that contrasted with the spiritual emptiness of life on the singles-bar circuit, life in pursuit of Mr. Goodbar. Sisterhood was indeed powerful. Released from competing with one another for the attention of men, women grew in self-confidence. And for some, the next step was obvious: blacks had not had to live, night and day, in the most intimate relationships with white people. Why should women have to be shackled to men by the force of mere biology?

Separatism produced new feminist models of sexuality based on a radical reassessment of the sexual revolution. *Anticlimax*, a 1990 critique by Sheila Jeffreys, who defines herself as a "lesbian and revolutionary feminist," recast the sexual revolution, in which "single women were conscripted into heterosexual sex" as "the freedom for women to take pleasure from their own eroticized subordination." The new liberty of women's exploration of their sexual selves was no more than a reinforcement of male dominance and female submission.[6] Heterosexuality is eroticized power difference, the expression of a political institution for the organization of male dominance that should cease to function: "The resurgence of heterosexual desire within feminism after a brief period in which it was questioned fits into the increasingly sadistic tenor of male-supremacist society."[7] This strikes me as an extremely blunt instrument with which to tackle the problems of sexuality. No mention is made in the book of reproduction, and the future is a vague and shadowy place in which, perhaps, the world has been transformed into two sectors—one in which women practice, with one another, "Bambi" or "vanilla" sex (the gentle, antierotic caresses that early lesbian separatism preferred), the other a wilderness of men trying to quell their nasty natures on their own. Somehow, were men left to their own devices, I doubt whether restructuring their sexuality to acceptable female standards would occupy much time in a male-only hemisphere.

Yet although radical feminism lacked conventional power because it usually did not work within existing structures, curiously, in the end, it was the campaigns of radical feminism—against rape, pornography, and domestic violence—that were to catch fire with women who had never thought through feminist politics at all. The streets obviously *were* unsafe; women *were* being beaten by violent men; and most women, in marriages and other relationships, trying by small degrees to make footholds at work or balance jobs and motherhood, loathed the insistent depiction of female sexuality in the form of pneumatic bimbos, their mouths in perpetual O-shaped pouts, just waiting to suck cock.

Pornography modeled men's violent fantasies and gave them independent status in the world. The women who appeared in pornography were by no measure real women. They were the male sexual fantasy of a woman. Porn legitimated those fantasies and turned them into images that could then shape reality. This is why porn makes women feel so one-dimensional, so degraded.

The campaign against pornography spread far beyond the organized women's movement. In 1986, the British MP Clare Short moved a Commons motion to outlaw from newspapers the notorious "Page-Three girls," topless lovelies that men were meant to drool over at the family breakfast table. Robert Adley, Conservative MP for Christchurch, objected: "The trouble with the hon. Lady, and those who think like she does, is that she tends to mix only with those who share her views. To suggest seriously, as she does, that these pictures are offensive to the overwhelming majority of women is inaccurate. I suggest they are offensive to the overwhelming majority of those with whom the hon. Lady is in touch, which is not the same at all."[8]

Adley was completely wrong. Thousands of letters poured in from all sorts of women in all parts of the country—housewives, policewomen, lawyers, teachers, schoolgirls, factory workers, nurses. Certainly Clare Short had tapped into a bedrock of Puritanism that had sat out the sexual revolution, increasingly outraged. But more significantly, the parliamentary debate revealed the extent to which the connection made by feminists between sex and violence had found a receptive audience among the *majority* of women, as this letter indicates:

> I am a middle-aged, fulfilled woman with a lovely husband and two well-adjusted normal daughters in their twenties and I agree with you completely (although a lifelong Conservative—but this really is above politics). . . . I'm not a prude or jealous or anything in that vein, just feel that anything that can be done to try and stop all these horrific sex (and other) attacks on women should be done, and anything that might eliminate it—such as Page 3 girls—bought for a few pence, because I realise there are other mags even more explicit, but they cost a lot more. Sorry this is a bit of a jumble but I just felt I had to write and give you my support.[9]

In the mid-eighties, a further excavation of the male sexual psyche unearthed its most distasteful find: child sex abuse. When phone lines for children were set up, thousands of calls were received every day. I suspect most people in the country looked back into their most submerged memories of childhood to remember if they had been abused themselves. And many had. Occasionally, women sexually abused their children. But the mother of an abused child was more likely to be in living terror of a violent man on whom she had a masochistic dependence.

The history of feminism from the seventies onward has been the articulation of a politics of male violence. The first book to express this sense of brutality being programmed into men was Susan Brownmiller's *Against Our Will: Men, Women and Rape*. It was published in 1975, a crucial year in American history, the year America definitively lost the war in Vietnam and in doing so was fatally wounded in its sense of itself as an uncomplex, active, and honorable presence in the world. Brownmiller was a mainstream journalist with close ties to Movement politics. Her book was a carefully researched history—of wars, pogroms, slavery, mob violence against blacks, serial killing. Her theme was that rape had nothing to do with sex: "From prehistoric times to the present, I believe," she wrote in her introduction, "rape has played a critical function. It is nothing more or less than a conscious process of intimidation by which *all men* keep *all women* in a state of fear."[10] This statement was to reverberate through the women's movement.

The world knew about the atrocities of My Lai and wondered what brief moment of psychosis could have induced such actions in ordinary American boys. *Against Our Will* showed that they were commonplace, everyday events carried out on groups of women. One account showed how casual they could be: a deserter had told a Toronto writer of an incident involving himself, two buck sergeants, and two other men who " '. . . took these four chicks in the elephant grass. . . . We balled these chicks. They were forcibly willing—they'd rather do that than get shot. Then one of the guys yelled some derogatory thing at the woman he balled. . . . He just reached for his weapon and blew her away. Well right away the three other guys, including myself, picked up our weapons and blew away the other three chicks. Just like that.' "[11] Sex was merely a way to generate fear in women; its links with violence were all too obviously provable, not just in Vietnam but in the growing numbers of serial killers who stalked the world—almost always men, almost always preying on women. All the jokes women used to tell—"Be careful, you might get raped," "I should be so lucky"—suddenly seemed sick indeed. Rape fantasies, which women undoubtedly had, were cultural conditioning, a mark of our male-induced masochism.

The desire of men for wholeness, their attraction with and repulsion from the Other, has been one of the single most important sexual themes of the twentieth century. But this quest for authenticity finally disintegrated during the Vietnam years, a decade in which men and women were driven to the extremes of two separate kinds of experience. While American GIs faced defeat in Vietnam, women were simultaneously constructing a new independent identity. The Vietnam War fractured the wholeness of the gaze. It was, in a way, a war fought against women. The fatal mistake America made was believing in the Madame Butterfly story of the fragile beauty, at once innocent and submissive, treating her man like a king yet possessed of the exotic sex secrets of the Orient: the impossible dream of the virgin and the harlot rolled into one in a land without feminism. Impossibly romantic, she rejects her own culture and dies for love. The first Vietnamese postwar performance of *Madame Butterfly* was not lost on audiences, who saw it as a parable of their own recent history.

In a mythic reading, the East is irredeemably female and passive and the West immovably male and dominant. It could take no account of Asian men except to assume their desire for submission to American foreign policy; to be less than male was to be no match for American military machismo. And if the Vietnamese had defeated the French in the previous decade, it was because the French themselves were hardly men—only twenty years before they had had to be rescued from the dominant military machismo of the Germans. The real Vietnam was, of course, a different place. Against the beef-fed might of the American GI was ranged a shadowy guerrilla army. They recruited women: one commando I met in Saigon had arrested her first American soldier at the age of seventeen. He was a foot taller than she was and she had to make him kneel down to put on the blindfold. Such images were depicted on Vietnamese postage stamps to symbolize the humiliation of the enemy: "He tried to bribe me with his fountain pen," she said. "But I told him, 'You cannot bribe me. I have my own fountain pen.'" Quite.

Much has been made of the youth of the GI in Vietnam, whose average age was nineteen. Many would have been virgins, far from home in a country whose existence they could hardly have been aware of before the war started. Sometimes, before they went, they looked it up on the map and were surprised to find out how far away it was. They had thought it was real close, like Panama. Twenty years later you can walk through the quiet grasses of Cu Chi, your eyes looking for and failing to find the trapdoors in the grass that led to the tunnels in which the Vietnamese lived and trained a subterranean army of guerrillas. You will feel what the GIs felt: their youth, their loneliness, their assault by an enemy they never quite caught sight of except from the corner of the eye. In this strange world, they came of age sexually. They did so in the brothels of Saigon, Bangkok, and Manila, the R&R centers for the troops. At the height of America's military deployment, there were 600,000 soldiers and 500,000 prostitutes, almost one for every GI. Far from the backseat fumblings of high school dating, the women must have fulfilled the GIs' every adolescent fantasy, giving them anything they wanted, asking only a few dollars in return. It was sex with no demands other than the economic. But even the prostitutes were not what they seemed. Many had been recruited as spies and efficiently passed information back to Hanoi. Either in bed or in the jungle, women were alien.

In Vietnam, what was a woman, exactly? Not someone with whom you would have a meaningful relationship, but an amalgam of body parts. What was the difference between a whore in a cathouse and a chick guerrilla or village woman? The total number of GIs convicted of rape between 1965 and 1973 was twenty-four.[12] The veterans returned to America deeply wounded: in their bodies, in their minds, and in their sex. If the women's health movement had come to see the body in a holistic way, the veterans could only find it in fragments. "Nudity was part of death there. It was nothing to see naked bodies, dead, cut up or whatever," a veteran told a counselor.[13] "Romantic love died in Vietnam, right next to my friends," said another.[14] For the combat-fatigued, sex in Vietnam became a mood-altering drug. In the jungle they may have literally shit themselves with fright. The heart could not bear up under it; in the cathouse, with a bar girl, they could at last feel a man again. One veteran wrote a poem about it in 1986, long after the war was over:

Come here, lie with me
And take away the pain
Then go away
I never want to see you again.[15]

A little research has been done into the long-term effects on the sexual lives of veterans. A POW was sexually abused by his guards. His mind filled with sadistic images as he thought about what he wanted to do to them if he found them again. When he made love to his wife, he thought of piercing her, ripping her. Some men could only have sex if it was staged in the props of the brothel, the wives dressed up in erotic outfits. There was no separating sex and violence. Death was real; combat-readiness the only hope of staying alive.[16]

The prom queens the men had left behind were disturbingly transformed by the sexual revolution. The sexualization of women's lives through magazines like *Cosmopolitan* had taught them some of the tricks of the bar girls of the East with a willingness to engage in men's sexual fantasies. To "real men," feminists are not "real women" but part man. Women's newfound independence, their fight for selfhood and separateness, had made them resemble the women of Vietnam in another way: they were the enemy in a man's own bed. Instinctively, even while the war was going on, Bernardo Bertolucci had understood this when he made *Last Tango in Paris:* the ritual acting out of sexual violence in that private place to assuage the pain of Paul's life outside the room; the final escape from it when, clothed, he offers himself to Jeanne and she rejects him, returning his violence. Vietnam and *Last Tango* were metaphors for the disintegration of the old sexual patterns, of the possibility that anything—even sex—could be real.

I would suggest that in losing the Vietnam War America not only lost its vision of the future and confidence in its preordained destiny but its sense of its own authenticity and wholeness. America's sexing of itself as male—in such guises as cowboy, soldier, fire fighter, cop (images that were later appropriated and parodied by gay men)—was questioned and its own reality lost. The action movies of World War Two and afterward had depicted heroism and comradeship. The films made after the Vietnam War sought to supply a set of costumes for the American male sexual identity to wear. In 1976, a year after the final ignominious withdrawal from Saigon, George Lucas's *Star Wars* was released, a film that inaugurated action movies with their crude battles between good and evil. The cult of high-technology violence and humor in the cinema reached its apocalyptic expression in the 1989 film *Die Hard*, which returned to Bruce Willis the prewar authenticity of man against a foreign enemy (British actors have become an all-purpose image in Hollywood of evil and its concomitant effeteness, the femininity that had defeated the U.S. in Vietnam). Only in violence could men find their realness, but even this was no more than a pose. Rambo fulfilled the male craving for the reintegration of male identity that experience could not supply when there was no war to fight and the Japanese were buying up America. I suspect that the image of the two-fisted Wall Street dealer for whom lunch is for wimps was another media-induced construct to help to fulfil that craving for male wholeness and authority.

The legacy of this loss of authenticity is an alienated, postmodern culture of sex as spectacle, which has been carefully chronicled by Bret Easton Ellis's *American Psycho,* a novel whose psychopathic antihero could indeed be Rambo gone rampant in New York. In Ellis's first novel, *Less Than Zero,* the narrator, Clay, gets up late. Duran Duran is playing in his mother's room. Inside, his sisters are "watching some porno film on the Betamax with the sound turned off." He wonders whose the film is. His mom's? His sisters'? A Christmas present? His own? One of the sisters says she hates it when they show the man coming. Later, at a friend's house, fourteen boys and two dogs watch another porno video. A naked fifteen-year-old girl is tied, spread-eagled, to the bedposts. A naked teenage boy is tied up and raped by a fat black man. The man then rapes the girl. Clay leaves the room, walks out onto the deck, and listens to the waves, the seagulls, the hum of telephone wires, the sound of trees shuffling and the girl and boy screaming on the video. Two boys come out onto the deck and argue about whether the chainsaw scene was real:

> "Yeah, I think it's real too," the other boy says, easing himself into the Jacuzzi. "It's gotta be."
> "Yeah?" Trent asks, a little hopefully.
> "I mean, like, how can you fake a castration? They cut the balls off that guy real slowly. You can't fake that," the boy says.[17]

This was bringing the war home in a way that had been unimaginable forty years before, when Hollywood was making such peacetime films as *The Best Years of Our Lives,* about a veteran struggling to come to terms with demobilization. The video culture Ellis describes was straight from

Vietnam, the war that had accompanied his childhood on TV. Ellis has identified himself as part of a lost generation, Generation X, morally neutral, basically unshockable, barely able to distinguish between the repetitive images of war on the nightly news and the slaughter at the movies—*Robocop, Total Recall, Die Hard 2*. He has spoken nostalgically of the sex of his parents' generation: "In life and movies, eroticism has disappeared from the sex scenes. . . . The sensuality of a movie like *Last Tango in Paris* was powerful not only because of its naturalness but also because there was no sense of inhibition. The times didn't call for it."[18]

A Safety Pin Stuck Through My Heart

One of the things Warhol was always talking about, and I was, too, was what you can do that hasn't been done before. Unexploited territory. Sado-masochism, transvestites—such things came in not only because they were novel but also theatrical . . . all image and display.

Ronald Tavel

The history of the sexual revolution since the late seventies has been the erosion of what previous generations would have defined as the "sexual." In a violent society, suffused by sexual violence, sex itself has come to parody violence, turning that old slogan, "Make love not war," on its head. What had been for Paul in *Last Tango* a moment of truth and piercing intensity, a no-bullshit domination of woman by man, came to rather more closely resemble the tango contest—only vestigially about sex.

The seventies were a backlash decade for the sexual revolution. A 1980 book, Gabrielle Brown's *The New Celibacy*, promised to reveal the truth of its subtitle: *Why More Men and Women Are Abstaining from Sex—And Enjoying It.* The author, who appended her name with her Ph.D. to affirm her "expert" status (then still needed in American publishing when sexual matters were concerned), thought she had spotted a "trend": *Penthouse Forum* of January 1979 had asserted that sex was too easy to have and had become a meaningless experience; *The New York Times* of May 1, 1978, reported a wave of asexuality sweeping the nation as an antidote to painful sexual experiences and traumatic divorce; the *Village Voice* of January 23,

1979, claimed that celibacy was the new chic and among those who had "come out" were Mick Jagger and Andy Warhol.[1]

As the Vietnam War was coming to an end, Britain was reaching a separate closure. Punk was, Brown rightly detected, an antisexual movement reacting against the excesses of the dinosaurs of sixties pop with its groupies and padded groins. Punk was about detonation, violence, rage. Johnny Rotten was supposed to have said that sex was just squelching, he'd rather have a cup of tea. Jon Savage, in his biography of the Sex Pistols, detects in their songs a "language of revolutionary millenarianism. . . . They embraced the struggle between authoritarianism and freedom which was now to be acted out in the country about which they spoke so passionately." Julien Temple had noticed that, " 'the Sex Pistols seemed to be the heirs to the Diggers and the Ranters. Rotten's lyrics had that millennial feel. He hadn't read the texts but he spoke in that language.' "[2] It was songs like "I Am the Antichrist" that must have triggered this memory, for the vision of punk was very far from a utopian one. Punk prophesied the destruction of Old England, of an England lost in the dream of its own history, particularly its great moment of glory when it had fought the last world war. The dead-end kids of London in the decade after the Swinging Sixties, the first teenagers since the fifties not to have known youth affluence, felt enslaved to the dole, hopelessness, and the ominous rise of the far Right in the form of the resurgent neo-Nazi National Front.

Punk was anything but futuristic. Sickened by all the fusions of rock with jazz and classical music, it demanded a return to the basic roots of rock and roll, its early barbarism. Savage argues that punk was the product of Luddite social realism, competing in the discos with a fusion of gay liberation and high technology and in the high schools with the ascendancy of Heavy Metal and its overblown macho sexuality. In America, it flourished not in San Francisco but Los Angeles, the most alienated urban landscape in the country.[3] But unlike the millenarian cults of the seventeenth century, it was joyless and without a program. It lived in real fear. By 1980 it seemed that nuclear war would be inevitable within the next five years. People in London were glad they lived near parks so they could run out into the nearest open space and be vaporized instead of enduring life in the post-nuclear wasteland. Punk detonated the remnants of the sixties in a revolutionary statement of nihilism that politicized some people in preparation for Rock Against Racism in 1978 and the miners' strike of 1984. But Thatcherism in Britain and Reaganism in America defeated those political aspirations. The most lasting legacy of punk concerned its sexual politics.

Malcolm McLaren and his girlfriend Vivienne Westwood were fascinated by the fifties and spent some years running a retro shop on King's Road until they ran out of retro images to recycle. McLaren the Jew made the Nazi regalia worn by Mahler's Aryan anima in Ken Russell's film about the composer: she was a " 'huge German Catholic creature with a Nazi helmet. . . . We used a Dominator bike-tyre T-shirt and the skirt was very short, in leather, and had a zip down the front of it. Either side of that we had this huge Jesus cross in brass studs. This was right down the centre of the crotch and then on the back was this huge swastika in brass studs.' "[4] McLaren was influenced by the New York Dolls, kids from Queens who toured Britain performing in drag and emulating Andy Warhol's glamorization of bisexuality. McLaren liked rubber, Christine Keeler, Valerie Solanis, and dominatrices, all sexual outlaws. The King's Road shop began to ransack the sexual underground for the paraphernalia of the S/M scene, and its walls were covered with a thin gray spongelike material from the Pentonville Rubber Company, graffitoed with phrases from fetish books and Valerie Solanis's SCUM manifesto. The goods were inflatable rubber masks, tit clamps, whips, chains, lacy rubber petticoats, and boots with foot-high heels. McLaren toyed with naming the shop after a quote from a porno mag: "The Dirty Stripper who left her UNDIES on the railings to go hitchhiking said you don't THINK I have stripped off all these years just for MONEY do you?"[5] Instead, he called it SEX. Its clientele were half fetish shoppers, half fashion victims.

Undoubtedly McLaren's aim was to shock. But unlike Jefferson Poland, who wanted his ideas to transform America into a better place, punks were marginals. Their T-shirts—a naked black footballer with a pendulous cock or an image of a small boy suggestively exhaling a cigarette, taken from a pedophile magazine—represented for Savage the first redefining of the sexual:

Printed on brown or pink, or red on green, these images were simple but complex: as McLaren and Westwood knew, there was a world of difference between an image in a brown-bag pornzine and a silk-screen blow-up worn in public display. The effect could be consciously asexual. Both McLaren and Westwood had strong elements of puritanism in their own sexual make-up, and their blow-ups of fetish imagery were polemical, a comment on the image's primary use. The overt sexuality became an abstraction of sex.[6]

Another T-shirt depicted a cutout of a photograph of a pair of breasts; when worn by men, it derailed any ideas of sexual liberation and turned them into an androgynous joke. As Andy Warhol in the fifties and sixties had appropriated images of the new consumer culture, McLaren and Westwood raided the vocabulary of the sexual revolution. A kind of anarchic conservatism in McLaren hated the inoffensiveness that sexual freedom had imposed on desire. He wanted to put the danger back into sex, the sense of prohibition, the power relations, the decadence, the theatricality. Hippie sexuality had mocked adults; if hippie chicks flaunted their breasts and the guys got out their cocks, it was only to say, "We're young and we're beautiful and we're having a great time. How about you?" Sid Vicious's version of "My Way," by comparison, took on the great phallic totem of the male ego. Johnny Rotten, according to fellow punk musician Jordan, was so prudish that when he had to spend the night at her place, he wouldn't take his trousers off until he had got into bed.[7]

McLaren and Westwood's attempts to shock were impersonal by comparison with the hippies, and the attempts had nothing to do with their own bodies. Above all, their fascination with S/M had as much to do with the novelty of the subject matter. Real sexual subcultures are separated from one another by rigid laws. The shoe fetishist is not going to be aroused by someone in rubber. McLaren and Westwood were not interested in the act but in the image, the costume you wore to do it in. For Poly Styrene, the song "Oh Bondage! Up Yours" "was about being in bondage to material life. In other words it was a call for liberation. It was saying: 'Bondage? Forget it! I am not going to be bound by the laws of consumerism or bound by my own senses!' It has that line in it: 'Chain smoke, chain gang, I consume you all': you are all tied to these activities for somebody else's profit."[8] And Derek Jarman saw in the images of sexual bondage the figures of bank robbers and terrorists in stocking masks and balaclavas, outlaws of crime and politics.[9] Sex for punk had everything to do with politics and very little to do with sex.

Punk, like every other youth cult, was a male-dominated movement, but women's places within it allowed unprecedented freedom. Lucy Whitman, who as Lucy Toothpaste produced a feminist fanzine called JOLT during the period, believes that "the role of women in punk was very different from anything that had gone before and that was because the ideas of the women's movement had already begun to filter through." It offered girls a place that had not existed for them in music before. To be in a group you certainly didn't have to have any talent; all you had to have was some daring: "There was definitely a feeling that girls weren't just going to be groupies. Women were setting up bands and there was a sort of sense of comradeship between the girls and the boys. The Au Pairs, the Slits, the Raincoats were all writing about sexual relationships, usually from a disillusioned, alienated view. Bands like the Slits would have rather dropped dead than say they were feminists because it would have seemed too prissy. They had a very aggressive, no-messing-with-us image." The presence of these tough, streetwise girls jolted feminism.

When Whitman became involved in the feminist magazine *Spare Rib*, she found herself in the position of defending punk against an older generation of feminists who found it frightening and misogynistic and failed to recognize that its use of imagery was largely ironic. Punk, Whitman had to explain, was a supremely tongue-in-cheek movement, reveling in visual puns and parodies. Like feminism, she thought, punk was about consciousness-raising, about jolting people out of their complacency, challenging conventional perceptions, breaking down stereotypes (though it also had to do with visual messages, with posing, about getting the right image and being seen at the right gigs): "Punk had a big effect on feminist fashion because at the beginning of it all most feminists were still wearing dungarees and the idea of dressing up in any way was frowned on. I remember going to women's events and other women looking at me askance because of my punky appearance and yet within a year nearly everyone was looking like I did. Punk gave us the chance to reject conventional feminine attire but have fun with our appearance at the same time."

Within punk, marginal sexuality was tolerated because sex itself was marginalized. To Whitman, it was very funny to see people struggle up the road with their legs tied together in their bondage trousers. "I saw it more as a metaphor for our confinement in a sexist capitalist society, and that's how I understood Poly Styrene's song 'Oh Bondage! Up Yours.' In those days people who actually practiced S/M kept it a closely guarded secret, whereas the punks who walked into Woolworth's wearing bondage clothes probably didn't have any interest in S/M as such. The clothes were just meant to be a challenge to conventional morality." Bondage wear was a reaction against sex as the be-all and end-all of existence, a deliberate sundering of form and content.

Although women like Jordan and Patti Smith made a point of coming out as bisexual, Whitman didn't think there was space to be lesbian or gay, certainly not right at the very beginning. But it was a good place to be if you were uncertain about your sexuality because punk wasn't interested in sex, so heterosexuality wasn't compulsory. "You could look quite dykey and say it was because you were punk. You didn't have to have a partner of the opposite sex for credibility and in the history of popular culture, that's unique."

Long after punks had become quaint figures, like Chelsea pensioners, on London's streets, to be photographed by tourists alongside bobbies and guardsmen, or dragging dogs about on lengths of string at New Age festivals, the images of punk continues to be incorporated into fashion. The designer Jean-Paul Gaultier spent the ensuing decade putting models into rubber corset dresses and multi-zipped cat suits, poking fun at the *haute bourgeoisie* sitting on gold chairs at the fashion shows by displaying on the catwalk images from the red-light district of the rue St. Denis or the gay S/M subculture. Why did the imagery of S/M become such a dominant motif in the eighties and nineties? Partly, of course, it had to do with safe sex. Penetration, thanks to AIDS, was out. Gay men in particular needed new erotic pathways, which they constructed through clothes, poses, alternative turn-ons. The abundance of sex gay men were able to have through an extensive club culture lowered the boredom threshold and required the eroticization of the whole body as a generalized site of pleasure. S/M invoked not orgasm but a form of catharsis—truthfully, sex in the head. S/M had long been a small sub-category of gay male practice. For Guy Hocquenghem, the author of *Homosexual Desire,* who was interviewed in 1980, the anal-centeredness of homosexuality was a liberation from the phallocentricity of homosexuality and a total denial of reproduction's role in sex:

> S-M is *the* scene: the kind we always desired from the time we became homosexuals, a sex game between real tough men—the theater of what male heterosexuals would be doing between themselves if they had sex together. It is also a very *fragile* theater, which is why it's a non-speaking arena; no critics allowed, actors perform only for a participating public. . . . Rather than expressing guilt—for breaking society's taboo against homosexuality—the S-M code expresses the 'sophisticated' pleasure of being a complete cliché, destroying oppressive social imagery of us by caricaturing it ourselves—perversion as the negation of neurosis, of the pleasure of punition subverting the moral code of painful guilt.[10]

For the lesbian sadist Pat Califia, S/M is a revolutionary feminist subversion:

> I wonder if any man could understand how this act, receiving sexual service, feels to me. I was taught to dread sex, to fight it off, to provide it under duress or in exchange for romance and security. I was trained to take responsibility for other people's gratification and pretend pleasure when others pretend to have my pleasure in mind. It is shocking and profoundly gratifying to commit this piece of rebellion, to take pleasure exactly as I want it, to exact it like tribute. I need not pretend I enjoy a bottom's ministration if they are unskilled, nor do I need to be ungrateful.[11]

It is harder, however, to decode the revolutionary nature of the masochist. The argument is that an S/M communication consists of two equal exchanges. Grace Lau, feminist photographer and S/M practitioner, explains S/M as a topsy-turvy world where the slave is the real master who is dictating the level of pleasure and pain. "He looks in chains but the master knows very well that the slave has a limit to what he can take. A lot of men who want to be abused happen to be in powerful positions. They want to negate all their responsibilities and pretend to be powerless and they want beautiful women to attend to them while they're powerless. But of course they still have power because they know this woman can't really hurt them and it is they who are dictating the level of pain. So in all ways they retain their power."

One of the most powerful women in the world is, of course, Madonna, the theme of whose book *Sex* is *safe sex*, which is why it opens with S/M pictures. In her version, S/M is reduced to a world of cozy protection and security: "There's something comforting about being tied up. Like when you were a baby and your mother strapped you in the car seat. She wanted you to be safe. It was an act of love."[12] Close up, the revolutionary potential claimed for S/M seems dissipated; bondage is reduced to something quite soppy, the degeneration to infantilism that Angela Carter detected in the activities of libertines.

The more S/M comes above ground and into the realm of fashion the less dangerous it becomes, and one suspects that the real sadomasochists must be waiting for their fifteen minutes of fame to pass so they can get back to having a good time without all the tiresome theorizing. But S/M is particularly eloquent with meanings, and its use as metaphor now pervades popular culture. The film *Basic Instinct* begins with an act of designer bondage. Its notoriety was caused by the apparent portrayal of a lesbian murderess. I don't see that Catherine is gay; she is someone for whom the whole body is an instrument of desire. She is polymorphously perverse. She ties up the old rock-and-roll star with whom she is having sex by binding his hands to the bed with a white Hermès scarf, then kills him, symbolically finishing off one of the principal icons of sixties sexuality. S/M—its costumes, its political discourse—is to me an expression of the powerlessness of radical politics in the Thatcher/Major—Reagan/Bush years. It implies the longing of a generation for real power, the kind exercised by Wall Street and the City in the eighties, but denied to the Left and to sexual outlaws in the decade of family values. It is hard not to find in S/M forms of real self-hatred, the failure of a generation to take charge of its own future. Power exhilarates and it disturbs; it upsets equilibriums that must be rebalanced in the internal life of our fantasies.

I detect too in S/M the resurgence of the Catholic imagination after its temporary defeat by science and futurism. The myth that Europe is a sophisticated, cosmopolitan society, free from repression and hypocrisy, that exists to this day in America is fueled by visits to the Continent. Even the peasant economies of the Mediterranean, dominated by the Church, celebrate a visual language of the erotic derived from a complex system of iconography. Incense, bright colors, bared flesh, and the interpenetration of religious ecstasy with palpable pain found in crucifixion scenes and depictions of the death of St. Sebastian induce a sensual syntax that permeates everyday custom. The same Latin sensuality, heightened by vestiges of Indian culture, saturates South America. The Catholic Church never succeeded in repressing eroticism; it was merely victorious in sublimating it so that it found new forms of meaning in art.

For Catholics the ultimate sin is disobedience. Listen to this fictional account of the acolytes of a fifteenth-century Spanish evangelist:

> All paused at the Stations of the Cross, beating themselves with scourges of twisted hemp twined into branches, with iron lashes, thick rods and briars. Some twisted their bodies so frenziedly that the great quantity of blood which gushed from the wounds wide as fingers made it necessary to take the whips from them, lest they kill themselves. . . . The thirsty knelt as a token of humility to drink the water offered by the compassionate. . . . The bells tolled an accompaniment to the human serpent in its wretchedness and agony. "The use of this penance was so widespread that wherever Master Vicente went, the silversmiths and other craftsmen set up booths with scourges as if they were having a whip fair," San Antonio wrote.[13]

Freed from the discipline of the Church, Catholics continue their dialogue with God, as Viva, one of Andy Warhol's "Superstars," makes clear: "The Factory was a way for a group of Catholics to purge themselves of Catholic repression . . . and Catholic repression in the Fifties was so extreme that the only way to liberate oneself from it was to react in the completely opposite direction, and then hopefully level off after that."[14] The Factory should best be expressed as a monastery, an enclosed place of devotion, work, art, spiritual experience, and adherence to a strict sexual code—in this case, what used to be known as perversion.

Catholicism is extraordinarily well-suited to postmodern times. It has a preexisting museum of images to raid. For Madonna as an adolescent, Christ was to be worshipped like a movie star. Judaism, as Camille Paglia, the philosopher of postmodern sex, has pointed out, is a word culture. So was Christianity until it had to retreat to pictorialism to convert the pagan masses.[15] The vivid, carnal colors of the peasant churches in Italy, Spain, Mexico, and Guatemala, the "pagan conflation of longing, lust, fright, ecstasy, resignation, repose . . . the daemonic sublime,"[16] the heightened dramatic rituals moving the soul with their tableaux of dominance and submission, form the creative impulses of Catholic art. And whenever Catholics break free from the external whip of sin and guilt, they break out into a spectacular display of hedonism. In Spain, Franco's fascism was reinforced by the Church. After his death, the country went mad in a sexual free-for-all whose chronicler was Pedro Almódovar, the filmmaker of gender ambiguity, revenge, murder, and high irony. In Poland, Warsaw's post-Communist Lent Ball was organized by a satirical magazine called No that specialized in offending the Church and had a circulation of one and a half million. Three upmarket call girls performed a moving tableau in which they danced to the disco beat of an updated Gregorian chant in front of three kneeling men who removed their clothes to reveal edible briefs that were instantly devoured.[17]

Catholicism's other postmodern characteristic is its lack of belief in the future. Why put any faith in progress if you have eternity? In Catholicism, desire is a timeless moment endlessly ritualized. The American artist Andres Serrano, brought up a Catholic, left the Church at thirteen but remains obsessed by "the theatrics, the drama, and the mystery."[18] Retaining the Catholic fascination with vestments and costumes, he photographs Ku Klux Klan wizards. Using his own bodily fluids, he imprisons Christ in a transparent casket in which the Messiah is viewed through the clear golden liquid of the artist's piss, like the glass orb of the alleged blood of

San Gennaro of Naples that is said to liquefy every year. The uneasy relationship Catholics have with the physical, constantly mindful of the interconnection between sin and death and the loss of eternal life, makes Catholic artists the ideal commentators on the plague years. Camille Paglia's war is with the millenarian Protestant vision to which feminism has succumbed: "Feminists grossly oversimplify the problem of sex when they reduce it to a matter of social convention: readjust society, eliminate sexual inequality, purify sex roles and happiness and harmony will reign," she writes.[19] Sex for Paglia is a dark power, the point of contact where human meets nature. Humane eroticism is impossible, for sex can never be free of anxiety and psychic shadows. The barbarism of lust emanates from anarchic nature. Women are chthonic, sluggish with hormonal impulses beyond our capacity to control, barely distinguishable from animals. Desire drives us. Politics are an illusion, a bold but futile attempt to escape our libidinal selves; women should not be deluded by the male program of social change into which feminism has trapped them: "The western idea of history as a propulsive movement into the future, a progressive or Providential design climaxing in the revelation of the Second Coming, is a male formulation," she writes. "No woman, I submit, could have coined such an idea, since it is a strategy of evasion of women's own cyclic nature, in which man dreads to be caught. Evolutionary or apocalyptic history is a male wish list with a happy ending, a phallic peak."[20] Could the sexual revolution have been more finally defeated than in this amputation of its most cherished belief, that of progress? Thus the Vatican's revenge against the renegade Catholic, the Jewish scientist, the feminist financier, and the eugenicist.

Witness

No Glove, No Love

13 January, 1992

Dear Ms. Grant
   Happy New Year!
   I'm sorry this has taken me so long to complete. I hope it's not too late for you to use in your research.
   I would like to thank you for giving me the opportunity to think at length about my sexual history. I remembered a lot of funny things that I guess I had suppressed. It was nice to sit down and think about myself, and how my sexuality has been shaped by my family, my peers, guys, Madonna . . .
   I am very excited to be contributing to your book, and I wish you the best of luck in 1992.
   Sincerely Yours,

——— ———

SEXUAL QUESTIONNAIRE

How old are you?
24

Where do you live?
California

When did you first experience sexual feelings?
When I was 13 years old I had a crush on a boy in my class and I would think about him when I was in bed. One night I started imagining kissing and

touching him, and all of a sudden my underwear was wet. I remember not thinking it was strange because we had just studied reproduction in my biology class and I knew what was going on because it happened to frogs.

When did you lose your virginity?
When I was 17

Under what circumstances?
I was a senior in high school, and my boyfriend was in college. Naturally all my friends thought the first thing we were going to do was have sex, since of course he must've been experienced in that area. We would make out pretty heavily, petting, dabbling in oral sex, and then one day he asked me if I'd ever had sex, and if I'd like to do it with him. I didn't feel pressured at all, but I did feel very strongly that if we were going to do it, we were going to on my terms. I'd been wanting to do it for some time, but I was a little frightened, so when he suggested it in such an open manner I said "Let's try it right now." My vagina was very tight, and attempts at having sex were painful, so we decided to ease into it through mutual masturbation and poking around. It took about three and a half months before I was comfortable and the pain subsided. After that I wanted to have sex all the time. I lost my virginity before my friends did. It made big news because up until that time, I'd never had a boyfriend, nor had I any dates. I never had any regret about having sex because I had been looking forward to it since my early adolescence. Also, even though it was at my boyfriend's suggestion, I was in complete control of the sexual situation, even down to what birth control we used. We used only condoms because I felt he needed to learn to respect my decision. We only had sex when I wanted to. The experience was very positive for me because I had learned to be assertive, creative and how to get my way.

How many sexual partners have you had?
5

Have you had one-night stands?
I almost did once, but he and I had nowhere to go. Had it not been so cold that night, we very likely would have had sex on the back of his scooter.

Have you ever initiated a relationship by making it clear to a man that you want to go to bed with him?

I have never initiated a relationship in that way, though I would suspect that if I were in need of a sexual partner today, I would probably be that direct. I have a sister and friends with HIV, and I think that the world needs to communicate more openly about sex.

Do you make it clear to your partner that you want your sexual needs fulfilled by indicating to him what you find arousing?

I think the second person I had sex with was very taken aback by my assertive manner. I didn't think I was "assertive" (why is that bad anyway?); I was just letting him know what I enjoyed. For example I would perform oral sex on him the way I would have liked him to perform on me, or I would try all sorts of crazy sex positions. Usually, though, unless I spelled it out, men had very little understanding of non-verbal communication, and just thought I was this crazy, hot little number. I found that after telling one guy what I found arousing, I had guys asking me out on dates all the time (I had never had one date in high school!). I was always a bit of a tomboy, and in college I experimented with having sex with whomever I wanted, and I soon found that women could not act that way. I knew it was taboo to behave like a guy, and that's why I did it. I wasn't considered a slut, but women and men felt threatened. I thought it was a fucked form of sexism. Double standards are stupid.

What forms of contraception have you used and what do you use now?

I have used condoms, sponges and I tried the Pill once. I turned into a monster when I was on the Pill, and I felt disgusting. I also had a philosophical problem with taking it. I thought, "Whom am I conveniencing with this synthetic drug?" I felt it was just a way of removing responsibility from men, and I stopped using it 2 weeks later. Even in high school I felt this tremendous need to teach men to be responsible for birth control. Sometimes, for spontaneity's sake, my boyfriend and I use the rhythm method; but by and large, my law is no glove, no love.

Are you or have you been frightened of getting pregnant?
One of the first times I had sex, the condom broke. I remember my boyfriend being freaked out, worrying about whether or not to tell his mom, where could we get the money for the abortion etc. I was less emotional about it. I thought, "Hey, if I'm pregnant, I'll just get an abortion." A few times recently I've been worried about being pregnant mostly because I'm a student, and the cost of an abortion is still pricey. I don't think it's a fear of pregnancy, as much as it is a fear of finances.

Are you worried about AIDS?
I was for some time because this guy I had slept with had a spotty drug past. I should probably get myself tested for HIV, just to know for sure. I have been in a monogamous relationship for the past 4 years, so although I no longer fear "catching" it, there is still the possibility that I may have the virus. I am scared to get tested.

How has this affected your sexual behavior?
When I was "free" (not promiscuous, just free to sleep with whoever suited my fancy at the time), I used condoms every single time I had sex, so you could say that I took precautions. I used condoms more for contraceptive reasons than for disease prevention. I wasn't really attracted to types that seemed to have a checkered, potentially threatening past, but then again, unless men tell you everything about themselves can you really know if they are "safe"?

Do you know anyone who has acquired AIDS through heterosexual sex?
Yes, my sister who is 23 contracted it from a boyfriend of hers in 1990. She said they only had sex once without protection and after they broke up she had premonitions that he had AIDS. He was her first boyfriend.

Would you consider being in an openly non-monogamous relationship?
I was once with three guys. I loved it; they were all jealous of each other. I thought, "Wow, this is greater than Jules et Jim." Eventually I got bored

with the lot of them. Currently having HIV positive friends and family, I would not even fathom an openly non-monogamous relationship. It is simply too dangerous.

Do you think all pornography should be banned?
No. I don't think so. Sometimes I like to use books to "get in the mood." Most of the time, I really have to concentrate though, because most pornographic reading is so utterly ridiculous that in order to get turned on, I have to shut off my brain. I don't think all pornography should be banned because after all, no one is forced to purchase it, and if there are enough people out there who like it and want it, then they should be able to buy it.

The problem is that most pornography is degrading to women because it represents them as either whores who love to suck (god, I hate that one) or women who just need the right man to help them let go and become whores who love to suck. Pornography is also oppressive because it continues to advance that image of the perfect woman, with the perfect body, usually blonde hair, tons of make-up—basically a Barbie doll with a big mouth. I watched some videos by Candida Royalle, a woman who purports to make pornographic videos from a woman's point of view, and those weren't too offensive. I guess I don't mind reading pornographic material because it allows you more freedom to fantasize and be creative (I guess you'd call it erotica—it sounds more tasteful).

If you are/were without a sexual partner would you use a male prostitute if one were available (with attractive, healthy, disease-free men, of course)?
No, because I can't help thinking it's depraved to offer sexual services for money. Sex is not a commodity that can be bought and sold like toasters.

What do you think of Madonna?
"Sex may not be a commodity to be bought and sold like toasters" . . . how can I say that and justify loving Madonna? I think because she sells sexuality, the idea of being a sexual, loving person which I feel is completely different from selling sex. It's liberating, not confining. In her videos, Madonna portrays a variety of women, from the headstrong teenager of "Papa Don't

Preach" to the peepshow dancer in "Open Your Heart" to a weak-willed woman in "Express Yourself." She is never belittled or abused by men. She isn't a sex object; she is a sex subject. I really admire the ideas she is exploring in her art form. In these days of AIDS, rape, sexual harassment, I feel her music and videos are very positive and educational. She may not be the greatest singer, dancer or actress but she has balls.

Who do you think has gained most from the sexual revolution?
Women have gained some ground, but not enough. We still aren't permitted to control our bodies!

Is your attitude toward sex different from that of your parents?
Completely. I can actually talk about it.

12

The Millennium: Sex in the Time of Virtual Reality

The idea is that a complex fabric of electronic sensors could be worn over the sex organs—a washable or disposable "dick sleeve" for Him, perhaps a "data bikini" for Her—and used to digitise sensual touching.
"High Tech Sex," *Marie Claire*, April 1993

When I began to write this book, there were two questions I wanted answered. Why, thirty years after the sexual revolution, had prostitution not withered away with women's greater sexual freedom? And, given that capitalism abhors a vacuum and must constantly seek out new markets, why was there no sex industry aimed at women? Jefferson Poland had thought it inevitable. But during the course of my research, something happened: 1992 had become The Year of the Hardbody, the raunchy, voguishly libertarian postfeminist woman who had turned her back on Andrea Dworkin to explore the adventure playground of sex. With bravado and condoms she stalked the club scene. Instead of *Cosmopolitan* she read *For Women* or *Ludus,* the new sex magazines for girls with attitude, critically appraising the pinups and cursing the law that penises can only be depicted in detumescence. It was a sudden and spectacular reversal from the late eighties, when the single girl was portrayed as a career woman who had traded intimacy and the family for success and an arid personal life, or the one-night stand from Hell that provoked a national bloodlust in audiences for the film *Fatal Attraction*. According to the media, everyone must have a sexual persona in the nineties. The sight of armies of secretaries, on a night out with the girls, jeering at a male stripper when he finally stepped out of his G-string to reveal a less-than-satisfactory organ, was the signal for the breaking of the spell that the wicked witch of the eighties had cast on us: the silencing of desire.

Two years before, there had been every indication that women had no interest in pornography and that there were crucial differences between male and female sexual behavior. The most insistent argument was that women found it virtually impossible to separate sex from emotion. That Harlequin Romances and Mills and Boon bodice rippers went as far as women were prepared to go along the road to sexual fantasy. In response to an article I wrote in the *New Statesman,* a number of readers sent me letters with biological theories that held women's role in reproduction to be so wired-in genetically that desire could never be sundered from nurture. Sexuality, it was argued, was so close to nature that it seemed to resist other explanations that would account for the distinctive cultures of male and female lust.

Many women I talked to felt that intimacy in relationships was structured into their consciousness, beyond conditioning or the accidental historical moment of their birth. At the 1991 San Diego sex convention, a workshop leader told me a story about a men's group he had run. For one session, he had asked its participants to bring their wives or girlfriends. The men and women were divided into two separate groups and asked to go away and come up with a list of questions each would like to ask the other. When they reconvened, at the top of the women's list was: "Why is it that when I try to get close to you, you act like I'm trying to take something away from you?" What the men wanted to know, on the other hand, was "How important is penis size?"

Nowhere are those two sexual cultures more evident than in the contrast between the world of gay men and of heterosexual women. In 1979 I went to San Francisco to see a friend from London, a painter who had moved there in part to live in the world's greatest gay capital, known at the time as "Clone City." He was working as a waiter in a restaurant and I dropped in there for dinner. He pointed to the man at the next table. Last night he had had sex with him at a bathhouse, he said. Now the man refused to recognize him, let alone acknowledge that brief moment of connection. "I'm getting a bit fed up with all this," my friend said.

"Sometimes, instead of having sex with them, I want to ask them if they'd like to come back to the flat for tea." The world he described made me gape. I tried to imagine a woman getting all dressed up on a Saturday night to go out for gloryhole sex—sucking a disembodied cock that was stuck through a hole in a wall. As someone who had wholeheartedly climbed on board the sexual bandwagon of the sixties and who was, at that particular moment, sleeping with two men (one a nineteen-year-old student I taught, nine years my junior), I found it impossible to imagine a city full of women that could duplicate San Francisco's disconnected sexual marketplace.

San Francisco, at that moment, regarded itself as in the vanguard of revolutionary sexual politics, a far more radical agenda than had ever been imagined by swingers, swappers, or participants in group marriage. John Rechy, in an early nonfiction account of the Los Angeles scene of the late sixties, saw homosexuals as radical outlaws for whom the sex hunt was an act of art and of sabotage. For Rechy, "an acceptance of homosexuality— including, importantly, its tendency towards promiscuity—would result in a traumatic questioning of what, in the extreme, becomes oppressive within the heterosexual norm." The homosexual, he argued, would cause the heterosexual to ask a series of questions that would ultimately lead to the exposure of conventional sexual structures as little more than stagnant conformity: Why one wife? One husband? Why not lovers? Why marriage? Why sex with only one person? Why not open sex, open relationships? Why, necessarily, children?[1] In this model, bathhouse sex was capable of overturning civilization as we now know it.

Even at the time, however, I was not convinced. The San Francisco gay scene of the late seventies, just before AIDS, seemed to me to resemble a male-only fantasy, what men would get up to if left to their own devices, without women making irritating demands about commitment. It had constructed a secular religion based on worship of the phallus. In Randy Shilts's book *And the Band Played On,* about the early political conflicts within the gay community about AIDS, there is a doctor who seems to have reached the same conclusion:

Joe figured that the attraction to promiscuity and depersonalization of sex rested on issues surrounding a fear of intimacy. Joe knew these were not gay issues but male issues. The trouble was that, by definition, you had a gay male subculture in which there was nothing to moderate the utterly male values that were being adulated more religiously than any macho heterosexual could imagine. . . . Promiscuity was rampant because in an all-male subculture there was nobody to say "no"—no moderating role like that a woman plays in the heterosexual milieu. Some heterosexual males privately confided that they were enthralled with the idea of the immediate, available, even anonymous sex a bathhouse offered, if only they could find women who would agree.[2]

The average AIDS patient in those early days had had around 1,100 sexual partners. A few counted as many as 20,000.[3] By comparison, a sex survey of 34,000 readers of the American magazine *New Woman* in 1986 showed that by a small margin the majority of respondents had had less than five.[4] To my own eye, the density of "meanings" that encrusted the simple pleasure of cruising hid the meaninglessness of these encounters. If cruising had any political content it was not revolutionary at all, but more like a capitalist utopian vision of a sexual shopping mall, offering endless choice.

Not that heterosexual men were entirely unserved. In 1991, Sir Allan Green, the Director of Public Prosecutions, was forced to resign after he was arrested for speaking to a prostitute in Kings Cross, a red-light district of London. He received a great deal of sympathy from the most serious newspapers. *The Independent* dedicated a leader to his plight, headed "A Sad Resignation, A Bad Law," that called for the legalization of brothels. The incident called into question the long-held belief that men pay for sex because they cannot get it elsewhere, or that prostitutes fulfil sexual predilections no self-respecting wife would countenance in the marital bed. Green was a powerful man with that attribute of success, a "lovely wife and family" (after initially sticking by him as long as the media cameras were trained on the Green home, his wife left him and subsequently committed suicide). In the decades following the publication of *The Joy of Sex*, it seems unlikely that she, or other wives of men who use prostitutes, regards sex as an obligation men place on women, to be endured not enjoyed.

For the Kings Cross Collective of Prostitutes, the explanation for the continuing growth of sex work lies in men's economic power. Men are used to buying things when they want them. Research conducted among seventy men who visit prostitutes, carried out by the Public Health Research Unit of the University of Glasgow, confirms that more than half were married and most were in long-term relationships. While a minority wanted "specialist" services like S/M, anal sex, or transvestism, the theme that runs through the Glasgow research is that of control. "For some men the unemotional nature of the sex is the attraction," Dr. Neil McKeganey, co-director of the project, told *The Guardian* the day after the DPP's arrest. "There are no continuing obligations, either emotional or financial. There is also the attraction of clandestine sex: the illicit thrill is part of the attraction."[6] One man the project interviewed compared going to a prostitute to having his car serviced—"you tell them what you want done, and if they don't want to do it, you go elsewhere."[7] There was a hunger among the respondents for younger and younger women: "I like them as young as I can find them," one man said. "Early twenties, beyond that I'm not interested," said another. Dr. McKeganey understood that "in the view of many of the clients the relationship between themselves and the prostitute was not one of equals but a marked power imbalance between those whose sexual needs are paramount and those who, for a price, are there to meet those needs." One client told him, "[It's] the fact that you've got a bit more dominance: i.e. you've got the money in your pocket, then you've got the dominance over them." Prostitutes, for the punters, were a tabula rasa on which they could write their fantasies. Yet despite the clients' wild overestimation of the possibility of HIV infection (some thought that HIV levels among female prostitutes was as high as 70 percent, when most European studies put the figure at less than 5 percent) they continued to take risks.[8]

Prostitution continues to grow, both in the cities of Western countries and in the vast sex industries of Southeast Asia. In the bars of Bangkok, prepubescent village girls simulate sex acts. The simulation is not only of the act itself but a crude approximation of what passes for "sexy." The girls imitate what a grown woman might look like if she was feeling turned on. Inside those bars, a woman in her thirties, at the height of her sexual powers, is a misfit. The overriding symbol of the sexual woman is the tiny young girl. And for the men who take their sex holidays there, in the arms of these young teenagers they find an escape from the demands of the feminist West. I suspect that the persistence and even increase in the numbers of men using prostitutes, ironically, has something to do with the sexualization of women in the mainstream of society. Sex between men and women has become a two-way engagement. It is harder for men to find women who will lie back and take anything they are given, who will fulfil male fantasies without asking for the gratification of their own. When Cathérine in Buñuel's *Belle de Jour* becomes an afternoon prostitute, she discovers that her job is not to live out the baroque sexual fantasies she carries around in her head, but to become an actor in those of the punters, which seem particularly sordid and banal compared with the glorious direction, camera work, lighting, and casting of the "movies" she creates out of her own unconscious.

So why do women not go to male prostitutes when there are plenty of them about, in the shape of the young boys who populate the meatracks of our cities? Logically, there ought to be a great demand. In New York in particular there are armies of single women, the kind depicted in the film *Fatal Attraction*, "career women" without a partner but with the economic clout to buy a tasteful man. Gigolos have long been a feature of the lives of older, upper-class women, but in almost all cases they are gay men who act as escorts rather than sex providers. Bubbles Rothermere, the London society hostess whose husband lived more or less permanently in Paris with a Japanese hand model, was never without a boy to light her cigarettes and be seen on her arm as she arrived at another party. Madonna, currently one of the most powerful women in the world, seldom lacks a crowd of gay admirers, they feasting on her fame and camp cachet, she voyeuristically consumed by their sexual subculture.

When Gay Talese conducted his ten-year investigation into the American sex industry, he spent several months working as the manager of a New York massage parlor. He gradually became aware that the phone had never once rung with a call from a woman asking for the services of a male masseur. Talese was convinced that throughout New York there must be plenty of aging widows, spinsters, neglected wives, and liberated female executives "who might welcome a midday massage with erotic delicacies, including oral sex, in a balmy and bountiful East Side ambience that would offer some of the pampering of an Elizabeth Arden salon or a ladies' luxurious health club." Yet there seemed to be no take-up. In the major cities of Europe he found the same indifference. One sex therapist he met told him that a woman regards the penis as an alien object trying to enter her body; if a man is a stranger to a woman, his penis is a stranger to her as well. To take it inside her is to be invaded. Only when it is part of someone she trusts, loves, and desires, can the penis become familiar and can she allow it to enter and become part of her.[9] It is always the man, after all, who has the power of withdrawal. Violent intercourse can penetrate the most unwelcoming vagina.

Thirteen years after Talese's study was published, stories do occasionally surface of classy escort agencies that provide hardcore services for wealthy women. The early-eighties film *American Gigolo* painted a portrait of a male prostitute, his identity formed by his extensive wardrobe, another post-Vietnam nail in the coffin of machismo and authenticity. But if such agencies exist, few know where to locate them. For the female seeker after male prostitutes, there are a number of practical dangers that probably make the risks outweigh the benefits. New York, for example, is one of the most dangerous cities in the world for casual sex. Many male sex workers are bisexual or drug users or themselves visit HIV-infected individuals. Women, unlike men, are conditioned to associate the sexual encounter with potential consequences, specifically pregnancy. Buying sex, if it is to have a modicum of taste or class to it, costs a lot more than something off the street, as men know. To avoid the chance of danger or being physically hurt, a woman even thinking of paying for sex would have to pay a great deal for it—and women never earn as much as men. Then there is the obvious problem of possible impregnation. If a woman gets pregnant she generally likes to have a name, phone number, and preferably a decent human being on the other end to offer emotional support. Sex and emotion, in this sense, may be inseparable. In the end, sex does tend to make women physically vulnerable.

None of these arguments, it should be noted, requires biological explanations, or even ones that go very deeply into female psychology. Women simply have good practical reasons for not duplicating male behavior. It is, however, possible to imagine a brothel for female clients. Picture a health spa: a country house set amid gardens, with heated pools, Jacuzzis, and saunas. A pampering program of exercise classes, massage, facials, light, delicious, nutritious food, a luxurious bedroom, the company of other women—a temporary escape from the cares of everyday life. And, perhaps, on the menu of services to the body one ticks out on arrival, an evening visit to one's bed of a handsome young man, vetted by the management for HIV or other vicious diseases, armed with the best condoms money can buy, prepared to provide the most exquisite of sexual pleasures, the charge discreetly included with the bill presented on departure. Would there be takers? After the first year or two, when the bravest had tried it and liked it, I think so. Word would go round about the expertise of the "boys" the way women today trade the names of their hairdressers. Top boys would be stolen (cock-hunted) by other establishments.

My hunch is that the only thing that would hold many women back would not be modesty or squeamishness but their own lack of self-esteem, the awareness that no image exists in the world of the sexy older woman (unless she has applied technology to herself and looks twenty years younger than her actual age). The women who would like the service most and who could afford it, I suspect, would be the ones who would find the greatest gulf between themselves and their potential partners. They would know that these boys had no real desire, were only doing it for money. And in that knowledge would be their humiliation. Women are attracted to power, men to youth and beauty. Men have an extraordinary capacity for self-delusion when it comes to the attentions of a young and penniless woman.

If then the only differences between male and female sexuality are either practical or cultural, there seems to be the promise of a wholly undifferentiated desire, the sexual revolution that many women would like to see brought to a triumphant conclusion. Disposing of biology, as I think we must, what one appears to be left with is a postmodern reading of sexuality that holds that there is no human identity, just a shifting series of discourses, of which "sex" is one.

Since Foucault, it has been customary among certain academics no longer to think of sex as a biological drive, but as a series of culturally determined systems of knowledge, or ways of fashioning the self. Thomas Laqueur, who holds that sex is an artificial construct, not part of nature, illustrates this idea with a tale originally told by an eighteenth-century doctor in a medical text.

A young aristocrat, driven by poverty into the life of a religious order, came upon an inn whose owners were prostrate with grief over the death of their daughter that day. The innkeepers asked the monk to watch over the body, and during the long night, struck by the corpse's beauty, he forgot his vows. The next day, just as the coffin was about to be buried in the ground, the girl was felt to stir in her wooden prison and was subsequently aroused from what had actually been a coma. The parents were overjoyed until it turned out that the girl was pregnant, though she protested her innocence. Later her seducer returned and they were married. The case aroused considerable interest. Jacques-Jean Bruhier, who published it, offered it as a moral tale for the necessity of scientific testing to establish death. But another surgeon, Antoine Louis, pointed out that the monk was perfectly correct in assuming that the girl was no longer alive, for if she had been, it was impossible that she should not have given some sign of her orgasm. In the eighteenth century, any medical text or book on midwifery would confirm that a woman could not conceive without sexual pleasure.

But within only a hundred years, Laqueur points out, "the old valences were overturned."[10] In 1871, William Acton, a doctor, was to write:

> The majority of women (happily for society) are not very much troubled with sexual feeling of any kind. . . . Married men . . . or married women . . . would vindicate female nature from the vile aspersions cast on it by the abandoned conduct and ungoverned lusts of a few of its worst examples. . . . The best mothers, wives and managers of households, know little or nothing of sexual indulgences. . . . As a general rule, a modest woman seldom desires any sexual gratification for herself. She submits to her husband, but only to please him; and, but from the desire of maternity, would far rather be relieved from his attentions.[11]

This was an astonishing ideological reversal, Laqueur argues, a triumph of mind over nature:

> The commonplace of much contemporary psychology—that men want sex while women want relationships—is the precise inversion of pre-Enlightenment notions that, extending back to antiquity, equated friendship with men and fleshliness with women. Women, whose desires knew no bounds in the old scheme of things, and whose reason offered so little resistance to passion, became in some accounts creatures whose whole reproductive life might be spent anaesthetized to the pleasures of the flesh.*[12]

In the nineties, women seemed to be about to revert to this pre-Enlightenment model of female sexuality. The most supposedly basic elements of human sexuality—the orgasm, the existence of the clitoris, even the exact role of the sperm (which was once thought to be a homunculus that the man deposited in the uterus, a mere receptacle for growth)—have all been treated to major reinterpretations throughout history, and to say that women have, in some sense, a "fixed" sexual nature is absurd. Women's monogamy and men's promiscuity are no more innate than a woman's tolerance for getting up four times in the middle of the night to soothe a crying baby.

In the past twenty-five years there has been a real transformation, inverting long-cherished ideas about the swinging dolly-bird of the sixties and the sexually terrorized woman of the nineties. If women have never displayed their sexual pleasure before, it was because they had had no public arena in which to do so. A girls' night out at a Chippendales show was perhaps the only place where women could lose their inhibitions and

---

*In the 1970s, the American Psychiatric Association voted to overturn its previously held medical opinion that homosexuality was a mental illness, which prompted Senator David Norris, elected to Parliament as an openly gay man in Ireland, a country where homosexuality was illegal, to wonder if it were possible to vote on cancer no longer being an illness so that all the people could get up from their hospital beds and go home. And the common cold could be cleared up while we were about it.

express naked lust, and with the joy and laughter always absent among the silent men with their newspapers who glumly watch strippers or adult movies. According to one observer, women love to see a small penis; it is their way of humiliating the husbands and bosses who belittle them at home and at work. The male size-terror is one of the few sexual weapons women have over men. A safe-sex club in London, Night of the Ultra Vixens, taught young women in flesh-busting Gossard Wonderbras how to put on a condom with their teeth. There were party games—spin the dildo, snogging rounds, and stud line, in which the Ultra Vixens lined up tasty-looking people for a spot of performance kissing before a celebrity judging panel that awarded points for style and performance. Single women were particularly encouraged to come with the avowed intention of picking up men. The credo of the club was safe sex in the age of AIDS and postfeminist values: "It's okay to be brazenly seductive without putting out Come to Bed signals," said "Bunny Vixen" (aka Rebecca Tomlinson). "On the other hand women are perfectly in order to initiate sex if they want to. This club is about women's freedom of choice and broadening their sexual script. It's about being able to say yes, no or wear a condom."[13]

In literature, Alina Reyes's erotic novel *The Bear*, about a young woman who has an intense sexual affair with a middle-aged butcher, ironically played with the idea of flesh. Julie Burchill's *Ambition* depicted a young woman journalist, greedy for power, who takes on seven sexual labors to achieve the editorship she craves. *Ambition* was a movement onward from the shopping-and-fucking novels of the seventies and eighties, like those of Judith Krantz, which had always included set-piece explicit sex scenes inserted into the text like so many plums in a pie and just as easily extractable if you pushed in a thumb. Susan Street, Julie Burchill's heroine, is "a creature without conscience or scruples"[14] (an ironic stab at the title of one of Krantz's books), a postfeminist who would prefer to take her chances in the free market and find her own way than be dragged down by women's libbers who fight for equality.[15] A minor character is a designer dyke and member of an international "Muffia." The designer dyke was another eighties icon, not unlike Thatcher herself in her independence from men and capacity to fuck women over. Susan Street, like Catherine in *Basic Instinct,* is multisexual. For ambition she will perform in a three-way sex act with two other women in a bar in Thailand or be tied up and gang-banged by two African men. Throughout her "ordeal" she engages in a dialogue with her tormenter that inverts the discursive narrative of de Sade's *Justine.* Here it is the "victim" who justifies her amoral sexual autonomy. The sex in *Ambition,* sold openly in bookstores and airports, is as pornographic or more so than anything one would find in a top-shelf magazine or X-rated video.

The only explanation that could account for this explosion of female sexuality was that throughout the eighties, when state repression of desire was at its most threatening, women were undergoing a radical psychological shift in their sexual makeup. The sexual revolution had not, in fact, stopped with the elections of Reagan and Thatcher. It had been internalized and developed in private. In 1973, Nancy Friday had charted the sexual fantasies of American women in her book *A Secret Garden.* It was an interior life that most men did not even believe existed. In her follow-up study, *Women on Top,* published in 1991, she argued that "the desire to initiate and control sex—indeed to continue sex until the woman's full sexual appetite is satisfied" was the underlying theme of the new fantasies.[16] In place of the old dreams of rape, there was Cassie, a twenty-nine-year-old MBA with a brokerage firm who found that when she "was in a competitive or supervisory capacity with guys, a real sexual tension entered into the situation."[17] Other women fantasized about tying men up or making love to a virgin.

Nancy Friday speculated that the rape fantasy had vanished because women no longer needed the psychological excuse of being "forced" to enjoy sex. Furthermore, they had a new erotic vocabulary and shared identity with which to articulate their sexual feelings. And even if the world was not a safe place in which to act out their erotic desires, in their fantasies they could liberate themselves. *Women on Top* demonstrated the distance that the sexual revolution had taken women—all the way, so that their fantasies were now barely distinguishable from those of men.

The nihilism of the eighties, the seductive attractions of death and closure, the canceling of tomorrow until further notice, was ended by the renewal of female sexuality, the vital force whose power men had always been wary of. Annie Sprinkle, *42nd Street* dancer, porno film star, prostitute in massage parlors, cable-TV hostess, porn-magazine editor, performance artist, and self-styled "Shirley MacLaine of Porn," issued her *Post Porn Modernist Manifesto,* which brought together the new sexual vision:

> Post Porn Modernists celebrate sex as the nourishing life-giving force. We embrace our genitals as part, not separate, from our spirits. We utilize sexually explicit words, pictures and performances to communicate our ideas and emotions. We denounce sexual censorship as anti-art and inhuman. We empower ourselves by this attitude of sex-positivism. And with this love of our sexual selves we have fun, heal the world and endure.[18]

I had heard this theme before, from a local government officer who loved control: "The sixties was the era of the free sexual spirit," she had written. "The nineties must be the era of the loving spirit. Free enough to give and receive love, but loving enough to care about the dangers of unrequited sex and to curb disease with mutual trust and technological understanding. . . . I feel that the nineties has a lot to offer the young in terms of sex."

The greatest post-porn modernist of them all is, of course, Madonna. What Madonna has demonstrated is that economic power gives women freedom that they cannot have if they are dependent. In other words, a woman has shown other women what it is like to be a man, with a woman's body and a dick in the brain. Madonna has broken free of the sexual conventions that rule women's lives. She and a buddy would go out to Danceteria, pick out the cutest boys, go right up and kiss them on the mouth, take their phone numbers, and, while they were watching, tear up the piece of paper. She would ambush men in elevators.[19] She would get her driver to take her cruising the Lower East Side picking up banji-boys, street-tough Puerto Ricans whom she invited into her car to be screwed while driven around the block. Then they were dropped off right where she found them. She liked them really young.[20] She would go up to Club Nine, where the requirement for admission was a nine-inch prick. She ran measuring contests—the boys would line up, unzip, and with great ceremony she would measure them and write down the results in her little black book.[21] She was known, in gay parlance, as a size queen. Her 1992 album, *Erotica,* begins ominously enough with the figure of Madonna as cult dominatrix, runs into the great old standard "Fever," and disintegrates, with a giggle, in an extremely funny song about oral sex, almost in the style of Mae West, raiding the vocabulary of the fried-chicken industry for its most famous slogan—"Finger-Lickin' Good." Criticized, she compared her sexuality to Mick Jagger's or Prince's and that shut people up.[22] I suspect that the enormous hostility Madonna generates is because she demolishes everyone's pet theories about female sexuality: that women can't separate sex from emotion and they won't do oral.

A frequent criticism of her book *Sex* was that it was just pornography and, priced at fifty dollars or twenty-five pounds, it would be cheaper to go down to a newsstand and buy a smutty magazine. Such a critique begs the question of what the book was *for.* It was not intended as a gallery of pinups for male Madonna fans to buy (though that was who formed the queues outside bookstores on the morning of publication), but a manual of postmodern, postfeminist sexuality. Its agenda is first to give women sexual permission and then to attempt to establish a female erotic language. Traditionally it has been understood that while the male sexual imagination is visual, the female equivalent needs to be satisfied in narrative form. Fetishism, Camille Paglia suggests, "a practice which like most of the sex perversions is confined to men, is clearly a conceptualizing of symbol-making activity. Man's vastly greater commercial patronage of pornography is analogous."[23] But literate narratives run counter to the nature of contemporary culture. Madonna, it is certain, can't write; she assembles her identity in performance, in the shape-changing enhanced by video technique that is the antithesis of the old modernist preoccupation with authenticity. If women are deprived of what Camille Paglia has called "eye culture," then they can have no access to the discourses of a sexualized postmodern medium. Women, Madonna understands, must come to an accommodation with porn, the huge and shadowy postindustrial empire that permeates contemporary imagery.

So alien is the idea of bald-headed lesbians with tattoos to the sensibilities of the average newspaper columnist that a verbal recounting of the pictures in *Sex* sounds like a description of postcards from hell. In fact the images are tamer, livelier, funnier than one might imagine. They draw, of course, on the stylish sex of S/M, but these photographs depict a women's world. Even Madonna can be shocked as one of the lesbians shows her her clit ring and laughs as the star grimaces with surprise and disgust. From a reading of Nancy Friday's nineties fantasies, there is no doubt that many women do work through, in their minds, the lexicon of images Madonna's ballsiness has given her the chutzpah to print (and make oodles of money from). Over and over, these visual fantasies play with ideas of power, from the subordination of the body by physical restraints to an appropriation of male dominance. The most winsomely erotic pictures in the book are of Madonna gently (but with a hint of teeth) kissing a boy with long curly black hair and a cross round his neck, or applying lipstick to him:

> Sex with the young can be fun if you're in the mood [she writes]. One of the best experiences I ever had was with a teenage boy. I think he was a virgin. He hardly had any pubic hair. He was Puerto Rican . . . he never went to school so I started to give him reading assignments. I'd make him read out loud. Like Henry Miller's the Tropic of Cancer or something really arousing. . . . Then one day his parents kicked him out of his apartment and he wanted to know if he could spend the night at my house. I told him he could but I only had one bed. So we both got in it and I couldn't sleep, so I had sex with him and it was really awesome because he was so young and in wonderment of it all. He was fearless. He would do anything. . . . I was so turned on it was probably the most erotic sex I ever had. But he gave me crabs. That's what you get. So you win some and you lose some.[24]

Was this pornography? No, not in the sense that Andrea Dworkin would understand it. Real live sex workers have not been economically and psychologically oppressed by the activity. By publishing *Sex*, Madonna triumphantly proved what porn stars, strippers, and prostitutes have always claimed—that in the end it is the paying customer, not the sex worker, who gets screwed. Many women's objections to pornography had been with the aesthetics of an industry geared to high turnover at low cost. Madonna's fame sprayed onto porn a glitz and a chic that it had never had before, even in the pages of *Playboy*, whose soft-focus, lip-glossed center-folds have a dated seventies look. But if you took away the poverty-stricken images, the harsh lighting, and the cheap makeup, hardcore porn could look like a spread from *Vogue*. In fact fashion had been borrowing from porn for years. Madonna didn't sanitize porn, she gave it authority. Pornography, Madonna has taught us, is the most potent postmodern entity. It is impossible to arrive at any universal definition of it. As Rosalind Coward has argued, pornography has no intrinsic meaning; it is not a thing but a "shifting regime of representations."[25] It is a blank slate onto which we write our desires. By feminizing porn, Madonna has lanced feminist anger against the sex industry as a clear visual expression of misogyny.

The Year of the Hardbody has given rise to the belief that a second sexual revolution is imminent, one that would accomplish three things: reassert the gains made in the sixties and vanquish the New Right; abandon the sex-negative cul-de-sac along which feminism had taken female desire in the seventies; and formulate an overdue sexual language for the clitoris. The reign of the phallus has been a very long one. It rears up throughout Greco-Roman culture. Phalluses used to be worn as good-luck charms or displayed at places of potential danger, such as corners, bridges, and entrances. They guarded fields in the form of herms—busts of gods atop a stone plinth with a penis jutting out from the unmodeled material. Phalluses were afforded respect, even worship. The phallus stands in for and is imbued with the qualities of its owner. In contrast, the vulva is rarely seen in real life and in art. The female genitals lack a convenient and well-designed shape.[26] There is a red-figure vase circa 430–420 B.C. in the British Museum's *secretum* of X-rated antiquities that depicts a woman watering a row of phalluses rising from the ground like a bed of asparagus. This female service of the visible totem of male sexuality and power has gone on long enough. A clitoris-and-vagina-centered sexual and cultural revolution is an inevitable next step. No sexual revolution can be fully accomplished without a proper equation between male and female sexuality.

Madonna has appointed herself to the vanguard of this next phase in the evolution of our sexual lives. But before we all follow her leadership and hail her as the harbinger of the new life, let us look a little more closely at her politics. First, Madonna, to herself, is not just the most successful evolution of women in pop. She is what you must be to be anyone at all in the East Village club scene she came out of: an Artist. If America had once offered the prospect of freedom to the pioneers and dissidents escaping repressive regimes in Europe and elsewhere, by the eighties that freedom was manifest only in capitalism itself, in the illusion of consumer choice that was no more than a variegated form of social control. There were other restraints: an increasingly bureaucratized government and the religious Right with its insistence on conventional morality. The only possible role left for the wannabe outlaw is that of the artist. Not the artist of the Renaissance with his patrons and indissoluble links to the Church. The artist from the eighties onward is like the child in nursery school; any attempt to impede self-expression is both damaging and akin to child abuse. Self-expression leads to "statements" that are sanctified because they are being made by artists. In the hands of dealers and managers, those statements usually amount to an expression of the artist's desire to make money.

Within such a climate, artistic freedom and sexual freedom became inseparable. The most inarticulate mumblings about sexuality are now statements to be treated as artistic products. In an interview with Andrew Neil (a representative of the New Right) in the *Sunday Times Magazine*, Madonna was asked, "Do you see yourself as being some kind of sexual revolutionary . . . with a messianic desire to spread this sexual revolution?" Absolutely, she replied, except that *this* revolution would be a human revolution; sexual repression was what was wrong with most "bad behavior." Didn't we go through that sexual revolution in the sixties? Neil asked. "Yes," she replied. "But everybody was high and I am doing it without the help of hallucinatory drugs, whatever." Her book had nothing to do with the social liberalism of the sixties, she asserted: "It's one on one, it's human beings learning how to love their neighbor and tolerate each other."[27] The final words of *Sex* are: "A lot of people are afraid to say what they want. That's why they don't get what they want."[28]

Americans have such a repugnance for history that it is hardly surprising that Madonna has a hazy idea about the drug culture of the sixties.

Which is why much of what she believes is new is merely a revival of the crude political justifications for swinging. Nothing Madonna has said about sexual freedom would have been startling to a meeting of Emanuel Petrakis's Sexual Emancipation Movement. Terry Garrity was popularizing oral sex two decades previously. What it boils down to is the message that if everyone fucked, the world would be a better place, as Richard Ogar and the Sexual Freedom League once believed. And there is no chance of this vision being co-opted by capitalism: Madonna *is* capitalism.

But a better place in what way? There is an absence here, a great hole where politics ought to be. She has thrown out of it "social liberalism," by which she must mean the idea of social programs for widespread change—the voter-registration campaigns, Lyndon Johnson's War on Poverty, equal pay, union organizing for the farmworkers—the great reforming vision of the sixties that genuinely believed concrete change could be accomplished. Madonna's programmatic platform for a better world is restricted to issues that affect her personally, such as abortion and censorship. Madonna's message, I was assured by a male intellectual fan, is that "women can do anything they want." But it is *not true*.

The world of *Sex*, Madonna concedes, is a perfect place, with no AIDS, no real violence, no pregnancy. Outside it is rape, abuse, disease, and a culture hostile to women's sexuality that is not expressed in acceptable forms. *Sex* is a utopia with no practice to get there. In place of politics we have ambition, selfishness, greed, and amorality—"If you're all as rich as me you too can make a fortune from your fantasies." In Madonna's pursuit of self at any price I detect the lost soul of a lapsed Catholic for whom morality is an oppressive external intervention that assaults the unconscious. The whole of morality must be rejected, because Catholicism never lets you think for yourself and construct your own version of ethics. "What the heart wants, the heart wants," Woody Allen has said in defense of his affair with his stepdaughter. Fuck what anyone else wants.

But a want is also a lack in another sense of the word. Madonna's sexual politics, everything to do with sex and nothing to do with politics, are merely a filling of a personal emptiness.

So it must be. Postmodernism's message denies that true conflicts of interest either exist or could be resolved if they did. If you don't believe in progress, conflicts of interest are simply semantics. The postfeminist woman is politically shaped by postmodernism. Like Madonna, the Ranters rejected the notion of sin, which they saw as part of the coercive power of the state. But, unlike Madonna, they lived in an age of mass action and the connecting up of issues. Sexual freedom was only part of a larger movement of social and political change that was taking place all about them—in the attempts to extend the franchise, the redistribution of wealth, the disestablishment of the Church. For all men and women to be passionate, to live out their desires, sex had to be unshackled from reproduction and the body liberated from poverty. They dreamed of a world of free men and women. Postfeminists cannot campaign because of their horror of being associated with what they call "victims"—feckless, hopeless, always whining about what they don't have. Postfeminists are easily bored. They can't run the risk of being feminists because it would require them to abandon the quest for perpetual self-transformation and have some real thoughts about real people. They would have to ask why having children drives women into poverty. They would be obliged to contemplate the fact that most women do dreary, unpleasant, unglamorous jobs for male bosses and little pay.

One of the germs of this book was in an article I wrote for *The Observer* on my quarrel with postfeminism. It provoked a reply from Carla Garapedian, a young American television producer living in London:

As one of those mini-skirted professionals, why did I stay silent? It was partly out of wishful thinking but also because, like other women, I didn't have anyone to follow. Nothing to rally around. No new battle cry. No new identification of the problems. Women coalesce around issues, but what are the issues for women in the nineties? We've lost our vigilance, the mental habit of thinking of gender as a political issue. Ask today's women what they talk about in the workplace. In my office, where almost all the women are under the age of thirty, we rarely talk about women's rights. If we do, it is always prefaced, shamefacedly, by "I'm not a feminist, but . . ." Feminism has gone out of the coffee-lounge and effectively underground. Postmodernism, and its progeny postfeminism, doesn't have any ideas about how to overcome the genuine conflicts between men and women but its real danger is in denying that the conflict itself exists. Its worst attribute is that it's made some of us believe, without quite knowing why, that social change is no longer possible.

Are we actually constructing a post-phallic sexual language? Across America, according to Nancy Friday, Catholic virgins are having fantasies that involve group sex, bondage and discipline, and alsatian dogs. How, one asks, can they know how to imagine it? The answer is the pornographic video, swapped on the school bus as cigarette cards once were or watched in groups at slumber parties. Contemporary young women are acquainted with an exhaustive variety of what used to be called deviance, explored twenty-five years earlier only by the prostitute and the hardcore sex industry. American as a packet of Trojans, Nancy Friday is unaware that fantasies express themselves in cultural languages. She believes that the increasing appearance of lesbian motifs refers to our unconscious desire to be once again at Mom's breast. There is an alternative explanation: that the expression of sexuality in America and Britain is depicted almost exclusively through the female body, which becomes a universal object of eroticized desire. She fails to discuss the role of pornography available at the newsagent in constructing fantasies. Why are so many of the ones she cites so unreadable, with their clichéd and conventional plotlines? Has porn robbed us of primal creativity? In Madonna's *Sex* we also see the poverty of the female sexual imagination. Erotica is an assemblage of sub-gay porn—gay, because in the milieu in which Madonna moves, that of the New York performance artist, that is the current fashionable expression of sexuality.

The raunchy woman is in part a media artefact because she represents a huge new potential market for capitalism. Sexual history from the mid-seventies onward is a chronicle of the advance of the male sexual imagination through pornography, not as the erotic expression of male/female sexual desire but the male attempt to reintegrate his world after the assault on it by a sexual revolution that challenged phallic jurisdiction. The sixties' sexual revolution had been all about authenticity, about throwing off inhibitions and hypocrisy, about doing one's own thing. Sexual freedom was posed as a series of civil liberties. The sex industry seized hold of part of that polemic. If a guy liked to beat off while looking at dirty pictures or dirty movies, then why not? The sexual revolution had given him that right. But the extension of pornography had a curious effect. Instead of becoming a minor adjunct to the main event, sex itself, it saturated external reality, becoming part of mainstream culture. Sex as image became far more significant than sex itself. It rapidly discovered that new technology would free it from legal restraint. Sex could take a multiplicity of forms, one of which is cyberporn. In the eighties, California had given way to Thailand as the capital of erotica. Now it is reasserting its supremacy. A San Francisco–based magazine called *Future Sex* is a primer on how to have sex with a computer. The sex industry was once tightly ghettoized in certain sections of cities, subject to close government scrutiny. Now anyone with an Apple Mac can access "Virtual Valerie," designed by Chicago-based Mike Saenz, a former illustrator for Marvel Comics. "Virtual Valerie," costing ninety-nine dollars, is described by her inventor as "a simulated human being," "a sexual date on a disc."[29]

Purists might argue that the problem with "Valerie" is that you can't touch her or fuck her. Valerie is to future cyberporn what the box camera is to the camcorder. Virtual Reality scientists are currently developing a sense of robotic touch through a Teletact glove, the product of experiments with pneumatic technology and pressure pads that will be used to allow people to manipulate objects through remote-controlled robots in dangerous situations like nuclear power stations.[30] This will undoubtedly be hijacked by the Virtual Reality cybersex industry. Valerie has had so much fan mail that Saenz has created a successor, "Virtual Valerie 2." But there is no "Virtual Victor" on the horizon. Saenz's creative department consists entirely of heterosexual males who, he admits, "have a hard time with other kinds of fantasies."[31] Men once had millennia to form their sexual dreams. Women have very little time to create ones independent of cybersex. Now that we're all plugged into the global communications fantasy, we don't have dreams anymore. MTV does that for us.

Can we imagine a future sexuality? While I was researching this book, I glimpsed it, ironically in the person of a woman already middle-aged when the sexual revolution began: Betty Dodson, who had been the victim of Germaine Greer's polemical assault. She was sixty-two when I met her, in the apartment where she had lived since she first came to New York in the sixties. She was born in 1929, in the Kansas Bible Belt. As a young girl she masturbated to fantasies of her wedding night and herself in an elegant nightgown walking toward a faceless bridegroom. As she unveiled her body in this fantasy, she came. She masturbated so much that when she finally saw her own genitals by the light of a window using her mother's ivory hand mirror, she was shocked by what she saw and believed that the lips of her vulva were deformities produced by self-abuse. She was married for a time but it was not until the sixties that she discovered, from a male lover, that all female genitals were like hers.

She began to reexamine romance. She decided that when she fell in love, she lost her center. She turned her self over to the relationship and for the time it went on, she was, she believed, temporarily insane. Then there would be the terrible period of breaking up and the anger and the frustration and the guilt and the misery and then she would go on to the next man and do it again. So she began to declare that what she was doing was mainlining emotions. In 1969 she swore off romantic love. It was bullshit, it was illusion. It was about her fantasy of the person, and of course the reality of the person would interrupt that fantasy. She threw herself into the alternative sexual society I have described in this book: she held group sex orgies in her apartment; she went out to California to take part in the Sandstone experiment and terrified many of the men there with her assertive female passions; she became bisexual; she visited the Vault, the S/M club from which many of the images in Madonna's *Sex* were excavated; she loves Madonna but dislikes porn videos—in the age of AIDS, she says, we're so frightened of sex that the only way we can involve ourselves with it is separated by a sheet of glass.

When she went into menopause she didn't at first identify the hot flashes. She was smoking some marijuana from Hawaii one day when suddenly she got a huge body rush: simultaneously she would feel heat and a rush in the pelvis that would move up to her forehead and form little beads of sweat, and she would take a deep breath and say, "Aaaaah, it's delicious." She called them her "heat orgasms." One day she described them to a friend, who said, "Betty, that's menopause." She could feel the aging thing taking her down into a depression. She saw herself on the dungheap of old age. So she said, "Fuck this shit, I'm going to turn my sixties into my most powerful dynamic decade and the sex will be different and I'm not operating with all those old images. I'd like to go through this lifetime with my own body and my own face, without hormones, without surgery." It was a blow when she had to get glasses and dentures, but she came to see the former as a fashion accessory and the latter as a sex aid: "When it comes to oral sex, I take out my teeth, honey, and you're going to get a blow job that'll take you on a trip. I have a little ritual that goes with it, I play different roles. I'm the masked bandit and I tie a silk scarf around my face because I'm not going to be seen without teeth, I can't handle it so you find your limits." She saw that the only answer to the problem of monogamy, sex, and aging was to be in community, to have a sense of fluidity of people coming in and out of our lives, of shift and change.

I know, I know. Romantic love is sure to retain its hold over us into any future that we can imagine. At sixty-two many people have given up sex completely for the greater pleasures of food or gardening or some hobby or spiritual contemplation, relieved to have got finally shut of those inconvenient desires that plague us. But this image of a woman still struggling to retain and affirm her sexuality is one that I hope will go with us into the next millennium.

Writing a book with a title like *Sexing the Millennium* puts one under the obligation of prescription, if not actual prophecy. When I try to imagine a future sexuality, it contains the overthrow of phallocentrism, an end to repressive laws on homosexuality and practices like clitorectomy. But it also attempts to understand how real people could have real sexual lives. I have been fascinated by how, beneath the manufactured political rhetoric of gay liberation, many gay men, it seems, have managed to structure long-term relationships that were confident enough to be non-monogamous. They did have love, companionship, and commitment; these were the qualities they worked at in their relationships. Sex was left to casual encounters, free to take place in an arena of adventure and danger. Gay male couples managed to preserve the excitement and the tension of sex within a form of nuclear family and they often succeeded in doing so without the jealousy, possessiveness, and insecurity that characterize heterosexual relationships. Christopher Lasch, in a critique of the notion of "progress," has argued for the social and psychological necessity of limits. I suspect that most people have neither the stomach, the time, nor the sex drive for revolutionary promiscuity. I do not, however, think that "traditional family values" will serve us into the next century either. With longer lifespans, we cannot be expected to sustain fifty years of monogamous married life. I think we will find some sort of accommodation with non-monogamy beyond the prohibitive activity of adultery.

And what about the future for women? I began by looking into the darkness with that question, "Has there *been* a sexual revolution?" The answer must be yes, though it is not complete. Fifty years ago people believed that technology would liberate sexuality. We now know there is never likely to be a birth-control method that is safe, fully effective, non-invasive, easy to use, acceptable to both men and women, and not offensive to any religious group. In that sense the future has turned out to be a big disappointment. But we have something and we could have abortion on demand as a safety net. Women have gained unprecedented sexual freedom as a result of greater control over reproductive choice. Sex is no longer "men's business." We are learning to take our pleasure rather than always give it. But the future still damages women. Postfeminism, my argument goes, is bogus, vacuous, and devoid of new ideas. Because a sense of time is absent, it is unable to predict its own future. What happens when the postfeminist hardbody hits forty, then fifty? Women have good cause to fear the breakdown of marriage. One of the most panting sexual agendas of the sixties was the sexualization of children. A decade that has witnessed the long-term effects on children of sexual abuse by adults has tarnished that particular dream. In place of it should be the eroticization of our whole lives beyond puberty. We live in a society in which single, divorced, and separated women over the age of forty are doomed to sexlessness because our phallic culture has turned the young girl into *the* cult object of desire. So many people are sexually off-limits—the old, the disabled, the ugly. For Madonna, the one perversion she draws the line at is sex with a fat person. When a man looks at an older woman, he sees how time ravages youth. When a woman looks at an older man, she sees maturity and, in it, his history. We need to defeat the male gaze. Time can be an erotic dimension.

The alternative is a future sexuality formed by the marketplace, the forward impulse of which would be the shifting basis of consumer demand. Ironically, electronic technology would rob us of the capacity to shape our own dreams. There has never been a time when people did not long for a more equitable reordering of social conditions. Nor, I believe, will we stop trying to create an ethical society in which we would act out the passionate adventure of our lives. Perhaps sex is just the ghost of freedom—but, until we have Utopia, it can speak eloquently of what the heart desires.

References

1 What Sexual Revolution?

1 Bret Easton Ellis, *American Psycho*, p. 370
2 Helen Zahavi, *Dirty Weekend*, p. 10
3 *Ibid.*, p. 185
4 *The Independent*, March 24, 1992
5 *The Independent*, March 14, 1992
6 *The Guardian*, February 26, 1992
7 *The Independent*, February 22, 1992
8 *The Times*, February 4, 1992
9 *The Independent*, December 14, 1991
10 *The Independent*, March 20, 1992
11 *The Times*, January 29, 1992
12 *The Guardian*, April 16, 1992
13 *The Observer*, March 8, 1992
14 *Law Society Gazette*, September 30, 1991
15 *The Guardian*, March 28, 1992
16 *Evening Standard*, November 24, 1992
17 *Suck*, 1972
18 Germaine Greer, *The Change: Women, Aging and the Menopause*, p. 2
19 Sheila Jeffreys, *Anticlimax: A Feminist Perspective on the Sexual Revolution*, p. 316
20 *Ibid.*, p. 311
21 *The Guardian*, October 13, 1992
22 Anaïs Nin, *A Spy in the House of Love*, p. 45
23 Camille Paglia, *Sexual Personae: Art and Decadence from Nefertiti to Emily Dickinson*, p. 3
24 Lawrence Osborne, *The Poisoned Embrace: A Brief History of Sexual Pessimism*, p. 235
25 *Ibid.*, p. 237

2 The Sexual Heresy

1 Christopher Hill, *The World Turned Upside Down: Radical Ideas During the English Revolution*, p. 70
2 Norman Cohn, *The Pursuit of the Millennium: Revolutionary Millenarians and Mystical Anarchists of the Middle Ages*, p. 13
3 Quoted in Hill, op. cit., p. 161
4 Quoted in Cohn, op. cit., p. 169
5 *Ibid.*, p. 151
6 *Ibid.*, p. 160
7 Hill, op. cit., pp. 184–5
8 *Ibid.*, p. 13
9 "A Fiery Flying Roll," *ibid.*, p. 170

10 *Ibid.*, p. 256
11 Richard Baxter, 1696, quoted in Cohn, op. cit., p. 291
12 Hill, op. cit., p. 259
13 Cohn, op. cit., pp. 299–300
14 Hill, op. cit., p. 257
15 *Ibid.*, pp. 258–9
16 Donald Pennington and Keith Thomas (eds.), *Puritans and Revolutionaries: Essays in Seventeenth Century History Presented to Christopher Hill*, pp. 257–8
17 *Ibid.*
18 Hill, op. cit., pp. 307–8
19 Gay Talese, *Thy Neighbor's Wife*, p. 341
20 *Ibid.*, p. 346
21 Steve Humphreys, *A Secret World of Sex*, p. 181
22 Elaine Showalter, *Sexual Anarchy*, p. 199
23 *Ibid.*, p. 39
24 Sheila Rowbotham and Jeffrey Weeks, *Socialism and the New Life: The Personal and Sexual Politics of Edward Carpenter and Havelock Ellis*, p. 10
25 *Ibid.*, p. 109
26 *Ibid.*, p. 85
27 *Ibid.*, p. 95
28 *Ibid.*, p. 120
29 Quoted in Marek Kohn, *Dope Girls: The Birth of the British Drug Underground*, p. 51
30 Daphne du Maurier, *Rebecca*, p. 284
31 H. C. Fischer and E. X. Dubois, *Sexual Life During the World War*, p. 161
32 Dora Russell, *The Tamarisk Tree*. Vol. I: *My Quest for Liberty and Love*, p. 69
33 *Ibid.*, p. 156
34 *Ibid.*, p. 198
35 *Ibid.*, p. 217
36 Norman Lewis, *Jackdaw Cake*, pp. 79–80
37 *The Independent on Sunday*, March 8, 1992
38 George Steiner, *In Bluebeard's Castle*, p. 44
39 Angela Carter, *The Sadeian Woman*, p. 147

3 The All-American Offshore Population Laboratory

1 Nora Ephron, "The Pill and I," in *The Sixties: The decade remembered now, by the people who lived it then*, pp. 71–2
2 Angus MacLaren, *A History of Contraception from Antiquity to the Present Day*, p. 27
3 John Guillebaud, *The Pill*, pp. 9–10
4 Richard Davenport-Hines, *Sex, Death and Punishment: Attitudes to Sex and Sexuality in Britain Since the Renaissance*, p. 18
5 John D'Emilio and Estelle B. Freedman, *Intimate Matters: A History of Sexuality in America*, p. 245
6 MacLaren, op. cit., pp. 181–2
7 *Ibid.*, pp. 216–17
8 *Ibid.*, p. 226
9 Alvin Toffler, *Future Shock*, p. 2
10 *The Guardian*, June 20, 1992

11 Quoted in Barbara Seaman, *Women and the Crisis in Sex Hormones*, p. 79

12 James Reed, *From Private Vice to Public Virtue*, p. 321

13 *Esquire*, December 1983

14 Reed, op. cit., p. 358

15 Annette Ramírez de Arellano and Conrad Seipp, *Colonialism, Catholicism and Contraception: A History of Birth Control in Puerto Rico*, p. 13

16 *Ibid.*, pp. 7–8

17 *Ibid.*, p. 17

18 *Ibid.*, p. 23

19 *Ibid.*, pp. 33–4

20 *Ibid.*, p. 47

21 *Ibid.*, p. 48

22 *Ibid.*, p. 49

23 Leonard Bernstein, January 6, 1949, "*West Side Story* Log," sleeve notes, *West Side Story*, Deutsche Grammophon, 1985

24 Ramírez de Arellano and Seipp, op. cit., p. 83

25 *Ibid.*, pp. 82–3

26 John A. Smith, *Ryder Memorial Hospital: An Unfolding Story of Health Care*, p. 2

27 Gregory Pincus Papers, Library of Congress (GPP)

28 GPP

29 GPP

30 Ramírez de Arellano and Seipp, op. cit., p. 116

31 GPP

32 GPP

33 GPP

34 *Time*, January 1, 1968

35 *The Observer Magazine*, April 19, 1970

36 Carl Djerassi, *The Politics of Contraception: Birth Control in the Year 2001*, p. 19

37 Susan C. M. Scrimshaw, "Women and the Pill: From Panacea to Catalyst," *Family Planning Perspectives*, Vol. 13. No. 6, Nov/Dec 1981

38 *Family Planning in the Sixties: Report of the Family Planning Association Working Party, September 1963*, Ch. 4, p. 1

39 *Ibid.*, Ch. 7, p. 13

40 *Ibid.*, p. 17

41 Barbara Seaman, *The Doctor's Case Against the Pill*, p. 65

4 The Country Run by Men in Dresses

1 Nell McCaffertey, *A Woman to Blame*, p. 164

2 *Ibid.*, p. 69

3 *Ibid.*, p. 87

4 Quoted *ibid.*, p. 28

5 Donnchadh O Corráin, "Prehistoric and Early Christian Ireland," in R. F. Foster (ed.), *The Oxford Illustrated History of Ireland*, p. 21

6 Quoted in Richard Ellmann, *James Joyce*, pp. 530–1

7 *The Guardian*, May 20, 1992

8 Uta Ranke-Heinemann, *Eunuchs for Heaven: The Catholic Church and Sexuality*, p. vii

9 *Ibid.*, p. 12

10 *Ibid.*, p. 13

11 *Ibid.*, p. 51

12 *Ibid.*, p. 59

13 *Ibid.*, p. 62

14 *Ibid.*, p. 46

15 *Ibid.*, p. 74

16 *Ibid.*, p. 104

17 *Ibid.*, p. 164

18 *Esquire,* December 1983

19 Reed, op. cit., pp. 353–4

20 Ronald Blair Kaiser, *The Encyclical That Never Was: The Story of the Commission on Population, Family and Birth,* p. 78

21 *Ibid.*, pp. 91–2

22 *Ibid.*, p. 95

23 *Ibid.*, p. 97

24 *Ibid.*, p. 129

25 *Ibid.*, p. 137

26 *Ibid.*, p. 145

27 *Ibid.*, p. 176

28 *Ibid.*, p. 223

29 *Ibid.*, p. 242

30 David Rice, *Shattered Vows,* p. 41

31 Kaiser, op. cit., p. 244

32 *The Observer Magazine,* January 18, 1970

33 Loretta McLaughlin, *The Pill, John Rock and the Church: The Biography of a Revolution,* p. 191

34 *Ibid.*, p. 230–1

35 "Offentenzeitung für die Katholische Geistlichkeit Deutschlands," October 1977, quoted in Ranke-Heinemann, op. cit., pp. 267–8

36 Rice, op. cit., p. 42

5 Our Age Buys a Fun Fur

1 *Time,* April 13, 1966

2 Jonathon Green, *Days in the Life: Voices from the English Underground 1961–1967,* p. 86

3 Christopher Booker, *The Neophiliacs: A Study of the Revolution in English Life in the Fifties and Sixties,* p. 109

4 *Ibid.*, p. 262

5 *Mail on Sunday,* April 21, 1991

6 Booker, op. cit., pp. 42–3

7 Brigid Keenan, *The Women We Wanted to Look Like,* p. 164

8 Valerie Steele, *Fashion and Eroticism: Ideals of Feminine Beauty from the Victorian Era to the Jazz Age,* p. 239

9 *Ibid.*, p. 241

10 Vance Packard, *The Sexual Wilderness: The Contemporary Upheaval in Male-Female Relationships,* p. 17

11 *Ibid.*, p. 165

12 *The Observer Magazine,* August 27, 1967

13 Nik Cohn, *Ball the Wall,* p. 293

14 *The Observer Magazine,* loc. cit.

15 Cohn, op. cit., p. 293

16 Quoted in Joel Lobenthal, *Radical Rags: Fashions of the Sixties,* p. 139

17 Cohn, op. cit., p. 281

18 *Ibid.*, p. 285

19 *Daily Mail,* August 8, 1968

20 Cohn, op. cit., p. 309

21 *Ibid.*, p. 311

22 George Carstairs, *This Island Now,* p. 55

23 Noel Annan, *Our Age: The Generation that Made Post-War Britain,* p. 461

24 *Ibid.*, p. 101
25 *Ibid.*, p. 103
26 *Ibid.*, p. 107
27 *Ibid.*, p. 116
28 *Ibid.*, p. 167
29 Brigid Brophy, *Don't Never Forget: Collected Views and Reviews*, p. 23
30 Brian Braithwaite, *The Business of Women's Magazines*, p. 35
31 *Nova*, October 1967
32 Braithwaite, op. cit., p. 38
33 *Nova*, September 1965
34 *Nova*, February 1966
35 *Nova*, October 1966
36 *Nova*, September 1968
37 Braithwaite, op. cit., p. 38
38 *Nova*, September 1967
39 *Nova*, April 1965

6 Fun, Fun, Fun

Note: References to *Cosmopolitan* magazine are to the U.S. edition except where otherwise stated
1 *Cosmopolitan* (U.K. ed.), February 1992
2 Helen Gurley Brown, *Sex and the Single Girl*, p. 7
3 *Ibid.*, p. 204
4 *Ibid.*, p. 209
5 *Ibid.*, pp. 210–11
6 *Ibid.*, pp. 2–4
7 Barbara Ehrenreich, Elizabeth Hess, Gloria Jacobs, *Remaking Love: The Feminization of Sex*, p. 2
8 *Cosmopolitan*, July 1965
9 *Ibid.*
10 *Cosmopolitan*, September 1966

11 *Ibid.*
12 *Cosmopolitan*, February 1968
13 *Cosmopolitan*, October 1965
14 *Cosmopolitan*, May 1969
15 *Cosmopolitan*, October 1969
16 *Cosmopolitan*, no date available
17 "J," *The Sensuous Woman*, pp. 122–3
18 *Ibid.*, p. 122
19 *Ibid.*, pp. 9–10
20 *Ibid.*, p. 27
21 Terry Garrity, *Story of "J": The Author of* The Sensuous Woman *Tells the Bitter Price of Her Crazy Success*, p. 53
22 *Ibid.*, p. 199
23 *Ibid.*, p. 83
24 *Cosmopolitan*, July 1971
25 Linda Wolfe, *The Cosmo Report*, p. 208
26 *Ibid.*, p. 209
27 *Ibid.*, p. 216
28 *Ibid.*, p. 229
29 *Ibid.*, pp. 303–4
30 *Cosmopolitan*, September 1987

7 A Clarion Call to the Strenuous Life
1 *The People*, November 1, 1964
2 Sexual Emancipation Movement Newsletter, No.22
3 SEM Newsletter, No.16
4 SFL Archive
5 SFL Archive (the last names of the bride and groom have been omitted at the request of the owner of the archive)
6 *Ibid.*

7 Herbert Marcuse, *Five Lectures: Psychoanalysis, Politics and Utopia*, p. 92

8 Quoted in Gerald Howard (ed.), *The Sixties: Art, Politics and Media of Our Most Explosive Decade*, p. 216

9 Paul Robinson, *The Freudian Left: Wilhelm Reich, Geza Roheim, Herbert Marcuse*, pp. 239–40

10 Jefferson Poland, *Sex Freedom Marchers*, p. 11

11 *Ibid.*, pp. 12–13

12 *Ibid.*, p. 14

13 *Ibid.*, pp. 14–15

14 "Free Speech Comes to Berkeley," Howard (ed.), op. cit., p. 132

15 Poland, op. cit., p. 16

16 *Ibid.*, p. 19

17 SFL Archive

18 Jefferson Poland, "Sexual Freedom League Grows Older," December 25, 1967, typescript, SFL Archive

19 SFL Archive

20 Poland, "Sexual Freedom League Grows Older"

21 *Ibid.*

22 *Ibid.*

23 SFL Archive

24 *Ibid.*

25 Richard Ogar, *San Francisco BALL*, No.6, September 18, 1970

26 *Ibid.*

27 Abe Peck, *Uncovering the Sixties: The Life and Times of the Underground Press*, p. 30

28 *Ibid.*, p. 211

8 Sister Kerista Saves the World

1 Krishnan Kumar, *Utopia and Anti-Utopia in Modern Times*, p. 15

2 *Ibid.*, p. 16

3 *The Independent*, August 18, 1991

4 Laurence Veysey, "Ideological Sources of American Movements," *Society*, January/February 1988

5 Kumar, op. cit., p. 36

6 *San Francisco Chronicle*, March 10, 1967

7 "The Erotic Evolution of Kerista: Pushing Out the Frontier of Sexual Liberation," *Kerista Journal of Group Living*, Winter 1987

8 "The Messianic Era," *Kerista Journal*, June 1984

9 "The Erotic Evolution of Kerista," loc. cit.

10 Larry L. and Joan M. Constantine, *Group Marriage: A Study of Contemporary Multilateral Marriage*, pp. 11–12

11 *Ibid.*, pp. 30–1

12 Dick Fairfield, "Harrad West," *The Modern Utopian*, Winter 1969, Communes USA edition, p. 146

13 *Ibid.*, p. 148

14 *Ibid.*, p. 149

15 *Ibid.*, p. 147

16 Constantine, op. cit., pp. 234–5

17 *Family Synergy Newsletter*, August 1991

18 "Carol" and "Tim," *The Swinger's Handbook*, p. 7

19 *Ibid.*, p. 18

20 William and Jerry Breedlove, *Swap*

Clubs: A Study in Contemporary Sexual Mores, p. 147

21 *Ibid.*, pp. 239–41

22 "Carol" and "Tim," op. cit., p. 80

23 *Ibid.*

24 Peter Roberts, *The Swapping Game*, p. 81

25 Derek Bowskill, *Swingers and Swappers*, p. 26

26 *Ibid.*, p. 22

27 *Ibid.*, p. 155

28 "Carol" and "Tim," op. cit., p. 187

29 June M. Reinisch and Ruth Beasley, *The Kinsey Institute New Report on Sex: What You Must Know to Be Sexually Literate*, p. 6

30 *Ibid.*, p. 33

9 The Future Has Been Postponed Until Further Notice

1 Gregory Pincus Papers, Library of Congress (I have omitted the name of the physician who attended the writer)

2 Barbara Seaman, *Women and the Crisis in Sex Hormones*, pp. 85–6

3 Barbara Seaman, *The Doctor's Case Against the Pill*, p. 18

4 *Ibid.*, p. 37

5 Barbara Seaman, *Free and Female*, pp. 159–60

6 *Spare Rib*, December 1975

7 Boston Women's Healthbook Collective, *Our Bodies, Ourselves*, p. 17

8 *Virginia Medical Monthly*, August 1968

9 Mary Daly, *Gyn/Ecology: The Metaethics of Radical Feminism*, pp. 9–10

10 Robin Morgan (ed.), *Sisterhood Is Powerful*, p. 405

11 Germaine Greer, *Sex and Destiny*, p. 133

12 Seaman, *Women and the Crisis in Sex Hormones*, p. 214

13 *Ibid.*, p. 215

14 Greer, op. cit., p. 134

15 *The New York Times Magazine*, December 16, 1990

16 *Ibid.*

17 *The Economist*, June 1, 1991

18 *The New York Times Magazine*, loc. cit.

19 *Ibid.*

20 *The Observer Magazine*, June 7, 1992

21 *The Independent on Sunday*, June 18, 1992

10 Vietnam Tango

1 *The New Yorker*, October 28, 1972

2 *Daily Express*, February 18, 1975

3 Henry Miller, *Crazy Cock*, p. 181

4 *Ibid.*, p. 157

5 *Ibid.*, p. 167

6 Sheila Jeffreys, *Anticlimax*, pp. 1–2

7 *Ibid.*, p. 30

8 Clare Short, *Dear Clare . . . This Is What Women Think About Page 3*, pp. xvii–xviii

9 *Ibid.*, p. 107

10 Susan Brownmiller, *Against Our Will: Men, Women and Rape*, p. 15

11 *Ibid.*, p. 30

12 *Ibid.*, p. 98

13 Aphrodite Matsakis, *Vietnam Wives: Women and Children Serving Life with Veterans Suffering Post-Traumatic Stress Disorder*, pp. 57–8
14 *Ibid.*, p. 62
15 *Ibid.*, p. 49
16 *Ibid.*, p. 98
17 Bret Easton Ellis, *Less Than Zero*, p. 75
18 *The Guardian*, April 9, 1991

11 A Safety Pin Stuck Through My Heart

1 Gabrielle Brown, *The New Celibacy: Why Men and Women Are Abstaining From Sex*, p. 3
2 Jon Savage, *England's Dreaming: A Biography of the Sex Pistols*, p. 357
3 *Ibid.*, p. 434
4 *Ibid.*, p. 56
5 *Ibid.*, p. 68
6 *Ibid.*, p. 100
7 *Ibid.*, p. 186
8 *Ibid.*, p. 32
9 *Ibid.*, p. 375
10 *ZG* magazine, issue 80
11 *Ibid.*
12 Madonna, *Sex*, unpaginated
13 Homero Aridjis, *1492: The Life and Times of Juan Cabezón*, p. 19
14 Jean Stein and George Plimpton (eds.), *Edie: An American Biography*, p. 226
15 Paglia, op. cit., p. 33
16 *Ibid.*, p. 28
17 *The Guardian*, April 22, 1992
18 *The Guardian*, September 14, 1992

19 *Ibid.*, Paglia, pp. 1–2
20 *Ibid.*, p. 10

12 The Millennium: Sex in the Time of Virtual Reality

1 John Rechy, *The Sexual Outlaw*, pp. 205–6
2 Randy Shilts, *And the Band Played On*, pp. 89–90
3 *Ibid.*, p. 126
4 *New Woman*, October 1986
5 *The Independent*, October 4, 1991
6 *The Guardian*, October 4, 1991
7 *The Independent*, June 9, 1992
8 Neil McKeganey, "Why Do Men Buy Sex and What Are Their Assessments of the HIV Related Risks When They Do?" Unpublished paper
9 Talese, *Thy Neighbor's Wife*, pp. 605–7
10 Thomas Laqueur, *Making Sex: Body and Gender from the Greeks to Freud*, p. 3
11 William Acton, *Functions and Disorders*, pp. 101–2
12 Laqueur, op. cit., p. 4
13 *Evening Standard*, March 20, 1992
14 Julie Burchill, *Ambition*, p. 17
15 *Ibid.*, pp. 142–3
16 Nancy Friday, *Women on Top*, p. 49
17 *Ibid.*, p. 57
18 Re/Search, *Angry Women*, p. 25
19 Christopher Anderson, *Madonna Unauthorized*, p. 75
20 *Ibid.*, pp. 124–5
21 *Ibid.*, p. 212
22 *Ibid.*, p. 110

23 Paglia, op. cit., p. 20

24 Madonna, op. cit.

25 Rosalind Coward, *Feminist Review*, No.11

26 Catherine Jones, *Sex or Symbol: Erotic Images of Greece and Rome*, pp. 62–72

27 *The Sunday Times Magazine*, October 18, 1992

28 Madonna, op. cit.

29 *Marie Claire*, April 1993

30 *Time Out*, May 27, 1992

31 *Marie Claire*, April 1993

Selected Bibliography

Acton, William. *Functions and Disorders*. London: John Churchill, 1862

Anderson, Christopher. *Madonna Unauthorized*. London: Michael Joseph, 1991

Annan, Noel. *Our Age: The Generation that Made Post-War Britain*. London: Fontana, 1991

Aridjis, Homero. *1492: The Life and Times of Juan Cabezón*. London: André Deutsch, 1991

Booker, Christopher. *The Neophiliacs: A Study of the Revolution in English Life in the Fifties and Sixties*. London: Collins, 1969

Bowskill, Derek. *Swingers and Swappers*. London: Star, 1975

Braithwaite, Brian, and Barrell, Joan. *The Business of Women's Magazines*. London: Kogan Page, 1988

Breedlove, William and Jerrye. *Swap Clubs: A Study in Contemporary Sexual Mores*. Los Angeles: Sherbourne Press, 1964

Brophy, Brigid. *Don't Never Forget: Collected Views and Reviews*. London: Cape, 1966

Brown, Gabrielle. *The New Celibacy: Why More Men and Women Are Abstaining From Sex—And Enjoying It*. New York: McGraw-Hill, 1980

Brownmiller, Susan. *Against Our Will: Men, Women and Rape*. New York: Simon & Schuster, 1975

Burchill, Julie. *Ambition*. London: Corgi, 1990

Carstairs, George. *This Island Now*. London: Hogarth Press, 1963

Carter, Angela. *The Sadeian Woman: An Exercise in Cultural History*. London: Virago, 1979

Cohn, Nik. *Ball the Wall: Nik Cohn in the Age of Rock*. London: Picador, 1989

Cohn, Norman. *The Pursuit of the Millennium: Revolutionary Millenarians and Mystical Anarchists of the Middle Ages*. London: Paladin, 1970

Comfort, Alex. *More Joy of Sex*. London: Quartet, 1975

Constantine, Larry L. and Joan M. *Group Marriage: A Study of Contemporary Multilateral Marriage*. New York: Macmillan, 1973

Daly, Mary. *Gyn/Ecology: The Metaethics of Radical Feminism*. London: Women's Press, 1979

Davenport-Hines, Richard. *Sex, Death and Punishment: Attitudes to Sex and Death in Britain Since the Renaissance*. London: Fontana Press, 1991

D'Emilio, John, and Freedman, Estelle B. *Intimate Matters: A History of Sexuality in America*. New York: Harper & Row, 1988

Djerassi, Carl. *The Politics of Contraception: Birth Control in the Year 2001*. Palo Alto: Stanford University Press, 1979

Du Maurier, Daphne. *Rebecca*. London: Pan, 1975

Ehrenreich, Barbara; Hess, Elizabeth; and Jacobs, Gloria. *Re-making Love: The Feminization of Sex*. New York: Anchor, 1986

Ellis, Bret Easton. *American Psycho*. London: Picador, 1991

———. *Less Than Zero*. London: Picador, 1986

Family Planning in the Sixties: Report of the Family Planning Association Working Party. London: Family Planning Association, 1963

Fischer, H. C., and Dubois, E. X. *Sexual Life During the World War*. London: Francis Aldor, 1937

Foster, R. F. *The Oxford Illustrated History of Ireland*. Oxford: Oxford University Press, 1991

Friday, Nancy. *Women on Top*. London: Hutchinson, 1991

Garrity, Terry, with Garrity, John. *Story of "J": The Author of* The Sensuous Woman *Tells the Bitter Price of Her Crazy Success*. New York: Morrow, 1984

Green, Jonathon. *Days in the Life: Voices From the English Underground, 1961–1971*. London: Heinemann, 1988

Greer, Germaine. *The Change: Women, Aging and the Menopause*. London: Hamish Hamilton, 1991

———. *The Madwoman's Underclothes: Essays and Occasional Writings 1968–1985*. London: Picador, 1986

———. *Sex and Destiny*. London: Secker & Warburg, 1984

Guillebaud, John. *The Pill*. Oxford: Oxford University Press, 1984

Haynes, Jim. *Thanks for Coming! An Autobiography*. London: Faber & Faber, 1984

Hill, Christopher. *The World Turned Upside Down: Radical Ideas and the English Revolution*. London: Temple Smith, 1972

Howard, Gerald (ed.). *The Sixties: Art, Politics and Media of Our Most Explosive Decade*. New York: Paragon House, 1991

Humphreys, Steve. *A Secret World of Sex: Forbidden Fruit, The British Experience 1900–1950*. London: Sidgwick & Jackson, 1988

"J." *The Sensuous Woman*. New York: Dell, 1982

Jeffreys, Sheila. *Anticlimax: A Feminist Perspective on the Sexual Revolution*. London: Women's Press, 1990

Johns, Catherine. *Sex or Symbol? Erotic Images of Greece and Rome*. London: British Museum Press, 1990

Kaiser, Robert Blair. *The Encyclical That Never Was: The Story of the Commission on Population, Family and Birth 1964–6*. London: Sheed & Ward, 1987

Keenan, Brigid. *The Women We Wanted to Look Like*. London: Macmillan, 1977

Kohn, Marek. *Dope Girls: The Birth of the British Drug Underground*. London: Lawrence & Wishart, 1992

Kumar, Krishnan. *Utopia and Anti-Utopia in Modern Times*. Oxford: Basil Blackwell, 1987

Laqueur, Thomas. *Making Sex: Body and Gender From the Greeks to Freud*. Cambridge, Mass.: Harvard University Press, 1992

Lewis, Norman. *Jackdaw Cake*. London: Hamish Hamilton, 1985

Lobenthal, Joel. *Radical Rags: Fashions of the Sixties*. New York: Abbeville Press, 1990

McCaffertey, Nell. *A Woman to Blame: The Kerry Babies Case*. Dublin: Attic Press, 1985

McLaren, Angus. *A History of Contraception: From Antiquity to the Present Day*. Oxford: Basil Blackwell, 1990

McLaughlin, Loretta. *The Pill, John Rock and the Catholic Church: The Biography of a Revolution*. Boston: Little, Brown, 1982

Madonna. *Sex*. London: Secker & Warburg, 1992

Marcuse, Herbert. *Five Lectures: Psychoanalysis, Politics and Utopia*. London: Allen Lane, 1970

Matsakis, Aphrodite. *Vietnam Wives: Women and Children Surviving Life with Veterans Suffering Post-Traumatic Stress Disorder*. Kensington, Maryland: Woodbine House, 1988

Miller, Henry. *Crazy Cock*. London: HarperCollins, 1991

Morgan, Robin (ed.). *Sisterhood Is Powerful*. New York: Vintage Books, 1970

Neville, Richard. *Play Power*. London: Faber & Faber, 1971

Nin, Anaïs. *A Spy in the House of Love*. London: Penguin, 1973

Obst, Lynda Rosen (ed.). *The Sixties: The Decade Remembered Now, by the People Who Lived It Then*. New York: Random House/Rolling Stone, 1977

Osborne, Lawrence. *The Poisoned Embrace: A Brief History of Sexual Pessimism.* London: Bloomsbury, 1993

Packard, Vance. *The Sexual Wilderness: The Contemporary Upheaval in Male-Female Relationships.* New York: David McKay, 1968

Paglia, Camille. *Sexual Personae: Art and Decadence from Nefertiti to Emily Dickinson.* New York: Vintage, 1991

Pasle-Green, Jeanne, and Haynes, Jim. *Hello, I Love You! Voices from the Sexual Revolution.* New York: Times Change Press, 1977

Peck, Abe. *Uncovering the Sixties: The Life and Times of the Underground Press.* New York: Citadel Press, 1991

Pennington, Donald, and Thomas, Keith (eds.). *Puritans and Revolutionaries: Essays in Seventeenth Century History Presented to Christopher Hill.* Oxford: Oxford University Press, 1978

Ramírez de Arellano, Annette, and Seipp, Conrad. *Colonialism, Catholicism, and Contraception: A History of Birth Control in Puerto Rico.* Chapel Hill and London: University of North Carolina Press, 1983

Ranke-Heinemann, Uta. *Eunuchs for Heaven: The Catholic Church and Sexuality.* London: André Deutsch, 1990

Rechy, John. *The Sexual Outlaw: A Non-Fiction Account, with Commentaries, of Three Days and Nights in the Sexual Underground.* London: Futura, 1979

Reed, James. *From Private Vice to Public Virtue.* New York: Basic Books, 1978

Reinisch, June M., and Beasley, Ruth. *The Kinsey New Report on Sex: What You Must Know to Be Sexually Literate.* London: Penguin, 1990

Re/Search #3. *Angry Women.* San Francisco: Re/Search Publications, 1991

Rice, David. *Shattered Vows: Exodus From the Priesthood.* Belfast: Blackstaff Press, 1991

Roberts, Peter. *The Swapping Game.* London: Everest Books, 1976

Robinson, Paul. *The Freudian Left: Wilhelm Reich, Geza Roheim, Herbert Marcuse.* Ithaca and London: Cornell University Press, 1990

Rowbotham, Sheila, and Weeks, Jeffrey. *Socialism and the New Life: The Personal and Sexual Politics of Edward Carpenter and Havelock Ellis.* London: Pluto Press, 1977

Russell, Dora. *The Tamarisk Tree.* Vol. I: *My Quest for Liberty and Love.* London: Elek, 1975

Savage, Jon. *England's Dreaming: A Biography of the Sex Pistols.* London: Faber & Faber, 1991

Seaman, Barbara. *The Doctor's Case Against the Pill.* London: Michael Joseph, 1970

————. *Free and Female.* Greenwich, Connecticut: Fawcett Crest, 1972

————, and Seaman, Gideon. *Women and the Crisis in Sex Hormones.* New York: Bantam, 1978

Shilts, Randy. *And the Band Played On: Politics, People and the AIDS Epidemic.* London: Viking, 1988

Short, Clare. *Dear Clare . . . This Is What Women Think About Page 3.* London: Hutchinson Radius, 1991

Showalter, Elaine. *Sexual Anarchy: Gender and Culture at the Fin de Siècle.* London: Bloomsbury, 1991

Smith, John A. *Ryder Memorial Hospital: An Unfolding Story of Health Care.* Humacao, Puerto Rico: Ryder Memorial Hospital, 1989

Steele, Valerie. *Fashion and Eroticism: Ideals of Feminine Beauty from the Victorian Era to the Jazz Age.* Oxford: Oxford University Press, 1985

Steiner, George. *In Bluebeard's Castle: Some Notes Towards the Redefinition of Culture.* London: Faber & Faber, 1974

Talese, Gay. *Thy Neighbor's Wife.* New York: Laurel, 1980

Toffler, Alvin. *Future Shock.* New York: Bantam, 1971

Wolfe, Linda. *The Cosmo Report.* New York: Arbor House, 1981

Zahavi, Helen. *Dirty Weekend.* London: Macmillan, 1991